THE HALL-MILLS
MURDER CASE

THE HALL-MILLS

MURDER CASE

The Minister and the Choir Singer

WILLIAM M. KUNSTLER

RUTGERS UNIVERSITY PRESS

NEW BRUNSWICK, NEW JERSEY

For Bruce Rae and Russell B. Porter
—newspapermen to the end.

Rutgers University Press acknowledges the cooperation of Judge Arthur S. Meredith in providing additional illustrations for this paperback edition.

Third paperback printing, 1996

Library of Congress Catalog Card Number 64-12043
ISBN 0-8135-0912-2

CONTENTS

(Illustration section between pages 152 and 153)

PART III

PART IV

INTRODUCTION

The urge to write this book had its genesis on a hot night in June 1961. During an interview on an all-night radio program I was asked whether I had any idea who had killed Edward Wheeler Hall and Eleanor Reinhardt Mills thirty-nine years earlier in a lovers' lane just outside of New Brunswick, New Jersey. In a moment of not uncharacteristic rashness I stated that I thought I did. Two days later I received a telephone call from a detective in the office of Arthur S. Meredith, the Somerset County prosecutor of the Pleas. He wanted to know whether I would be willing to discuss the case with the prosecutor. I told him that I would be delighted to do so.

It wasn't long before I found myself sitting in Mr. Meredith's fourth-floor office in the ultramodern Somerset County Administration Building in Somerville, New Jersey, an attractive rural community some thirty-five miles southwest of New York City. I soon realized as I talked to the earnest young district attorney that my knowledge of the famous unsolved mystery was far from extensive. But my curiosity had been stimulated, and I resolved that I would set about the task of learning more about the mysterious deaths of the handsome Episcopal rector and his passionate choir singer on the night of September 14, 1922.

I harbored the intriguing hope that my labors might result in identifying once and for all the murderer or murderers. But as I dug deeper into the records of the crime, I began to realize that the passage of time was a formidable obstacle. Even the most spectacular murders have a way of losing their immediacy.

The desire to solve the double killing was soon coupled with an equally compelling desire to re-create one of the most fascinating murder stories in American history. The combination of wealth, social prestige, adultery, and sudden death proved to be as irresistable to me as it had been to the news media of the time.

Surprisingly, the New York *Times*, which in 1922 (as it does today) normally eschewed the gory details of sensational murders served up by its less restrained competitors, devoted more space to the case than did any other American journal. When publisher Adolph S. Ochs was once asked why his paper occasionally outdid the tabloids in its coverage of certain crimes, he replied, "The yellows see such stories only as opportunities for sensationalism. When the *Times* gives a great amount of space to such stories, it turns out authentic sociological documents."

It is my earnest hope that I have succeeded in presenting not just another murder story, but a "sociological document" of possibly the only era in our history when such a crime could have caused the stir it did. I have tried to depict the drama, the pathos, the tragedy, and the comedy inherent in the most notorious double homicide in the annals of American crime since Lizzie Borden's father and stepmother were mysteriously hacked to death thirty years earlier.

As for my solution, it is supported by more logic and at least as much evidence as the many that have been proposed during the four decades since the discovery of the couple's bodies under an isolated crab apple tree.

I owe more than I can say to the following persons and institutions who helped, in one way or another, to bring this book into being: Franklyn S. Adams, the Association of the Bar of the City of New York, Joanna Bukszpan, Katherine B. Carter, the late Clarence Case, United States Senator Clifford Case, Arthur Charpentier, Sam D. Cohen, Frank M. Deiner, Lawrence Hughes, Renate Knispel, Jane B. Kunstler, Susan Y. Kunstler, Frederick G. Marks III, Arthur S. Meredith, the New York Public Library, Frank M. O'Connor, the Pace College Library, Timothy N. Pfeiffer, the late Russell B. Porter, the late Bruce Rae—and last, but hardly least, my usually patient and always understanding wife.

William M. Kunstler

September 15, 1963

ADDENDUM

It has been some sixteen years since I finished this book. I am as convinced as ever that it was the Ku Klux Klan which ended the lives of the minister and the choir singer. If I ever doubted this thesis, the events of the last few years, including cross burnings in New Jersey and elsewhere as well as the murders of five civil rights activists in Greensboro, N.C. by Klansmen, have reinforced my conviction that Reverend Hall and Mrs. Mills met their deaths at the hands of self-righteous zealots determined to impose their moral concepts on everyone else. It is my profound hope that the reissue of this book will remind new readers that there is little more dangerous in society than groups or individuals who believe that their way is the only right way and who will kill to prove that point.

W.M.K.

January 13, 1980

PART I

Chapter 1

THE DISCOVERY

(Saturday, September 16, 1922)

On the morning of Saturday, September 16, 1922, fifteen-year-old Pearl Bahmer,[1] a factory worker in New Brunswick, New Jersey, had a date with Raymond Schneider, a local youth some eight years her senior. Because it was a mild, sunny day, the couple decided to go for a walk, and headed out of town on Easton Avenue. Just as they crossed Mile Run, the little brook that was the dividing line between Middlesex and Somerset counties, Schneider suggested that they turn left into De Russey's Lane, a dirt road that skirted the abandoned Phillips farm.

It was exactly ten o'clock.

They had been walking down De Russey's Lane for several minutes when they noticed an isolated driveway leading off to the left. "Let's try this one," Schneider said. After scrambling over a low embankment that partially blocked the entrance to the path, he and the girl picked their way through the ankle-deep grass that choked the little-used thoroughfare. They had gone about five hundred feet when Pearl noticed something lying between the left-hand edge of the road and a nearby crab apple tree.

"Wait a minute, Ray," she cried, "there's two people lyin' there!"

[1] A complete list of the dramatis personae may be found on pages 335–344.

3

Pearl walked gingerly toward the crab apple tree. "Come here!" she called excitedly. "The people ain't breathin'!" Schneider, who was by now more than twenty feet away, turned and walked back to where Pearl was standing. He took a long look at what she had seen. "Let's get out of here!" he told the now thoroughly frightened girl.

The couple raced across the field to the home of Edward Stryker, who lived next door to the Francis G. Parker Memorial Home for the Aged on Easton Avenue. After listening to their story Grace Edwards, Mr. Stryker's niece, telephoned the New Brunswick police.

It was ten thirty that morning when Lieutenant Dwyer, who took the call at police headquarters, ordered Patrolman Edward Garrigan to go to De Russey's Lane and investigate Mrs. Edwards' report. The police officer left the building, crossed Bayard Street, cut through the courthouse, and walked to Spring Street. Just before he reached the railroad station, he stopped a car being driven by one George Cathers.

"I'm going to the Easton Avenue end of De Russey's Lane," the policeman said. "Will you drive me there?"

Cathers agreed, and turned left onto Easton Avenue and headed toward the west end of town. When they reached the Bristol Street intersection, Garrigan picked up Officer James Curran, another member of the New Brunswick Police Department.

Five minutes later the two policemen arrived at De Russey's Lane. Pearl and Ray, who were anxiously waiting for them, guided the officers to what shortly became the most famous crab apple tree in the country. Ordering the young people to remain in the path, Garrigan and Curran knelt down in the tall grass. They were horrified to discover the bodies of a man and a woman sprawled on the ground.

The couple, whose feet were pointing toward the crab apple tree, were lying on their backs, with the woman's head resting on the man's right arm. The latter's face was covered

by a Panama hat, and a small card was leaning against the
heel of his left foot. The woman's left hand was resting on
her companion's right knee, and a brown scarf covered the
lower portion of her throat. Some torn pieces of paper were
scattered between the bodies.

While Curran went to call headquarters, his partner took
a closer look at the dead man and woman. He noticed, as he
later testified, that the woman's throat was "a mass of maggots from ear to ear, right down to her chin." Near the
bodies he saw a man's dark leather wallet lying open on the
ground. By bending over he was able to see that it contained
a driver's license, which had been issued to one Edward
Wheeler Hall of 23 Nichol Avenue, New Brunswick. Although he saw no signs of a struggle, the grass around the
bodies appeared to have been trampled down recently.

Several minutes after Curran had left, reporter Albert J.
Cardinal of the New Brunswick *Daily Home News* joined
Garrigan. The newspaperman was intrigued by the card
propped up against the dead man's left foot. "He asked me
if he could pick the card up and look at it, and I told him
yes," Garrigan later said. Its Gothic letters spelled out the
name of Reverend Edward W. Hall, the pastor of the Episcopal Church of St. John the Evangelist in New Brunswick.
Before Cardinal replaced the card, Garrigan made a note of
it in his report book.

Curran called Lieutenant Dwyer from a house on Easton
Avenue. On his way back to the Phillips farm he stopped a
car driven by Dr. E. Leon Loblein, a veterinarian, who was
returning to New Brunswick from Bound Brook, and told
him that they needed someone to identify the body of a
man believed to be Reverend Hall. Loblein, who knew the
minister, accompanied the policeman to the crab apple tree.
When Garrigan raised the Panama hat which obscured the
dead man's face, Loblein nodded. "That's Reverend Hall,
all right," he said.

As the veterinarian was leaving, Detective George D. Tot-

ten of the Somerset County prosecutor's office arrived at the
scene. A half hour earlier news of the double murder had
spread to New Brunswick, and a number of curious spectators had already flocked to De Russey's Lane. It became impossible for Garrigan to control them, and by the time
Totten drove up, the crab apple tree had been stripped of
much of its bark, the calling card passed from hand to hand,
and the underbrush trampled down.

Because the bodies were lying in Somerset County, the
New Brunswick Police Department had alerted Totten's
office in nearby Somerville at eleven that morning. It had
taken the detective, Sheriff Bogart F. Conkling, and County
Physician William H. Long more than forty minutes to drive
the twelve miles from the county seat to the Phillips farm
because they had misunderstood their directions and gone to
the wrong end of De Russey's Lane.

"There was some delay there in making inquiries because
we realized we were on the wrong road," Totten was to tell
a Somerset County Jury in 1926. "After making some inquiries we rode down De Russey's Lane to Easton Avenue,
where I believe we met a gentleman from the New Brunswick Police Department who gave us the correct location
of where the bodies lay."

As he surveyed the scene, Totten was far more perceptive
than Garrigan. "The bodies were lying on their backs," he
noted. "The lady was on the right of the gentleman. The
gentleman's right hand was extended partly under the lady's
shoulder and neck; the clothing on the bodies was perfectly
arranged. The man had a hat, a Panama hat, partly conceal-
ing his face. His eyeglasses were on. I observed from under
the rim of the hat that his eyeglasses were spotted. There
were letters and cards lying on the ground between the two
bodies. The lady's hat lay off to her right on the ground and
a scarf was partly around the lady's neck. There was a wound
in the lady's neck which was entirely filled with maggots."

The calling card that Garrigan and Cardinal had examined was no longer leaning against the dead man's foot when Totten first saw it. It was now standing on its edge, some eight inches away from where Garrigan had originally seen it, supported by a tuft of grass. The detective noticed that the printed side was facing the feet of the dead woman. It contained what he thought looked like "flyspecks."

A card case and a number of letters were lying on the ground between the bodies. The card case contained a driver's license, an automobile registration, and Masonic and YMCA membership cards, all issued in the name of Edward Wheeler Hall.

Totten asked Conkling to pick up the card case and the letters. When the sheriff had collected these articles as well as a Peters .32-caliber cartridge case which had been discovered near the bodies, he wrapped them in a sheet of brown paper. He also picked up a two-foot piece of iron pipe that was lying a few feet away from the dead man and woman.

The letters, which were scrawled in pencil on cheap stationery, fairly sizzled. "There isn't a man who could make me smile as you did today," one of them read. "I know there are girls with more shapely bodies, but I do not care what they have. I have the greatest of all blessings, a noble man, deep, true, and eternal love. My heart is his, my life is his, all I have is his, poor as my body is, scrawny as they say my skin may be, but I am his forever."

The handwriting, Totten surmised, was that of a high school girl.

While the Somerset County officials were completing their preliminary search of the area, a green sedan drove into De Russey's Lane from Easton Avenue. The vehicle, which contained Edwin R. Carpender, a first cousin of Mrs. Edward W. Hall's, and former Middlesex State Senator William E. Florence, a New Brunswick attorney, parked near the entrance to the Phillips farm. After looking at the two corpses both men confirmed Loblein's identification of the man's as that of Reverend Hall, St. John's pastor.

White-faced and shaken, Carpender and Florence drove off at once.

Around two o'clock Samuel T. Sutphen, a Somerville undertaker who had been summoned by Dr. Long, drove up the lane. In the dead man's pockets he found two handkerchiefs and sixty-one cents in change. After turning the money and the handkerchiefs over to Sheriff Conkling, he and an assistant carried the bodies to his hearse.

"Better get them out of here in a hurry, Sam," Dr. Long told him. "They've been dead at least thirty-six hours."

As soon as Sutphen arrived in Somerville, he took the two bodies to his morgue. While he was removing the dead man's coat, a bullet fell to the floor. Because of the decomposition which had taken place, it was necessary for him to rip the shirt from the body. It was then that he had noticed a discoloration on the man's right hand.

The woman had been shot between the eyes. When Sutphen unwrapped the scarf around her neck, he saw that her throat had been cut from ear to ear. In addition, one of her arms had been bruised, and there was what appeared to be a small wound on her upper lip.

Later that afternoon he was informed by Dr. Long that John V. Hubbard, a New Brunswick undertaker, had been given permission to pick up the man's body. At 7 P.M., Hubbard arrived at Sutphen's morgue. With the latter's assistance the corpse was carried to the waiting hearse and then driven to New Brunswick. The following morning it was formally identified by Dr. Edward I. Cronk, the New Brunswick health officer, as that of Reverend Edward W. Hall.

Chapter 2

THE LIVING AND THE DEAD

But long before Dr. Cronk had made it official, there were very few people in either Middlesex or Somerset counties who did not know who the dead couple were. There had been gossip about Reverend Hall, the pastor of the fashionable Church of St. John the Evangelist, and Mrs. James F. Mills, one of his choir singers, for several years. If there was anybody in New Brunswick who wasn't aware that the minister and the soprano were deeply involved with each other, he was a rare bird indeed.

Hall had been born in Brooklyn in 1881. After graduating from Brooklyn Polytechnic Institute in 1898 with a liberal arts degree, he had attended General Theological Seminary in Manhattan. He had been ordained as a minister at Grace Church in New York and then served as the curate of its east side Chapel. In 1907 he had become the assistant pastor of a church in Basking Ridge, a small community near Bernardsville, New Jersey. Several years later he had been installed as the rector of St. John's in New Brunswick.

On July 20, 1911, he had married Frances Noel Stevens, the only daughter of one of New Brunswick's most prominent families. At the time of their marriage Hall was thirty and his bride thirty-seven. The couple had met when Miss Stevens, who attended Christ Church, became a teacher at

St. John's Sunday school. Like many of Hall's female communicants, she had been instantly attracted to the personable
bachelor.

Mrs. Hall had been born in Aiken, South Carolina, on
January 13, 1874. On her mother's side she was related to
the founders of the surgical supply firm of Johnson & Johnson. Several years after her marriage Mrs. Hall and her two
older brothers, William and Henry, were reported to have
inherited almost two million dollars between them from
their mother and an aunt.

After their wedding the Halls lived in a large two-story
red-brick mansion on the corner of Nichol Avenue and Redmond Street, just a few blocks from St. John's. One of the
finest houses in New Brunswick, it had belonged to Mrs.
Hall's family for many years. At the time of her husband's
death the household had included her eccentric brother,
known to everyone in town as Willie, and a number of
servants.

The couple led an orderly, if unexciting, life, which was
completely circumscribed by church activities. "We always
had breakfast together," Mrs. Hall was to testify four years
later, "and then he was very apt to stay in the house during
the morning, in his study; not always, of course, and more
apt to go out in the afternoon for calls or whatever might be
needed; and then we always had our supper together about
half past six, and he was out very often in the evening
through the winter to different meetings in the church."

Five blocks away from the Hall residence the family of
James Francis Mills occupied the second floor and attic of a
ramshackle frame house at 49 Carman Street. Mills, a mild-
mannered ex-shoemaker, had married fifteen-year-old Eleanor Reinhardt in 1905. A pretty brown-haired girl with a
thin but adequate soprano voice, Mrs. Mills had been associated with St. John's choir since her fourteenth birthday.
After the birth of the second of her two children in 1910,
she had become very active in the church's Ladies' Auxiliary,

and at the time of her murder was one of its most energetic members. In 1920 her husband, who had been employed in a New Brunswick rubber factory, quit his job to become the sexton of St. John's and an assistant janitor at the nearby Lord Stirling Public School.

Jimmy Mills was hardly what anyone would call a good catch. A meek, unambitious man, who had never made more than thirty-eight dollars a week in his life, he had not been able to provide his young wife with any but the barest necessities of life. For a time Eleanor Mills was able to assuage her frustrations by devoting herself to Charlotte and Danny, her two children. But as they grew less dependent upon her, she had turned to romantic novels and church activities as antidotes to her squalid home life. During the two years before her murder it was an extremely rare day when she couldn't be found at St. John's.

As Eleanor began to spend more and more of her time at the church, her friendship with the pastor gradually deepened until it had turned into a full-fledged love affair. Perhaps it was not surprising that the handsome Episcopal minister was attracted to Eleanor. During his first few years in New Brunswick, Hall had been unofficially engaged to one of her younger sisters. In any case, the affair quickly became the talk of the congregation. "The rector can't find time to call on me once a year," one elderly parishioner complained, "but he manages to call on Mrs. Mills eight or nine times a week."

By the end of 1919, Hall was a frequent—and always welcome—visitor at the Millses' four-room apartment. Apparently flattered by the minister's attentions to his wife, Mills went out of his way to be cordial. In return, Hall persuaded the St. John's vestrymen to hire him as its sexton.

"Dr. Hall[1] was my best friend," Mills told a reporter shortly after the murders. "When I was down-and-out this

1 Although the minister had never received his doctorate in divinity, members of his congregation referred to him as if he had.

summer, he came and took me to the hospital. He took care of me like a father. He was the kindest man I ever knew, and his heart was tender for anybody in trouble."

In December 1921, Mrs. Mills had begun to complain of excruciating pains in her back. The diagnosis was a malfunctioning right kidney, and the following January it was removed by Dr. Arthur L. Smith at Middlesex General Hospital. Because Mills was unable to meet the surgeon's bill of two hundred dollars, Hall had arranged to pay it in small monthly installments.

Mrs. Hall had seemed oblivious of any romance between her husband and Mrs. Mills. There was gossip that she had once ordered her rival out of the church summer camp at Point Pleasant, but she often told acquaintances she was sure her husband was not one to disregard his marital vows. "I would trust him more than I would myself," she said.

If there was any bad blood between the two women, it had never been apparent to anyone in New Brunswick. In fact, it was Mrs. Hall who had driven Mrs. Mills to the hospital a day before the kidney operation. During the choir singer's convalescence the rector's wife had visited her frequently. When Mrs. Mills had been discharged, Mrs. Hall had taken her back to her Carman Street apartment.

Just three weeks before the removal of her kidney Mrs. Mills had received a single red rose from Reverend Hall. "This red, red rose," the minister had written in the note that accompanied the flower, "is but a symbol of love, devoted, faithful, true. For love is like a rose, dear heart, fresh as the early morn. God took the beauty of the skies, the glory of the dawn, the fire of passion, the calm of evening, the golden glow and, with the mystery of the stars, he made the love we know. So in this rose you find me, dear, the love it can impart; love, loyal, true, and absolute, the offering of my heart."

Unfortunately, love had only eight months and twenty days to run.

Chapter 3

THE FUNERALS

(Sunday, September 17, through
Tuesday, September 19, 1922)

On Sunday, the day after he had gone to Somerville for Hall's body, undertaker Hubbard returned to pick up that of Eleanor Mills. Just before the hearse pulled up in front of Sutphen's Funeral Home, County Physician Long opened an incision in Mrs. Mills' abdomen. After examining her uterus briefly he closed the wound with a running suture.

When Hubbard arrived back in New Brunswick, Dr. Cronk issued two burial permits to him. Although the undertaker also acted as the Middlesex coroner, he did not think it necessary to order an autopsy on either corpse.

Because of the poor condition of the bodies Hubbard had not been able to embalm them fully. There had been so many breaks in the couple's circulatory systems that the embalming fluid could not flow freely. "If there is a break in the circulatory system or arteries," he later explained, "that disturbs the embalming, and the portions not reached by the circulatory system are not embalmed." In view of the extensive decomposition that had taken place, he warned both families that early burials would be advisable.

Edwin R. Carpender was in charge of the minister's funeral arrangements. At Hubbard's request, he went to the Hall residence, which was across the street from his own, and picked out one of the dead man's suits. Since it had been decided to bury Hall in his ecclesiastical vestments, Carpender was asked by Mrs. Hall to go to St. John's with Minnie Clark, one of its Sunday school teachers, and select the appropriate garments. With Mrs. Clark's help, he chose a stole, a cassock, and a white surplice.

Shortly after Hubbard had finished embalming the two bodies, he received a telephone call from Senator Florence. The lawyer, who represented the estates of Mrs. Hall's grandfather and aunt, asked him to have Reverend Hall's remains officially identified by some physician who had known him, and suggested Dr. Smith, the surgeon who had operated on Mrs. Mills the preceding winter.

Twenty minutes later Hubbard called back and asked Florence whether Dr. Cronk, who had just walked into his establishment, would be satisfactory. Mr. Florence replied that he would.

When he entered Hubbard's embalming room, Cronk seemed far more interested in Mrs. Mills than in the minister. After locating three bullet wounds in the dead woman's head the physician pulled out Long's running suture and opened the wound. Before leaving the funeral home he instructed Hubbard's assistant to close the incision.

Late in the day there was an emergency meeting of the church's vestrymen. After some heated discussion a motion for a vote of confidence in Hall was approved by the group. "We have explicit faith in our dead rector," one vestryman later told the waiting reporters. Similar sentiments were expressed in a telegram received from the Protestant Episcopal Convention which was being held in Portland, Oregon.

Hall's funeral was scheduled for Monday, September 18. At 11 A.M. that Monday, Hubbard drove the minister's body over to St. John's. The small stone church on George Street was jammed with more than two hundred mourners, most of whom were women, while scores of late-comers filled the sidewalks outside. Shortly before noon a heavily veiled Mrs.

Hall, flanked by her two brothers, entered the building. She paused for a moment beside the closed coffin, which was covered by purple asters, orchids, and carnations, and then walked slowly to her pew. "Mrs. Hall showed remarkable self-possession," one reporter noted. "She did not break down and could not be seen to shed tears."

The short Episcopal service for the dead was conducted by Bishop Albion W. Knight of Trenton, New Jersey. In place of a eulogy Bishop Knight read a somewhat guarded endorsement of the dead man by the twenty-nine ministers attending the funeral. "In view of the unfortunate mystery surrounding his death," it stated, "we do not hesitate to maintain our confidence in his character, entirely unshaken by the evidence so far revealed by public report."

At the conclusion of the services the casket was returned to Hubbard's hearse for transportation to Greenwood Cemetery in Brooklyn. The three-car procession arrived at the Stevens family vault in New York, via the Staten Island Ferry, at 4:30 P.M.

"My instructions," Hubbard later recalled, "were to place the body of Mr. Hall next to Mrs. Stevens, the mother of Mrs. Hall, and the suggestion was that that would leave room for Mrs. Hall alongside of Mr. Hall. When we got in the vault, we found there was room only for one body next to Mrs. Stevens." The problem was solved by placing the minister's casket on the unoccupied lower rack of the vault.

Funeral services for Eleanor Mills were held the next morning at Hubbard's. Sixteen-year-old Charlotte Mills, the dead woman's daughter, was in charge of all the arrangements. The handful of people who showed up at the small chapel on Bayard Street were surprised to learn that Mrs. Hall had sent a wreath which had been placed on the dead woman's casket.

The services were interrupted several times by Charlotte, who tried unsuccessfully to have the coffin opened so that she could see her mother's face once more.

Chapter 4

THE MISSING HOURS

*(Thursday, September 14, through
Saturday, September 16, 1922)*

Jimmy Mills couldn't have been more co-operative. Not only
did he cheerfully accede to all of the numerous requests of
Somerset County Prosecutor Azariah Beekman to come to
Somerville and answer questions about the case, but he
agreed fully with Beekman's initial theory that the murdered couple had been killed elsewhere and then brought
to the Phillips farm. "From what I know about Reverend
Hall," he told newspapermen, "I don't think he was killed
where his body was found. He was such a heavy man and
had asthma so badly that he couldn't have walked all the
way there from the trolley line. He must have been carried
there."

Mills, who was quickly classified by reporters as a mild-
mannered simpleton,[1] did not share the general consensus
that his wife and Hall had been having a love affair since
late 1919. "I can't explain," he said naïvely, "why he and
my wife were together there or wherever else they must have
been, unless it was to talk over some church matters." He
was certain that robbery and not jealousy had been the

---

[1] "He is such a man," Damon Runyon later wrote, "as you might
imagine to be a henpecked husband at home, a man bullied by his children
and by all the world, a man anybody could push out of their way without
protest from him, a harmless, dull little fellow."

cause of the minister's death. "I think some robbers killed
him for his gold watch and his money. He always carried a
large sum of money with him, and lots of people knew it."

At five forty-five on the afternoon of the murders, Thursday, September 14, he had dropped in at St. John's, he told
Prosecutor Beekman, to sweep up wood shavings left by the
carpenters who had been repaneling the vestibule of the
Sunday school room. Because the sweeping had taken a little
longer than he expected, Mills had not returned home until
six fifteen. "You are late for your supper," Eleanor had complained.

After supper the sexton had gone out on the back stoop
to work on some window boxes that needed new slats. While
he was hammering away, his wife left the house to make a
telephone call at a nearby candy store. She had explained
that on her way home from the church that afternoon a
neighbor had told her that Reverend Hall had telephoned,
and she wanted to return his call. Ten minutes after their
mother had gone to the candy store, Charlotte and Danny
left to visit an aunt.

Mrs. Mills had returned shortly before seven thirty.
"When she came back from telephoning," Mills recalled,
"she put her hat and shawl and scarf on and went out, and
that was the last I saw of her."

As his wife flounced down the front stairs, Mills had asked
her where she was going. "Follow me and find out!" she had
retorted. He had shrugged his thin shoulders and returned
to his carpentry work.

At nine o'clock Mrs. Elizabeth E. Kelly, who occupied the
basement and first floor of 49 Carman Street, had complained
about the noise Mills was making. "I was hammering and
she asked me what I was pounding on, and I said I was
making some window boxes." When it became too dark to
work outdoors, Mills had brought several boxes onto the
gaslit back porch, where he had continued to work until
nine forty-five. After finishing he had sat for a few minutes,

reading that evening's New York *World*. As he flipped the pages, he noticed that someone had torn out one sheet.

Charlotte and Danny had come home at ten thirty. A few minutes later Mills had decided to go to the church and look for his wife, who, he informed Prosecutor Beekman, "was always home about ten, as a rule." On his way to St. John's he had stopped at a neighborhood stationery store for a glass of soda water.

It had been eleven five when he arrived at the church. After turning on the lights he had closed the side windows. Fifteen minutes later he had returned home. "I went to bed," he said, "and left the light burning in the kitchen and fell asleep."

He had awakened at 2 A.M., and when he saw that the kitchen light was still on, had gotten dressed. He had stood outside the door of the attic bedroom, which for more than two years had been shared by Mrs. Mills and her daughter, and asked Charlotte where her mother was. "She just made a mumbling noise, about half asleep. She didn't say anything else, and I pushed the door open and she was not there."

Because he was worried that his wife might have had "a fainting spell," he had walked back to the church and looked for her in the pews. Failing to find her, he had locked up and returned home.

The next day he had arisen at 5:45 A.M. and gone to the corner grocery, where he bought some buns for breakfast. After preparing his children's meal he had left for his job at the Lord Stirling School, across the street. Although his wife had not returned home, he did not report her as a missing person to the New Brunswick police or inquire at any of the local hospitals. "My wife used to go away sometimes a day or two away from the house, and that is why I did not pay any attention to it," he explained to Beekman.

At eight thirty that morning Mills had gone to the church. As he was opening the windows in the rector's study, Mrs.

Hall had entered the room. "She says to me, 'Good morning, Mr. Mills.' I said, 'Good morning, Mrs. Hall.' She said, 'Did you have any sickness in your home last night?' I said, 'No.' She said, 'Mr. Hall did not come home all night.' I said, 'My wife did not come home all night.' And as something cropped up, I said, 'Do you think that they eloped?'[2] And she said, 'God knows. I think they are dead and can't come home.'"

Before she left, the minister's wife informed the sexton, according to his story, that she had "that morning early telephoned to police headquarters without giving her name and asked if there were any casualties."

He had next seen her at his house at noon, while he was eating his lunch. When she asked him if he had heard anything about the missing couple, he had answered, "No, Mrs. Hall, I haven't heard anything." She had returned at 5 P.M. to repeat her question. "If I hear anything," he had assured her, "I will let you know."

He had seen Mrs. Hall once more that day. After opening the church for choir practice at eight that evening, he had gone to the Hall residence. He had had a brief conversation with Mrs. Hall, who was sitting in a wicker chair on the front porch.

"I asked her, I said, 'Mrs. Hall, I don't know what to make of this. I can't get anywhere at all. I am just lost at sea on it.' And she said to me, 'I am looking at a blank wall before me.'" As he was leaving, the minister's wife had called after him, "They must be dead or they would come home."

While he was in Hall's office that morning, Mills had noticed a page from the New York *World* lying on the rector's desk. He assumed it was the page that had been missing from the paper he had read the previous evening after finishing his carpentry work. He had glanced at the sheet only

---

2 Mills' allusion to a possible elopement was surprising in view of his earlier statement to reporters that the couple must have been discussing "church matters." This discrepancy was later to plague him at the trial.

long enough to see that it contained an article about a prominent Episcopal minister's views on divorce.

On Saturday, Mills had had an early lunch with Mrs. Augusta Tennyson, one of Eleanor's four sisters. Shortly after Mills left the house, a little girl ran after him and told him Mrs. Tennyson wanted to see him again. A reporter had telephoned to inform his sister-in-law that the bodies of Reverend Hall and an unidentified woman had been found near De Russey's Lane. "I guess it must be Eleanor," Mrs. Tennyson had said.

Mills had been so "puzzled" by the news that he became confused about where the bodies had been discovered. "I didn't know whether they said Ryder's Lane or De Russey's Lane," he told Prosecutor Beekman, "and I started to Ryder's Lane, over toward the other side of town."

But in the end he hadn't gone to either street. After stopping at his own home, where a tearful Charlotte told him that the dead woman had been positively identified, he had rushed over to the Hall residence. By the time he had traveled the five blocks to the minister's house, he had become so nauseated that upon his arrival Mrs. Hall had been forced to give him some spirits of ammonia.

Charlotte Mills told a story that corroborated most of what her father had said, and added some new details. She informed the prosecutor that on Thursday, September 14, she had arrived home from school at 4 P.M. After supper she had seen her mother cut a clipping out of the New York *World*. "It was a clipping," she said, "on Percy Stickney Grant of his church in New York, on the divorce question."

Mrs. Mills had told her daughter that she was going to the church to leave the clipping on Dr. Hall's desk. Unknown to her husband, she had left the house at seven o'clock and returned fifteen minutes later. It was then that she had gone out once more, this time with her husband's knowledge, to make the telephone call to Hall that Mills had already described to Prosecutor Beekman.

As Charlotte explained it, "She went around the corner to phone and told me to wait for her, and that was the last I saw her."

Since the Millses had no telephone, it had been their custom to make their calls from the home of spinster Millie L. Opie, a dressmaker and milliner who lived next door. On this evening, however, Mrs. Mills had told Charlotte that she was going to use the pay telephone at a candy store around the corner. The fact that she had made such a call was later corroborated by the police. Shortly after Mrs. Mills had gone to call the minister, Charlotte, disregarding her mother's request to wait for her, had left the house with her brother, Danny, to visit an aunt.

She and Danny had returned home at ten thirty. "The light was lit, and the doors were unlocked," she said. "We came in and I went right up to my room."

Sometime during the night she had been awakened by her father's voice. "I don't know what time it was, I know it was quite late—my father called to me and told me that my mother had not gotten in yet and did I know where she was, or was she upstairs with me. And I just sort of grunted some kind of an answer, because I was very sleepy and I just barely made out what he said, and I immediately fell asleep again."

Other witnesses were to give Prosecutor Beekman further information on the activities of Eleanor Mills during "the missing hours."

On the night of September 14, John J. Meaney had been the motorman on the trolley that ran from Commercial Street to the end of Easton Avenue. He had started his run at eight o'clock, and when he reached the corner of George and Carman streets, Mrs. Mills had boarded his car. She had ridden to Buccleuch Park, the end of the line. Because she

was the last passenger to get off, Meaney noticed that she
had walked toward De Russey's Lane.

A few minutes later Agnes Blust and her children, who
had been walking out on Easton Avenue, had been passed
by Mrs. Mills. "She was on Easton Avenue, going out toward
the Parker home," Mrs. Blust told Beekman. "We met her
at the last entrance to Buccleuch Park. We had to move
kind of out of the way." Mrs. Mills, who was walking at a
leisurely pace, had smiled as she stepped around the Blusts.
"Good evening," she had said cheerily.

The choir singer, who was wearing a dark dress with polka
dots, had been carrying a small parcel in the crook of her
arm. Mrs. Blust thought that it had been "wrapped in a
yellow paper." She was certain that no strangers had been
following the choir singer because she had not seen another
person on Easton Avenue for the next fifteen minutes.

But on her way back to New Brunswick, she had passed
Hall, who was headed in the same direction as Mrs. Mills.
The minister, who was walking at a brisk pace, had looked
at his watch as he approached Mrs. Blust and checked it
with the clock on the Easton Avenue Vocational School. He
had then pushed by the Blusts and strode rapidly toward the
county line. No, no one had been following him.

And what had the St. John's rector and his family been
doing previously on that fatal day?

Shortly before ten in the morning on September 14, the
Halls, Willie Stevens, and ten-year-old Frances Voorhees, the
minister's niece who was visiting her uncle, had gone mar-
keting in the family Dodge. After lunch the rector had left
for a PTA meeting at nearby Berdine's Corners and Mrs.
Hall had gone to the kitchen to make some preserves. During
the early part of the afternoon Mrs. Minnie Clark, the St.
John's Sunday school teacher, had come in for a few minutes.

A little later Hall had driven by to pick up Frances Voorhees. He wanted the child to accompany him while he distributed flowers at a local hospital.

A few minutes after the minister and his niece had left, Mrs. Hall answered the telephone. It was Mrs. Mills. After being informed that Hall was not at home, the choir singer left a message for him. "You tell him," she directed Mrs. Hall, "that there is something about the doctor's bill for my operation that I do not understand." When Hall returned home at six thirty that evening, his wife told him of Mrs. Mills' call.

As soon as supper was finished, Mrs. Hall and young Frances had gone out on the piazza for a breath of air. While they were there, the telephone had rung. "I didn't go in to answer it," Mrs. Hall explained to the prosecutor, "because I thought there were others in the house; and then it rang the second time and I went in the house and took the receiver off, and at the same time I heard Mr. Hall upstairs." When she heard her husband answer, she had replaced the receiver and rejoined Frances on the porch. She was certain that the call had come about seven o'clock.

Mrs. Hall and Frances were playing a card game in the library when the minister came downstairs. He was going out, he told his wife, to check on Mrs. Mills' medical bill. "I might as well see what it is about," he had said. He had left the house "between seven and half past." At nine o'clock Mrs. Hall had put Frances to bed and returned to the library, where she played solitaire for the next two hours. Her brother Willie, who had gone to his room after supper, came downstairs sometime during the evening to say good night.

When she retired, Mrs. Hall had left a light burning in the hall. "When anyone was out," she explained, "it was lighted until whoever was out came in." She had gotten into bed, but had been unable to fall asleep. After reading for a while she had begun to worry about her husband. Although he was out almost every night on church business, he was usually home by ten o'clock. "I could not sleep because I kept wondering when Mr. Hall would come in," she said.

She was destined to spend a restless night. "I got up in the night and came downstairs to see if by any chance he had come in and I had not heard him, and I looked around the house just to see if there was anywhere I had missed him coming in, and about half past two I was perfectly frantic about it—I did not know what could have happened."

It was then that she had awakened Willie and told him she was going to the church to see if her husband "had possibly fallen asleep there."

She had dressed in a gingham dress, a light gray coat, and a brown hat, and accompanied by her brother, had walked to George Street. As they passed the open garage, Mrs. Hall had noticed that the family's two cars were parked inside. When they arrived at St. John's, they had found the church dark and the front door locked.

Because she remembered that Hall had mentioned Mrs. Mills' medical bill, she decided to walk past the Mills house. "I thought there was some possible chance that someone was ill there and he might have gone there." However, the Mills apartment had been dark, and she and Willie had walked home. The whole trip had taken "less than half an hour."

She had entered her house through the front door and gone directly to her room, where she had undressed for bed. As far as she knew, Willie had also retired. She had not been able to sleep (it was now Friday, September 15), and toward morning had called the police.

"I asked if any casualties had been reported—the one thought in my mind was that there might have been an auto accident, and my husband might have been injured and unable to communicate with me, and I asked that question, and they said nothing had been reported." She hadn't given her name or that of her husband because the gruff policeman who answered the telephone hadn't asked for them.

After breakfast Mrs. Hall had once again gone to St. John's. There she found Mills and learned for the first time that his wife had vanished, too.

Upon returning to her house she had telephoned Fannie H. Voorhees, her husband's sister and Frances' mother, in Jersey City. When she told Mrs. Voorhees that the rector was missing, his sister had said, "I'll take the next train to New Brunswick." Mrs. Voorhees and Theodora Bonner, another of Hall's sisters, who lived in New York, had arrived at noon, and Mrs. Hall had met them at the station. It was when she drove up Carman Street that she had noticed James Mills sitting on his porch.

"Have you heard anything?" she asked.

"No, I have not," replied the sexton.

After lunch Mrs. Hall had telephoned Mr. Florence and asked him to come to the house as soon as he could. The lawyer had arrived shortly after three o'clock, and Mrs. Hall told him that her husband had gone out the night before and failed to return home. "I asked if he would get in communication with the police if he considered that the proper thing to do. He said he did." Later that day Florence reported the rector's disappearance to the police.

At seven in the evening that Friday, Mrs. Hall had telephoned Agnes W. Storer, St. John's organist, to ask her to superintend that evening's choir practice at the church. "Will you take care of the choir rehearsal tonight," she had asked, "as Mr. Hall will not be there?" When Miss Storer asked if the rector was ill, Mrs. Hall replied quickly, "No, he is out of town."

At eleven the next morning (Saturday, September 16, the day on which the bodies were to be discovered) Mrs. Hall had called Reverend Thomas Anderson Conover, the rector of St. Bernard's Church in Bernardsville, New Jersey, some twenty miles north of New Brunswick. Prior to his elevation to the pulpit of St. John's her husband had been Conover's assistant at Basking Ridge. "Edward has disappeared," she had informed the minister. When she pleaded with him to come to her house at once, he had told her that he would leave Bernardsville as soon as he could.

Twenty minutes later a reporter for the New Brunswick *Home News* had called Mrs. Hall. "He asked me if Mr. Hall was home and I said no, and then he said, 'Well, where is he?' Could I give him his address? I said, 'No.' Then he asked again when would he be back. I said, 'Why are you asking me these questions?' I was in a very nervous and frantic state at this time, and he said, 'Well, we fear something has happened to him,' and I think I said then, 'Well, don't tell me over the telephone—come here,' or something of that kind."

The reporter's call had so frightened Mrs. Hall that she asked her cousin Edwin Carpender to visit the newspaper. "I went downtown again," he later testified, "to the Home News Publishing Company to see what they wanted, and they told me that the body of Reverend Hall and a woman who they thought was Mrs. Eleanor Mills had been found murdered out near De Russey's Lane. I said, 'I want you to tell this to her lawyer, Mr. Florence,' and I went up to Mr. Florence's office and brought him back to the Home News Publishing Company, and they repeated the same thing to him."

It was then that Carpender and Florence had driven out to the Phillips farm and identified the dead man's body.

Mrs. Hall first learned of her husband's death from Carpender's wife, Elovine. The latter had gone home for a few minutes at lunch time. One of her maids had informed Mrs. Carpender that her mother-in-law had called and left a message that the minister's body had been found near De Russey's Lane. She had immediately told Mrs. Hall the news.

"She broke down completely for a few minutes," Mrs. Carpender said, "and then I told her that there were some people downstairs to see her." Quickly regaining her composure, Mrs. Hall went downstairs to greet the first of a steady stream of condolence callers.

The grisly news had spread quickly, and soon a number of people came forward to tell their stories.

One of them was Cedric A. Paulus, a student at New Brunswick High School. At 1:15 A.M. on September 15 he had walked past the New Brunswick Trust Company. Fifteen minutes later he had arrived at St. John's. He was surprised to see that two windows in the Sunday school portion of the church, which faced George Street, were brightly lit. The boy had not stopped to investigate. "I went home and went to bed," he said.

William Phillips, the night watchman of the New Jersey State College for Women, was next. About 2:30 A.M. that same morning he had heard a dog barking near the Hall residence and decided to investigate its cause. As he neared the big house, he had seen a woman enter the Hall house. "I saw her go through the driveway of Redmond Street," he told Beekman. "I noticed that the lights of the Hall house had been on all night, which was rather unusual."

Another volunteer was a New Brunswick milkman. Shortly before dawn Harry A. Kolb had driven his horse and wagon into the Hall driveway. As he approached the back porch, he had noticed that a side door had swung open so that it blocked his path. "It was open so far that I had to run ahead of it and close it or my left front wheel would have struck it." He had then left four quarts of milk on the top of the kitchen steps.

Of particular interest was the story told by one of the Halls' maids whose account of Mrs. Mills' telephone call on the evening of the murder was slightly more detailed than the story Mrs. Hall had told Beekman.

Pretty Louise Geist had been employed by the Halls since October 1921. After supper on September 14 she had been in her second-floor bedroom when the telephone rang. "When the phone first rang, I did not answer it. We never answered the phone if some member of the family was in. When it rang the second time, I answered it and the person on the other end of the wire asked for Mr. Hall." She recognized the caller's voice as that of Mrs. Mills.

"Just a moment, I will get him," she had said. Thinking that the rector was in the library, the girl had gone to the banister to call him.

She had seen Mrs. Hall at the downstairs extension. "She was coming in and had just lifted the receiver off the hook, had it halfway up her body. I said, 'This is for Mr. Hall, Mrs. Hall. Is he downstairs?' She said, 'No, Louise, isn't he upstairs?' "

At that moment the minister, who was in the bathroom, had asked if the call was for him. "Oh, it is all right," Louise had informed Mrs. Hall. "He is up here." Her mistress had then replaced the downstairs receiver and walked back to the piazza.

Louise had heard part of Hall's conversation with Mrs. Mills. "Yes, yes, yes," the rector had told his caller, "that is too bad. I was going down to the church a little later. Can't we make arrangements for later, say, about a quarter after eight?"

A few minutes afterward she had seen Hall go downstairs. "I heard him tell Mrs. Hall he was going out, he had to go out for a little while. He was going out to see about the Mills bill." She had last seen him walking around the side of the house toward Redmond Street.

Shortly after nine thirty the maid had heard a bell ring. "I knew that was the bell to close up the house," she told Beekman. She had gone downstairs and closed the shutters in the dining room and the library. When she entered the living room, she had seen Mrs. Hall playing solitaire. After saying goodnight the girl had gone to bed.

Early the next morning Louise had been awakened by the sound of the downstairs shutters. Since Hall had often opened the shutters as a signal to her that he wanted an early breakfast, she had dressed and gone to the dining room, where she saw a somewhat distraught Willie Stevens. "What are you doing up so early?" she had asked him. "I would rather not tell you," he had replied nervously. "I would rather have Mrs. Hall tell you." When the maid repeated her question, he had informed her that "something terrible happened last night, and Mrs. Hall and I have been up most of the night. Don't tell Frances I told you."

Scottish Barbara Tough had been the Halls' upstairs maid since 1916. Thursday, September 14, had been her day off, and after visiting a friend at the Parker Memorial Home, she had had supper with a cousin. She had returned home "about ten o'clock."

When she entered the house through a side door, the lights had been on in the library, the halls, and the kitchen. She had gone immediately to her third-floor bedroom without seeing any member of the family. During the night she had heard Mrs. Hall moving about. "I was wide awake, and I heard her walk from her own room to the bathroom and from the bathroom back again, and it was only a few minutes then I heard the big clock downstairs strike two." Miss Tough had then fallen asleep.

Early the next morning Mrs. Hall had told Barbara that the rector had disappeared.

Chapter 5

FIRST DAYS

*(Saturday, September 16, through
Thursday, September 28, 1922)*

As reports of the double murder spread through New Brunswick, it quickly became the only topic of the day. The fact
that Mustapha Kemal Pasha and his Turkish Nationalists
had just massacred two thousand Greek residents of Smyrna
faded into insignificance next to the tantalizing news emanating from De Russey's Lane. The newspapermen who had
begun to flock into town from all over the United States
added to the general excitement, and it was a rare citizen
who was not interviewed at least once by enterprising reporters looking for a different angle.

And indeed there were plenty of new stories, most of them
about the torrid relationship between Mrs. Mills and the
rector.

Jimmy Mills, however, assured one inquisitive newsman
that he took no stock in any of the juicy stories that were
making the rounds. As far as he was concerned, his wife's
interest in Hall had been sublimely platonic. That was why
he had never discussed the frequency of her dates with the
minister. He was certain that Reverend Hall was not one to
steal another man's spouse. Besides, he had always been of
the opinion that Mrs. Hall had usually accompanied the
couple on their many afternoon drives.

As for Frances Hall, she insisted that she did not know why her husband had met Mrs. Mills on Thursday evening. She was certain, however, that he had not been romantically involved with the choir singer. "I worshiped Mr. Hall and trusted him absolutely," she said fervently. "I still believe in him. He did nothing wrong. His only aim was to help other people."

On Sunday, September 17, Somerset Prosecutor Beekman paid a call on Mrs. Hall at her home. Then on Monday he suddenly announced to the press corps that he was now working on what he termed "a solid lead."

Since four people who lived near De Russey's Lane had informed him that they had heard shots or women's screams at midnight on Thursday, the prosecutor reasoned that Hall and Mrs. Mills might have been killed by a jealous couple. As he saw it, the unknown assailants had followed the minister and the choir singer to the Phillips farm. The scratches on Hall's arms had occurred when the clergyman threw himself between Mrs. Mills and the other woman.

Because of the careful way in which the bodies had been arranged, the police, however, still inclined to the theory that the couple had been murdered in New Brunswick and taken across the county line. As time passed, this theory was to result in a tremendous amount of confusion over which county and which prosecutor was responsible for the investigation.

Early Monday afternoon, September 18, at a conference in Middlesex Prosecutor Joseph E. Stricker's office in New Brunswick, it was decided to transfer the investigation's headquarters to that city. Accordingly, Beekman ordered Detective Totten to turn over to Stricker the exhibits which he and Sheriff Conkling had found near the bodies. On Tuesday, the nineteenth, Totten received a receipt for two large pocket handkerchiefs, a pair of men's eyeglasses, a driver's license, an automobile registration, Masonic and YMCA membership cards, a calling card, and sixty-one cents in change.

With Stricker now in command, it was widely predicted that an arrest could be expected momentarily. This rumor was strengthened by the fact that late Monday night a carload of five detectives had left New Brunswick for an undisclosed destination. The reporters, who were instructed not to follow the officers, were told that one of the Hall servants was to be interrogated.

The consensus among the newspaper fraternity was that Willie Stevens, who had just been questioned and admitted owning a .32-caliber revolver,[1] was the prime suspect. He had hated the rector, local gossip had it, because Hall had refused to increase his allowance under a trust created for him by his brother, Henry Stevens, and sister, Mrs. Hall.

Although the reporters had been led by an overexuberant member of Stricker's staff to believe that the anticipated arrest would be made by nine thirty on Tuesday morning, the hour came and went without any comment from the prosecutor. But Stricker took advantage of the news lull to announce that the extensive publicity the investigation had received had hurt the police in their efforts to solve the crime. "If you would leave us alone," he complained peevishly to the reporters who constantly dogged his footsteps, "we would do a lot better."

Earlier that same Tuesday, while services for Mrs. Mills were being conducted at the Hubbard Funeral Home, the September terms of the Somerset and Middlesex Grand Juries began in Somerville and New Brunswick respectively. "You are to treat the crime as occurring in this county," Justice Charles W. Parker ordered the Somerset jurors. But in Middlesex County, Justice James J. Berigan told the new

---

[1] It was later discovered that the weapon had not been in working condition for more than a year before the murders.

panel, "The honor of the county is involved, and it is necessary to take every possible action to reach a solution."

On Thursday, September 21, Mrs. Hall released her first statement to the press. Miss Sally Peters, who had been the maid of honor at the Halls' wedding, told the reporters she had been authorized to say that it was the widow's opinion that robbery had been the motive for the double slaying. Not only had the rector been wearing his valuable gold watch, but he had also carried about fifty dollars in his wallet with which to pay for Mrs. Mills' operation. Neither the money nor the watch had been found on Hall's body by the police.

The next morning—Friday, the twenty-second—Charlotte Mills, not to be outdone by Mrs. Hall, told the reporters that like Beekman, she believed that jealousy and not robbery had been the cause of her mother's death. "Some women in the parish," she volunteered, "did not like to see the pastor giving her so much responsibility and placing so much dependence upon her."

Furthermore, the girl stated that she did not particularly like the austere Mrs. Hall, who had once been her Sunday school teacher. Not only had Mrs. Hall insisted on remaining on the porch whenever the Halls visited the Millses, but she had disapproved of Charlotte. "Mrs. Hall does not like flappers," Charlotte explained, "and I'm a flapper."

Charlotte recalled that her mother had attended a tea at the Halls' several weeks before the murders. When Mrs. Mills returned home, she had become deathly ill. "If it was not for the fact that it happened at the house of Mrs. Hall, who is such a good friend of mine," Mrs. Mills had told Charlotte, "I would have suspected that someone was trying to poison me."

Sunday, September 24, was a hot and humid day. As New Brunswick's burghers were reading of Georges Carpentier's surprise knockout in Paris by a Senegalese fighter named Battling Sik, Pearl Bahmer, the girl who had found the bodies in De Russey's Lane, was being arrested on a charge of incorrigibility filed by her father. At the same time Stricker was questioning Ray Schneider, her companion on that fateful morning eight days earlier, about his activities on the night of the murders.

Schneider, an unemployed roustabout who lived near Buccleuch Park, had spent the early evening hours of Thursday, September 14, with Pearl. After walking down Easton Avenue as far as Landing Lane the youth had taken Pearl home at nine thirty. He had then met two friends—Clifford Hayes and Leon Kaufmann—and the three boys had walked through Buccleuch Park. Although they reached a spot a half mile away from where the bodies were to be found some thirty-six hours later, they had not heard any screams or shots.

Jim Mills passed the long Sunday, the second since the murders, puttering around the church. He still disclaimed any knowledge of the many rumors that his wife had been the cause of trouble in St. John's choir. But his views were not shared by many. For example, according to the church's music director, it had taken all of Hall's diplomacy to keep peace in his choir. On one occasion Mrs. Mills had been badly scratched by a contralto colleague when both women tried to pick up the same Book of Psalms.

The new week was to prove no more productive than the preceding one. Instead of a solution, it succeeded only in producing more questions—as well as a host of confusing answers.

Stricker spent all of Monday morning continuing his interrogation of Pearl Bahmer. The girl, who had first told the prosecutor the day before that she had seen a gold watch and chain near the minister's body, now insisted that she had been mistaken. The police were also perplexed by her statement that she had not recognized Hall's body when she first saw it. She had been baptized by the minister in 1921, when her family transferred from St. Peter's to St. John's. In fact, Hall had visited her home three times in order to complete her transfer papers.

Pearl's home life had not been placid. She had not gotten along with her stepmother, and several weeks before the murders had moved in with a next-door neighbor. On September 11, three days before the crime, she had written a letter to her stepmother, ordering her to leave the house in two days or she would live to regret it. When Mrs. Bahmer failed to take the threat seriously, Pearl had thrown a brick through the living room window. It was this incident that had led to her arrest as an incorrigible minor.

Although the girl was scheduled to be arraigned shortly in Children's Court, Stricker ordered her released when her father suddenly withdrew his charges. At an impromptu press conference on the courthouse steps the prosecutor revealed that neither Pearl nor Ray Schneider had touched the bodies before the police arrived. He was firmly convinced, he said, that the young couple were telling the truth. But whether they were or not, one thing was certain: the investigation had ground to a frustrating halt.

Then suddenly on Tuesday morning Millie Opie, the Millses' obliging—and observant—neighbor, gave the newspapermen a field day. Her statements put the killings back in the headlines, crowding out the news from Greece that King Constantine had abdicated in favor of Crown Prince George. Hall and the choir singer, Miss Opie told reporters, had been meeting at the Mills apartment three or four afternoons a week. The minister usually drove up Carman Street and parked his car across the way from the house.

According to the dressmaker, the Millses had quarreled frequently. On one occasion Miss Opie had been talking to

Mrs. Mills when the latter's husband came home from work. Seeing that his wife was dressed to go out, he had barked, "Now, where are you going? Over to the church again, I suppose?" Mrs. Mills had appeared irritated. "Yes, I'm going to the church!" she had snapped.

When her husband complained that she did more for St. John's than she did for him, Mrs. Mills said angrily, "Well, why shouldn't I? I care more for Mr. Hall's little finger than I do for your whole body!"

Residents of New Brunswick looked knowingly at one another when they read the story. Hadn't they known it all along!

While Miss Opie was entertaining the press, Mills had been questioned once again by Stricker's staff. When he left the courthouse, the sexton complained bitterly at the grilling he had received. "They made me go over my story again and again," he said. "Two or three detectives would ask me questions until they got tired, and then they would turn me over to two or three more who would ask me the same questions. They kept that up all day, but I didn't change my story. I'm innocent, and they can't get anything on me."

When asked about Miss Opie's statement that his wife had said she cared more about the minister's little finger than her husband's entire body, he retorted angriy, "I don't remember her saying that."

"What would you have done if you found out that Mrs. Mills and Hall had been intimate?" one reporter asked him.

"I would have gone to Mr. Hall and spoken to him about it," was the phlegmatic reply.

"And what would you have done about Mrs. Mills?" the reporter persisted.

"I would have told her that she would have to quit or I would get a divorce."

Stricker, who was resting his hopes of a quick solution on finding the rector's missing watch, revealed that he had not been able to learn its number or make. The heavy gold timepiece, which had been given to Hall after his ordination, had been enclosed in a hunting case. Originally wound by a key, it had been converted by him into a stem-winder. Descriptions of the watch had been sent to all pawnshops in the area, but none had reported seeing it.

On Wednesday, September 27, Somerset County Prosecutor Beekman was back in the news. Obviously annoyed by Stricker's growing prominence in the case, he called a noon press conference. "Twelve days of investigation," he told the score of reporters who responded to his invitation, "have not produced the slightest evidence of the identity of the slayer or the motive for the crime."

Because of this stagnation he had decided to assume a more active role. "I have applied to Supreme Court Justice Charles W. Parker for authorization to exhume Mrs. Mills' body," he revealed. "Maybe an autopsy will tell us more than we know now."

The Somerset prosecutor also disposed of several theories as to the motivation for the crimes. There was no indication, he asserted, that the murdered couple had been killed by either thieves or blackmailers. As for the persistent rumors that the Ku Klux Klan had been back of the slayings, he tried to scotch them once and for all. "We have no evidence to that effect. We have had reports of that, and we have devoted part of our investigation to such theories, but nothing has developed to justify such a belief."

An hour later Charlotte Mills, who also felt that twelve days of investigation had proved very little and who showed every indication of being as strong-willed as her mother, gave reporters copies of a letter which she had just sent to Governor Edward I. Edwards.

"Dear Governor," the girl had written, "I am Charlotte Mills of New Brunswick. My mother, as you know, was murdered two weeks ago, and it seems to me that the investigation is not bringing results. I have received letters from strangers saying that the political gang is running things. Can that be true? As we have no means whatever to get legal help, is there not some way, dear Governor, to help me find the murderer of my mother?"

The next morning—Thursday, September 28—Middlesex County's Board of Freeholders voted to offer a reward of one thousand dollars for information leading to the arrest and conviction of the murderer. There was one string attached— the money was not to be paid if the crime was shown to have taken place outside of Middlesex. In announcing the decision the Board urged Somerset County to offer a similar inducement. "It's about time something like this was done," Jim Mills commented.

While the freeholders were voting, Mrs. Hall and Willie Stevens were being questioned again by Stricker. They were brought to the prosecutor's office in such secrecy that the reporters did not learn of their visit until they were about to leave the courthouse.

Willie flared up as the eager newsmen surrounded him. "I want you fellows to understand," he shouted, "that I don't want to be referred to as 'Willie' any more. I'm not a half-wit, as you have been saying, and I'm not a sissy." To prove the latter point, he pulled out a briar pipe and shoved it under one scribe's nose.

The rest of the day also proved eventful. In the early afternoon Justice Parker signed an order authorizing the exhumation of Eleanor Mills' body. Several hours later the rector's will, which had been executed on June 17, 1920, was offered for probate in the Middlesex Surrogate's Court. As expected, it left everything to Mrs. Hall.

Chapter 6

THE AUTOPSIES

(Friday, September 29, through Thursday, October 5, 1922)

Two weeks had now passed since the double killing. The officials of two counties were still investigating. The principals in the case to date were still being questioned without any appreciable results. The case itself was being edged off the front pages of the newspapers by the political maneuvers in New York, where the State Democratic Convention was preparing to nominate Alfred E. Smith for governor. Where to turn?

One place was to the victims themselves. Perhaps they could reveal something to point to their own murderers.

On Friday, September 29, Mrs. Mills' body was disinterred at Van Liew Cemetery and taken to Hubbard's funeral parlor. Two physicians—Runkle Hegeman of Somerville and Arthur L. Smith of New Brunswick—who had been appointed jointly by Beekman and Stricker, performed the autopsy.

"I found," Hegeman reported, "that Mrs. Mills had been shot three times in the head, each bullet having penetrated the brain, one having passed through the brain and out the other side, and the other two lying in the skull cavity."

The choir singer's head had been all but severed by some sharp instrument. "The throat had been cut apparently from left to right," Hegeman observed, "a very long, deep cut, severing all of the skin of the neck except four inches in the mid-line in the back. The muscles were cut down to the spinal column. Both large arteries and veins carrying blood to and from the brain were severed. The windpipe was severed and the gullet, or esophagus, was severed."

When the wound in Mrs. Mills' throat was opened, it was noticed that the larynx was retracted upward. Hegeman was convinced that the cut, which was so deep that the woman's backbone could easily be seen, had been inflicted with a very sharp knife. "The line of the skin cut," he observed, "was smooth and not jagged, as it would be if it were a dull or nicked instrument."

Dr. Smith turned over the two .32-caliber bullets he and Hegeman had found in Mrs. Mills' skull to Detective Totten as soon as they had been removed. The only other marks he had noticed on the body were a wound on the upper lip and scratches on both arms below the elbow. When the two physicians had finished their examination, copies of their joint report were promptly forwarded to both Beekman and Stricker.

Governor Edwards was jubilant over the results of the autopsy. Things would now move, he prophesied. He revealed that he had ordered Beekman and Stricker to co-operate with each other in investigating the crime. "The situation has been confusing," he told reporters, "because of the fact that the bodies were found just over the county line in Somerset County, and no one knows where the crime was committed. This has made it difficult for the authorities of each county to go ahead, but from now on there will be closer co-operation."

Edwards also distributed copies of a letter he had written to Charlotte Mills, in reply to hers, in which he promised that he would "leave no stone unturned" to solve the mystery of her mother's death. He had ordered the superintendent of the New Jersey State Police to assist the two county prosecutors in every way he could, even if it meant putting the whole force on the case. As for Charlotte's charges that the investigation was being stalled by politics, he assured the girl that "the shocked conscience of the State of New Jersey will never be satisfied until the murderer or murderers of your mother are apprehended."

But Charlotte Mills was apparently not the only one who was dissatisfied with the way the case was progressing. On the same day that Mrs. Mills' body was disinterred, it was learned that Mrs. Hall had retained Timothy N. Pfeiffer, a former assistant district attorney of New York County, to investigate her husband's death. Mr. Pfeiffer, a tall, bespectacled young man with a serious mien, had been associated with Samuel Seabury in the celebrated Lockwood banking investigation.

Not to be outdone by Beekman, Stricker had decided to hold an autopsy of his own. But on Sunday, October 1, a Brooklyn Supreme Court justice refused to permit the Middlesex prosecutor to exhume Hall's body because the corpses had been found in Somerset County. The justice suggested that the request for the exhumation order be submitted by Beekman.

While the latter, influenced by the governor's order to cooperate with his Middlesex confrere, was preparing the required papers, Mrs. Hall asked for permission to have a representative present at the autopsy. Her request was immediately denied.

The Phillips farm was a busy place that day. In addition to the usual Sunday crowds, county detectives, aided by the New Brunswick police, were raking the leaves in a desperate search to find the murder weapons. They were hindered in their efforts by the hordes of curious bystanders who flocked to the area.

"Some of them tore down the front porch of the old house, while others ripped apart the platform at the rear," one reporter noted. "One literally tore out a windowpane, entered, and opened the front door. Hundreds of persons went through the rooms, all furnished, and in the search for souvenirs, destroyed a quantity of furnishings."

There was a flurry of excitement on Monday morning when it was learned that after the murders Mrs. Hall had sent some clothing to Philadelphia to be cleaned and dyed. A detective was immediately sent to Bornot's cleaning and dyeing plant in that city. He was told by one of the firm's clerks that some garments had been received from Mrs. Hall on September 20 and returned to New Brunswick four days later. However, they had contained no stains and they had been dyed black, not cleaned.

During the day Charlotte, who was attending classes at New Brunswick High, was taken to Stricker's office. "They sent for me," she said later, "merely to ask me why I had complained to Governor Edwards about the manner in which the investigation was being handled. They asked me if I did not believe they were doing all that could be done in the matter, and I told them that I did not feel they were. I said I wanted the murderer of my mother arrested, and I went to Governor Edwards to ask him to assign Detective Ellis Parker of Burlington County[1] to run him down."

She had been informed that it was impossible for Parker to be sent to New Brunswick because he was assigned to another county. "Then I told those men at Prosecutor Stricker's office that I did not propose to permit them to annoy me any longer by sending for me to ask me silly questions." She also revealed that she had just retained a woman lawyer by the name of Florence M. North "to protect me."

At noon a reporter asked Beekman whether he had thought of searching the two wells on the Phillips farm for the missing murder weapons. "No," he replied, "but by gum,

---

[1] Parker, who was later to assume an unusual role in the investigation, enjoyed a nationwide reputation for solving difficult murder cases.

that's a crackerjack idea! I never thought of that before!"
But by the time a well digger, who was immediately hired
to drain the cisterns, could get to work, reporters armed with
shovels, rakes, and axes had done the job for him. No weapons were found.

On Tuesday afternoon an order directing the trustees of
Greenwood Cemetery to permit the disinterment of Hall's
body was finally signed. The directive also authorized an
autopsy and removal of any organs that might be helpful to
the New Jersey authorities. A Middlesex detective who had
gone to Brooklyn for the proceeding left immediately to
serve a copy of the order upon the cemetery officials.

Two days later the metal casket bearing Hall's remains was
chipped out of the brick and mortar that sealed the Stevens
crypt in Greenwood Cemetery. A Brooklyn patrolman escorted the exhumed body to the Kings County Hospital
morgue, where Drs. Hegeman and Smith were waiting. Because of Beekman's objections no newsmen were present
when the autopsy began at two forty-five that afternoon. A
little more than an hour later the two doctors finished their
unpleasant task.

As the reporters thronged around him, Hegeman stated
that the autopsy had not been very enlightening. "We found
nothing particularly new," he explained. "Dr. Hall was
killed by a bullet which entered his head near the right temple and came out at the back of the neck on the left side.
The point of exit was three and a half inches lower than the
entrance. The bullet went through the brain and was apparently .32-caliber. There were no other bullet wounds on
the body."

However, a series of abrasions had been found on both of
Hall's hands, particularly on the back of the right index
and left little finger. "On the ulnar side of the left palm,"
Hegeman said, "is a small abrasion, one eighth inch in
diameter, with clotted blood. On the palm surface of the

wrist, one inch above the palm, is an abrasion, with ecchymosis or scab formation, triangular in shape, five eighths inch long. Three inches above the wrist is a triangular abrasion three quarters by one half inch." Another small bruise was noted on the tip of the left ear.

On the right calf, five inches below the knee joint, Dr. Hegeman had found "a perforating wound, one quarter of an inch in diameter, with the skin abraded above and below." Unlike the abrasions on the dead man's hands, this was "a sort of a puncture wound, going into the fat, but not extending down to the muscle." It was his opinion that it had been caused either by a blunt instrument or by a fall on a tree stump. As for the abrasions, "they might have been caused by contact with bushes or in a struggle."

Although the doctors were of the opinion that Mrs. Mills had been killed last, her body had been more decomposed than that of the clergyman. "When I examined the body of Mrs. Mills," Hegeman noted, "the outer skin had softened due to deterioration following death. It rubbed off at slight touch." He attributed this to the fact that the embalming of her body by Hubbard "had not been very successful."

As the minister's body was being returned to Greenwood Cemetery, copies of the Hegeman-Smith report were sent to both Beekman and Stricker.

Chapter 7

AN ARREST AT LAST

(Friday, October 6, through Thursday, October 12, 1922)

The fall of 1922 was producing more than its share of macabre news. On Friday, October 6, most people in New Brunswick were diverted from the Hall-Mills case by an Associated Press report that Bennie Swim, a twenty-year-old New Hampshire youth, had just been hanged twice for the murders of his cousin and her husband. The boy was still living after the first drop, and it had been necessary to hang him again.

Perhaps because the city's attention was temporarily focused elsewhere, Beekman and Stricker decided to spirit Willie Stevens away from his home for further questioning. At seven that evening, while Mrs. Hall was conversing with a group of St. John's ladies in her drawing room, three cars filled with detectives drove up to her house.

Middlesex County Detective Ferdinand David, who was in the first vehicle, pulled into the driveway and rang the rear bell. When Willie opened the door, the detective ordered him to enter his car. He was not even allowed to notify Mrs. Hall of his departure.

Willie was driven at once to the tower of the Somerset County Court House, where he was interrogated by Beekman and a squad of plain-clothesmen until two in the morning. During his questioning he was shown the clothing that his brother-in-law and Mrs. Mills had been wearing on the night of their deaths.

It was not until bedtime that Willie's absence was noticed by his sister. At midnight she asked Sally Peters to report his disappearance to the police. Miss Peters drove down to headquarters and notified the desk sergeant that Willie could not be located. While a half dozen patrolmen were combing New Brunswick for a trace of the missing man, Detective David brought him back to Nichol Avenue.

At nine the next morning Timothy Pfeiffer, Mrs. Hall's new attorney, complained bitterly to Beekman about the cavalier treatment Willie had received. He informed the prosecutor that Mrs. Hall was under the care of her physician and asked whether she could expect "the same kind of treatment."

Beekman was less than apologetic. "Why, of course we wouldn't treat a woman the same way," he retorted sharply.

As Pfeiffer left Beekman's office, he was surrounded by the waiting reporters. The lawyer castigated "the bunch of Turks" who had kidnaped Willie. "That kind of investigation is all right when they are beginning to work on a solution," he told the newsmen, "but William Stevens has been at his home all the time since the murders were committed. He was given the third degree. The detectives only stopped short of force. Stupidity having fallen flat, they are now using brutal methods."

Beekman, who maintained that Willie had been "treated courteously," characterized Pfeiffer's outburst as belying his promise to co-operate with the authorities. However, although he claimed that Willie had supplied some new information, the Somerset prosecutor still didn't expect any immediate arrests.

But Governor Edwards did. At noon on Saturday he announced, "This murder must be cleaned up. There has been too much time lost already. I have sent Colonel

Schwartzkopf[1] to New Brunswick to get the murderer. He has been ordered not to come back until he does. The next time I see him, I expect that the murderer will have been arrested."

It was a bold statement, but fortunately, for the governor, soon forgotten because of the events that were to follow it.

On Sunday, October 8, the out-of-town reporters, who had hoped to see the last game of the 1922 World Series between the Yankees and the Giants, changed their plans abruptly when Assistant Middlesex Prosecutor John E. Toolan informed them that a break in the case could be expected before the day ended. "I think that we will have something to give out late tonight," he prophesied.

Earlier that morning Raymond Schneider, Clifford Hayes, Leon Kaufmann, and Pearl Bahmer had been brought to Stricker's office. Schneider and Pearl were, of course, the New Brunswick couple who had found the murder victims. The other two were acquaintances of Schneider's.

After grilling Schneider and Hayes for twelve hours, the detectives concentrated on young Kaufmann. The sixteen-year-old boy had an interesting story to tell about some events on the night of the murder.

He had met Schneider and Hayes in front of the Rivoli Theatre on George Street at 10:30 P.M. on September 14. He had joined the two young men, who were busy following Pearl Bahmer and a drunken man. "As we neared Seminary Place and George Street," he told Stricker, "Schneider took his coat off and said that he was going to fight the man. I understood he was going to fight him over Pearl Bahmer."

As Pearl and her unsteady companion walked toward the Raritan River, Kaufmann was surprised to see that Hayes was armed. "He took a pistol from a holster which he carried

1 Colonel H. Norman Schwartzkopf, the superintendent of the New Jersey State Police Constabulary, who was, a decade later, to play a prominent role in the Lindbergh kidnaping case.

under his sweater and started to follow them," he said. When
Schneider warned Hayes that the man was a bad actor,
Hayes had pointed to his pistol and said, "Don't mind, we're
protected with this."

At that moment the man had turned around and snarled,
"What are you doing here?" Hayes' pugnaciousness had vanished abruptly. "I want to put in a couple of hours of sleep
here," he had stammered.

Pearl and her escort had walked back to George Street and
then headed toward the west end of the city. When the three
boys reached the College Avenue entrance to Buccleuch
Park, the couple had disappeared. "We walked farther west
on George Street until we were opposite the old pavilion
near the Raritan River in the park. Then Schneider and
Hayes started into the park. I followed them. They walked
about one hundred yards to the house occupied by Christ
Huebner, the special policeman in the park. They said they
were looking for Pearl Bahmer and the man."

After walking around Huebner's house the youths had left
the park "at the old entrance on College Avenue between
Huntington Street and the culvert." Failing to find Pearl or
her companion in the neighborhood, they had walked back
to the park. "That was about eleven o'clock," Kaufmann
said, "and I went home." He didn't know what Schneider
and Hayes had done after he left them.

Pearl Bahmer, who had been waiting in the anteroom
while Kaufmann was being questioned, was next. She said
that Schneider had brought her home at nine thirty on the
night of the murders. Her father had met her on the stoop of
her house and ordered her to accompany him as he walked
off a drunk.

"Several times during the walk," she recalled, "I caught
glimpses of three youths following us. After a while I recognized them as Raymond Schneider, Clifford Hayes, and Leon
Kaufmann. They came up to us and began to abuse my
father. Raymond took off his coat, and after abusing my

father, said that he was going to give him a thrashing. But
he didn't carry out his threat."

It was 12:45 A.M. when Pearl left Stricker's office. An hour
later one of the prosecutor's aides sent a note to the tired reporters who had been waiting all day for a news break. "We
are working on a definite lead," it read, "but do not wish
to divulge the nature of same at this time. When the matter
is fully worked out, we will give out the news."

As a large crowd began to form around the courthouse, it
was rumored that Schneider had signed a statement accusing
Hayes of killing the minister and the choir singer. The
couple had been shot under the mistaken impression that
they were Pearl Bahmer and her father.

At noon on Monday, October 9, a press release was distributed to the newspapermen in New Brunswick. "Upon information in the prosecutor's office, obtained from Schneider
and other witnesses, we feel obliged under the situation to
prefer a charge of murder against one Clifford Hayes. Raymond Schneider will be held as a material witness awaiting
further developments in the case." An hour later Hayes was
on his way to the Somerset County Jail.

Beekman, who was now in full charge of the case, had
very little to say. As he emerged from Stricker's office, he
was besieged by the revitalized reporters.

If the killings were the result of mistaken identity, why
was Mrs. Mills' throat cut?

Where were the murder weapons?

Why were the slain woman's love letters scattered around
the bodies?

Why had the corpses been laid out so carefully?

Had Hayes confessed?

Outside of admitting that it had been Schneider's statement that had led to Hayes' arrest, the Somerset prosecutor
refused to answer any questions.

An hour after Hayes' arrest his father and an attorney

visited him in his cell. "He appeared to be exceptionally
cool in the face of the grave charges against him," the lawyer
said. "He asked me, 'If I killed Mr. Hall and Mrs. Mills, do
you think that I would be fool enough to stay around New
Brunswick for three weeks?' "

The boy had been bitter about Schneider's reported accusations. "I can't understand how he could have said those
things about me," he had complained to his father. "If he
really did say them, he lied. Schneider knows I had nothing
to do with the murders. I can't believe that he was in his
right mind when he made this alleged confession.

"I am unable to say what they did to Schneider before he
signed the paper in which it has been reported he accused
me of doing the shooting. They kept me awake all night.
They would ask questions every few minutes so that I could
not sleep. I am innocent. Those officials know it and so does
everybody else in town."

Almost everyone in New Brunswick agreed with him.
James Mills said he was convinced that Hayes was not guilty.
"I know how long periods of questioning can break a man
down," he explained. "I've gone through it myself."

The suspect's twenty-four-year-old brother was sure that
the police were barking up the wrong tree. "They may swing
my brother for the crime," he told reporters, "but they'll
never prove he killed Rector Hall or Mrs. Mills. I slept with
him on the night of this murder, and he slept as sound as a
baby. It looks to me that the governor got after these officials
and they had made good by arresting somebody and they
made my brother 'the goat' on Raymond Schneider's word."

By Tuesday morning resentment against Hayes' arrest
had become widespread. Its principal target was Frank F.
Kirby, the Middlesex detective who was credited with in-
ducing Schneider to make his statement. When Kirby returned by train to New Brunswick from Somerville at 10
A.M. after a fruitless attempt to obtain a confession from

Hayes, he was met at the railroad station by an angry group of local residents. By the time he had walked the four blocks to the courthouse, the crowd had swelled to such proportions that it was impossible for the detective to reach his destination.

Frightened by the threats that filled the air, Kirby suddenly turned on his heels and ran back toward the railroad station. The crowd followed him, throwing loose paving stones, rocks, and bricks at him. Miraculously untouched by the flying missiles, the detective reached the depot and barricaded himself in its baggage room. Several railroad employees rushed over and begged the crowd to disperse. Within a matter of minutes New Brunswick's entire force of eight policemen arrived and escorted the beleaguered man to headquarters.

Shortly after Kirby's rescue Prosecutor Beekman released Schneider's statement to the press. It had been obtained, he boasted, after thirty hours of almost continuous interrogation. Although the young man had told two untrue stories prior to his implication of Clifford Hayes, Beekman assured the reporters that the latest version would stand up in court.

Schneider's statement flatly accused Hayes of killing Hall and Mrs. Mills. "I and Clifford Hayes," it read, "left the Rivoli Theatre about 10:35 P.M. Thursday night and followed Mr. Bahmer and his daughter, Pearl, up George Street, then to Easton Avenue, where we lost sight of them. Hayes and I went through De Russey's gully and when, about three quarters of the way up, we came across a man and woman, Hayes said to me, 'There they are,' and pulled a gun from his pocket and fired three or four times."

As soon as he heard the shots, Schneider had run toward De Russey's Lane. When he reached the dirt road, he slowed down to a walk and headed in the direction of Easton Avenue. It was then that Leon Kaufmann had driven up and asked him to go for a ride. "I told him that Hayes was coming, and we waited. Shortly Hayes came along and we all then drove down to Buccleuch, when Hayes and I got out, Kaufmann going home. Hayes and I remained together a short time and we parted, Hayes going home, and I, too."

Although he had been only four feet away from Hayes when the shooting started, he did not know what had happened to his friend's gun. He had run away as soon as the firing started. "All I am sorry now," he concluded, "is that I did not report this sooner." The short statement was witnessed by two detectives.

But neither the statement nor Beekman's enthusiasm over it succeeded in convincing many people in Middlesex County that the case was closed. Assistant Prosecutor Toolan reflected the general consensus of Middlesex opinion. "This murder has not been cleared up," he said. "We have not quit our efforts to learn whether the families of Mr. Hall and Mrs. Mills know more than thus far they have seen fit to tell us."

Stricker was just as emphatic. "We have only scratched the surface of this case as yet," the Middlesex prosecutor told reporters who expressed doubt that the real killer was languishing in the Somerset County Jail.

It was soon obvious to everyone that the two counties were in total disagreement as to the wisdom of Hayes' detention. Despite Stricker's strenuous objections, Somerset County Prosecutor Beekman had insisted on arresting the boy. When skeptical newsmen pointed out to him that without the murder weapons and the rector's missing watch he would have to rely squarely on the testimony of a chronic liar, he snapped peevishly, "We have other witnesses, but I'm not telling you who they are."

"Have you eliminated the Hall and Mills families?" he was asked.

"I'm not going to sit here and discuss this case any further," he retorted.

As more than two hundred people called at the Hayes home to express their sympathy, the creation of a "Justice Fund" to pay for the prisoner's legal defense was announced.

Saturday, October 14, was designated as "Hayes Tag Day," and all residents of New Brunswick were urged to wear pasteboard tags embossed with Ruskin's maxim, "The truth in one's heart does not fear the lie on the other's tongue."

Shortly before noon Hayes was officially charged with the murders of the clergyman and the choir singer by Justice of the Peace William R. Sutphen. As soon as Sutphen had completed the legal formalities, Hayes was interviewed by his lawyer in the visitors' room of the county jail. "Hayes said he was not anywhere near the Phillips farm on the night that Schneider charged he shot Mr. Hall and Mrs. Mills," the attorney told the press after the conference with his client. "He accounted for every minute of his time on the night the rector and Mrs. Mills were killed."

An hour later the reporters rushed back to New Brunswick. Nicholas Bahmer, Pearl's father, had just been lodged in the Middlesex County Jail on his daughter's claim that he had had sexual relations with her.

Although he denied the incest charge, the tall, fair-haired saloonkeeper readily admitted that he had been carrying a .45-caliber revolver on the night of the murders. He had borrowed the weapon from a man, whom he refused to identify, for the purpose of "gunning for Schneider," whom he believed was the author of some threatening letters he had recently received.

The newsmen who crowded around Bahmer's tiny cell asked him if he believed that Hayes had shot the murdered couple. "I could get down on my knees and swear that Hayes didn't kill them," he answered fervently.

If Hayes wasn't the guilty party, who did he think was the murderer? "I have an opinion," he said, "but I don't want to say anything about it."

Five minutes later he lost his reserve and identified Schneider as the killer. "I know that boy," he explained simply.

As soon as Pearl's incest complaint against her father had been filed, Stricker decided that in view of her repeated threats to kill herself, she, too, would be better off in jail. Accordingly, he revived the incorrigibility charge against her and scheduled a hearing seven days hence.

When she flounced into the Middlesex County Jail, she was wearing three rings that Schneider had given her and carrying an armful of cheap magazines. "I'll be out of here in a jiffy," she forecasted as her cell door clanged shut behind her.

A lot of people were suddenly going to jail, but none of the incarcerations seemed to be moving the Hall-Mills case toward a solution—and very soon at least one of the prisoners would be free.

It was not until the evening of Wednesday, October 11, that Detective Totten, who, unlike Beekman, did not believe Schneider's statement, visited the youth in his cell, where he was being held as a material witness. For more than two hours he tried to convince Schneider to change his story. Shortly after nine thirty the detective, a strong believer in the theory that confessions come easier in the dark, turned off all the lights in the cell.

The stratagem soon paid dividends. An hour later Totten called out to Warden James Major, "Jim, come here! Ray has admitted that he lied!"

Schneider said that he had decided to tell the truth when he saw Mr. and Mrs. Hayes visiting their son earlier in the day. "I could see them from my cell, where I stood looking through the bars. When I saw Mrs. Hayes with that big pie and Mr. Hayes and Joe with a lot of other things for Cliff, all the good times Cliff and I had together since we were kids came back to my mind and I thought what a skunk I was, framing him like that. And when I saw in the papers that my own mother had taken it as hard as Mrs. Hayes, I felt very badly."

Beekman immediately contacted Hayes' attorney and volunteered to release the boy at once. However, since the lawyer insisted on a formal hearing to clear his client's name, Beekman scheduled one for one thirty the next afternoon. The proceeding, from which the press was barred, was held in the reception room of the county jail. After Justice of the Peace Sutphen had read Schneider's sworn retraction, he dismissed the charges against Hayes.

Just before leaving the courtroom Hayes walked over and held out his hand to his erstwhile accuser. Schneider, who had recoiled in fear as his long-time friend approached, pumped Hayes' hand vigorously when he saw that he was not going to be attacked.

In less than an hour Cliff Hayes was back in New Brunswick. As the car in which he was riding pulled up in front of his home, the street was jammed with the delirious denizens of the Sixth Ward. With his collie Rex barking joyously at his heels, Hayes fought his way through the crowd to climb the stairs to his front porch, where his parents and brother were waiting for him.

Schneider's father, who was sitting in the Hayes living room, told the boy that he and his wife had prayed that their son would eventually tell the truth.

Chapter 8

OLD CLUES AND NEW LEADS

(Friday, October 13, through Sunday, October 22, 1922)

Friday the thirteenth!

More than four weeks had passed since the murders without a single important clue having been unearthed. All that
the monthlong investigation had produced was one short-
lived arrest, a wealth of contradictory statements by the authorities, and periodic shifting of responsibility between
Middlesex and Somerset counties. Everyone's patience was
strained to the breaking point.

Tim Pfeiffer was the first to vent his spleen in public. On
Friday afternoon the lawyer called a press conference. When
all the reporters had filed into the spacious living room of
the big house on Nichol Avenue, Pfeiffer distributed copies
of a letter he had sent to Governor Edwards earlier in the
day.

The sharply critical communication called for "a thoroughly comprehensive, intelligent, and coherent investigation of the hideous crime." What he termed "the bungling
stupidity of the officials of two counties" had not only failed
to solve the murders, but had resulted in public resentment
against Mrs. Hall.

"The evidence is unmistakable," he had written, "that
the authorities of one county are at odds with the authori-

ties of the other county, with the efforts of the state troopers, standing between the two, rendered abortive."

The lawyer, for whom brevity apparently held little charm, called on Edwards "to take such action at once as may be necessary to cause the conduct of this investigation to be under the exclusive authority and jurisdiction of a competent and fearless officer of the state who will not be subject to county limitations, political entanglements, or petty disputes between rival detective forces, but who will be of one mind and determination to establish the truth and to bring the guilty to speedy justice."

Stricker was not happy about Pfeiffer's letter. The Middlesex prosecutor insisted that in view of the fact that the murders had taken place in Somerset County, he had gone beyond the call of duty in helping Beekman. "My position in this case has been to voluntarily assist the Somerset officials. I did not legally have to take upon myself this duty."

As for Pfeiffer's suggestion that the governor appoint a special prosecutor, Stricker pointed out that if New Jersey Attorney General Thomas F. McCran intervened he would do everything in his power to assist him.

Beekman shared his colleague's view on that score. "I'd be grateful for any help I could get in this case from the attorney general or anyone else. The one thing I want to do is to solve this case as soon as possible so that I can get back to the many other cases awaiting my attention in Somerset County, which I had to set aside in order to devote all my time to the Hall-Mills case," he said somewhat peevishly.

Earlier in the day Middlesex County Judge Peter F. Daly had issued two warrants for the arrest of Raymond Schneider. The youth was accused of perjury in the Hayes matter and the statutory rape of Pearl Bahmer. He was brought back to New Brunswick by Detective Totten.

As Totten's car pulled up in front of the Middlesex

County Court House, Detective Ferd David of Stricker's staff
was waiting with a pair of handcuffs. The manacled defendant was taken immediately to Judge Daly's courtroom,
where he was arraigned on the two charges. After Daly set
bail at eight thousand dollars, Schneider was driven to the
county jail.

Saturday, October 14, promised to be a slow news day
until the reporters discovered that Beekman and Stricker
had met with Supreme Court Justice Charles W. Parker in
Newark and had asked him to order the attorney general
into the case. Beekman emphasized that he and Stricker had
gone to Newark on their own initiative. "It is a mistaken
idea to think that the governor can have anything to do with
this matter." Politics were obviously beginning to play a
larger role in the month-old case.

Attorney General McCran, who was interviewed at his
home in Paterson, said that he was ready to go to New Brunswick if Justice Parker ordered him to do so. "All I know is
what I have seen in the newspapers," he told reporters, but
implied that if he took over the investigation he might draft
Burlington County Detective Ellis H. Parker to assist him.

Later in the day Ray Schneider was taken from the county
jail to the Middlesex General Hospital for the lancing of
an infected finger. As the car in which he was brought to
New Brunswick entered the city, Schneider saw hundreds of
girls and women selling the yellow tags that had been hurriedly printed to raise money for the no longer needed
"Hayes Justice Fund." By 8 P.M. more than five thousand
dollars had been collected, which would be divided equally
between St. Mary's Orphanage and the Children's Industrial
Home.

The new week was marked by a welter of fresh exhibits,
a report of a mysterious eyewitness, and the usual predictions of imminent arrests.

On Monday, October 16, the New Brunswick police announced that two bloodstained handkerchiefs which had been found on the Phillips farm a month earlier had just been turned over to them. One, a large white linen cloth, bore no identifying marks. The other, a small woman's handkerchief with a lace border, was initialed in one corner with the letter *S*.

Over the weekend Charlotte Mills had made a discovery of her own. Florence North, her attractive lawyer, told reporters that the girl had found a packet of letters from the minister to the choir singer in a handbag hanging behind a door on the second floor of the Mills apartment. The bag had also contained a diary kept by Hall during his summer vacation in Islesford, Maine, a month before his death.

This find, Miss North said, had been sold to the New York *American* for five hundred dollars. "The prosecutor refused to co-operate with me," she said bitterly, "so I didn't co-operate with him. I didn't want him to bungle the letters and the diary the same way officials have bungled the whole case."

In the furor created by the two revelations, Nicholas Bahmer's arraignment on his daughter's incest charge went almost unnoticed. Pearl was the only witness against her father, and after her somewhat confused testimony Bahmer's attorneys moved to dismiss the charge. County Judge Daly denied the motion and ordered the defendant held in ten thousand dollars' bail for the action of the grand jury.

Tuesday, October 17, started out with a rush. With Justice Parker apparently delaying his appointment of a special prosecutor until the local authorities had time to check out their latest leads, Beekman and Stricker took quick advantage of their new lease on life. A large room on the second floor of the Middlesex County Court House was hastily set up as an interrogation room, and detectives were ordered to round up Mrs. Hall, her two brothers, and Charlotte

Mills. For the first time since the investigation had started, reporters were not permitted in the white stone building.

Mrs. Hall's older brother, Henry Stevens, who had driven up from his home in Lavallette, New Jersey, was the first to appear. The erect, deeply tanned man, who bore a strong resemblance to his brother, Willie, walked swiftly from his car to the front entrance of the courthouse. Refusing to talk to the waiting reporters, he entered the building and was escorted by a detective to the second floor, where Beekman and Stricker were waiting for him.

For more than an hour the two prosecutors questioned him about his handkerchiefs. He readily admitted that one, a present from his mother, bore the letter S in one corner.

At 11:20 A.M. a detective escorted Mrs. Hall and Willie Stevens up the courthouse walk. The widow, who was dressed in deep mourning, pushed her way through the horde of reporters and cameramen who had all but made passage impossible. The fur collar of her long coat was up around her neck, and her face was completely obscured by a heavy veil. "Let me through!" she cried in a nervously strident voice as photographers swarmed around her.

When Mrs. Hall arrived upstairs, Beekman asked her to remove her black coat and hat and to put on the gray coat she had been wearing on the early morning of September 15, when she and Willie had gone to St. John's to look for the rector. Seconds later a door opened and a poorly dressed woman entered the room.

"Please stand up, Mrs. Hall," Beekman snapped. The new arrival stared at the widow for several minutes and then sat down abruptly. When Mrs. Hall followed suit, the woman peered intently at her face before quickly leaving the room.

Shortly before one o'clock a state trooper escorted Charlotte Mills into the building. Fifteen minutes later a breathless Timothy Pfeiffer raced up the courthouse steps, and shortly thereafter emerged with Mrs. Hall, whom he escorted hurriedly to a sedan that was waiting with its motor running. They jumped into the car, pulled down its curtains, and were driven off before the reporters could catch up with them.

Minutes later Willie Stevens appeared at the courthouse door. As he walked slowly down the marble steps, he was besieged by reporters. "What did they ask you, Willie?" one of them shouted. "Oh, a few questions," the bushy-headed eccentric replied. "They asked me did I see anyone leave the Hall house on the night of the murder, but I can't discuss that."

Henry Stevens left the building at two fifteen and drove at once to his sister's house. When the reporters arrived, they were met by Pfeiffer on the front porch. He informed them that because of Mrs. Hall's nervousness after her sojourn with Stricker and Beekman, she had been forced to cancel a scheduled interview with the press. As groans of disappointment filled the crisp fall air, the lawyer promised that he would arrange to meet with the reporters after conferring with his client.

One hour later Beekman issued a mimeographed statement. "Prosecutor Stricker and I have today examined Mrs. Hall and her brothers, William and Henry," it read. "These examinations were prompted by some new information received which cannot be disclosed. We do not intend the arrest of any person today, and any other statement than the above is unauthorized."

Pfeiffer was far more voluble when he held his promised press conference at 5 P.M. After detailing the questions which had been asked of Mrs. Hall and the Stevens brothers, he predicted that none of his clients would be arrested "unless some evidence is manufactured against the Hall family." He was positive that no new evidence had been received by either prosecutor. "The only thing that could be construed as the new information referred to by Mr. Beekman in his statement, I would think, was an attempt to identify Mrs.

Hall by a woman said to have seen her on the Phillips farm on the afternoon before the murders," he said.

Early the next afternoon Dr. John F. Anderson of E. R. Squibb & Sons released his analysis of the soil around the crab apple tree. It threw cold water on Beekman's pet theory that the dead couple might have been murdered elsewhere. "The fact that only 0.08 of a pint of blood was found in the soil upon which the bodies of Reverend Hall and Mrs. Mills were found," the chemist said, "is very good evidence that Mrs. Mills was shot before her throat was cut. Nor is it likely that we would have found 0.08 of a pint of blood in the soil if the bodies had been brought to the spot after the murders."

According to Anderson, a 129-pound woman would normally lose 6.1 pints of blood if her throat were cut while she was alive, but less than a half pint if she were already dead.

Reporters, who were eager to find out what Beekman and Stricker thought of the chemist's report, were unable to locate either man. The two prosecutors, who had learned to recognize a dead end when they saw one, had no desire to be cornered by the packs of story-hungry newsmen who prowled through the streets of Somerville and New Brunswick.

On Thursday, October 19, the news of Lloyd George's resignation as England's Prime Minister had little difficulty in overshadowing the now thoroughly stalled Hall-Mills investigation. But the case, despite its momentary lull, was growing in the public's imagination, and more than one hundred out-of-town reporters were now assigned to it. If news wasn't forthcoming, they would find it.

They soon did in the person of Florence North, who caused a stir with a report that relations between Mrs. Hall and Mrs. Mills had deteriorated during the summer of 1922. The coolness had developed when the rector's wife called to pick him up at the end of the two-week church camp at Point Pleasant in July. Mrs. Hall had started back to New Brunswick without waiting for the choir singer, who stopped the car by running in front of it.

On August 20, Hall had written to Mrs. Mills, urging her to forget his wife's rudeness. "Her remarks at Point Pleasant," he said, "were foolish and entirely uncalled for. I don't blame you for being hurt—you know how I feel about them. Dearest, don't let it trouble you."

But the apparently warm friendship that had once existed between the Mrs. Hall and the choir singer was never reestablished. After the Halls returned from Islesford on August 25, the two women refused to speak to each other in public, and during the last ten days of Mrs. Mills' life her references to the minister's wife were extremely bitter.

After talking to Miss North the reporters drifted over to St. John's to pump Jim Mills about the letters his wife had written to Hall. The sexton admitted that he had seen the notes wrapped in her brown scarf on September 13. "I just glanced at them," he said. "I took it for granted the letters were about church affairs."

Had he noticed the word "Honey" on some of the letters? He had. "Didn't that make you suspicious?" one of the newsmen asked him. "No," he replied, "I didn't think there was anything to worry about that." He now realized that he had been cuckolded. "They certainly made a sucker out of me," he said bitterly.

Friday, the twentieth, opened with the startling pronouncement by Beekman, who was now apparently in full charge of the investigation, that he had discovered a new witness—a woman who had seen a couple murder Hall and Mrs. Mills near the crab apple tree on the Phillips farm. Although this information had been in the possession of the authorities since Monday, the Somerset prosecutor had waited until today to release it. It was the unidentified woman's story that had given rise to the weeklong predictions that several arrests were about to be made.

Beekman's new eyewitness, who had blundered on the crime as she took a short cut across the Phillips farm, was reported to be a local socialite. A member of Hall's church, she had been reluctant to contact the police earlier. According to local scuttlebutt, she had seen three men and one woman kill Mrs. Mills and the minister.

At ten thirty Beekman and Totten appeared before the Somerset Grand Jury, which, like its Middlesex counterpart, had been sitting expectantly since the middle of September. An hour later the Somerset prosecutor drove to New Brunswick, where he closeted himself with Stricker. Just before lunch he heeded the reporters' frenzied pleas and made a short statement.

"It must be remembered at all times," he emphasized, "that the proceedings of a grand jury are absolutely secret, and therefore no questions, affirmative or negative, will be answered in respect to the proceeding. The investigation is far from a standstill, and we are satisfied with the progress of the last few days."

In Jersey City, Governor Edwards, who was becoming increasingly irritated by persistent questions as to when he would answer Timothy Pfeiffer's "bungling stupidity" letter of October 13, said that he had no intention of doing so. "I have not replied to Mr. Pfeiffer's letter," he snapped, "and what is more, I do not intend to reply to it. That letter was published in the newspapers before I received it. Therefore I shall not answer it. I am not shielding anybody. It is not my duty to interfere in the investigation—that is a matter for the Supreme Court."

With the Somerset Grand Jury scheduled to meet again on Monday or Tuesday, the sixth weekend since the murders promised to be a slow one as far as the army of reporters now

assigned to the case were concerned. Because of the shortage
of reliable information every rumor found its way into the
columns. In addition, a letter in the New Brunswick *Daily
Home News,* signed "For the Public," suggested that an
unidentified married couple, who had been sparking in De
Russey's Lane, might be helpful to the authorities.

On Saturday morning a group of bored reporters decided
to visit the Millses again. They found Mrs. Elsie P. Barnhardt, one of Charlotte's aunts, trying to calm her niece who
had just had a bitter quarrel with her father. "When I was
ordered to appear at the prosecutor's office," the girl raged,
"my father insisted that I say nothing about the quarrels he
had with Mother. If I was of age, I would leave home at
once. I'd like to live with relatives."

Mrs. Barnhardt told the newsmen about an auto trip she
and her sister-in-law had taken with the Halls to an Episcopal home for the aged at Bound Brook in early September.
During the ride Mrs. Hall had offered a toast. "Here's to
our sweethearts and wives," the minister's wife had proposed. "May our sweethearts be our wives and our wives our
sweethearts." Mrs. Mills had suggested an alternative one.
"May our sweethearts and wives never meet," had been her
contribution. Mrs. Hall had not shared her husband's amuse-
ment at Eleanor's sally.

Over at the Hall residence one of the widow's relatives insisted that the rumors of trouble between the minister and
Henry Stevens were "absolute rot." Although the two men
did not share common interests, she said, their relationship
had been cordial. "Henry liked hunting and fishing, and the
rector did not. That was the only reason the relations between the two were not more intimate."

It was true that Mrs. Hall's mother, and not Henry, had
given her away in marriage. The explanation was a simple
one. "Frances was an elderly bride, and it is only natural
that her mother should have acted for her."

The fact that it had been more than five weeks since the murders had not lessened the public's interest in the Phillips farm. Crowds began to flock to De Russey's Lane early on Sunday morning, and by noon more than three hundred cars were parked in the vicinity. Traffic soon became so heavy that a policeman was sent to the scene to keep the automobiles moving.

The whole case, as far as the public was concerned, had taken on the aspect of a carnival. Vendors hawking popcorn, balloons, peanuts, and soft drinks near the murder site were so numerous that according to one observer, "The scene resembled a circus lot more than a farm."

With the comparatively newsless weekend drawing to a close, the reporters drifted over to Stricker's office. When they asked him why he hadn't subpoenaed Hall's diary and letters before they had been sold, the prosecutor replied that he had no authority to do so. "It has been established," he explained, "that the crime was committed in Somerset County, so it is up to Beekman to take any action with regard to getting possession of this evidence."

Stricker denied that there had been an eyewitness to the murders. "I'm getting tired of denying stories sent out by the hordes of amateur crime solvers now in the city," he complained. "The eyewitness yarn appears to be one of these. It probably had its origin in the fact that on Friday afternoon I went to see a woman whose name has appeared several times before in the case."

He ended the brief interview by referring his interrogators to Beekman. "He is my colonel," he said pompously. "You and I are only privates in the ranks, and you must go to my superior officer for answers to these questions."

But at eleven o'clock the next morning Justice Parker finally ran out of patience.

Chapter 9

THE STATE TAKES OVER

(Monday, October 23, through Friday, October 27, 1922)

As the reporters filed into Attorney General McCran's Trenton office on Monday morning, they were handed a statement. "The Attorney General's department," it read, "has been requested by Mr. Justice Parker of the Supreme Court to take over the Hall-Mills murder case at New Brunswick. The Attorney General has deputized Wilbur A. Mott of Essex County, who for eighteen years has been Prosecutor and Assistant Prosecutor in that county, as Deputy Attorney General in special charge."

Mott, a distinguished-looking man in his early sixties, was known throughout the state as an astute lawyer and a clever cross-examiner. Prior to his long stint as Essex County prosecutor he had served as a police judge in Newark. A Republican, he had resigned as prosecutor in May in order to permit Governor Edwards to appoint a member of his own party. For the last five months he had been practicing criminal law in Newark.

The New York *Times* man scored a minor scoop by getting to Mott before his competitors, but the new prosecutor proved to be a very cautious man. "I have not as yet gone over the case," he said. Although he made it quite clear that he intended "to work, not talk," he promised that he would

hold daily press conferences "to let the public know whatever developments there may be which the press and the
public are entitled to know."

Stricker and Beekman immediately promised to work with
Mott if he needed their services. Pfeiffer assured the new
prosecutor that "Mrs. Hall and all the family are ready now,
as they have been, to make available to him all the information within their knowledge regarding the case."

Jim Mills said that he was very happy to hear of the new
appointment, but didn't think that it would do much good.
"What is needed is someone to solve the mystery," he said.
"They ought to have Ellis Parker here, but even he would
have a hard time finding out anything now, because so much
time has gone. It has rained two or three times since the
murder, and any evidence has been destroyed."

He ended with a somewhat startling thought. "What
should have been done was to arrest the whole Mills family
and the whole Hall family and then let us fight our way
out."

Mott's first official act was to name James F. Mason, the
chief Essex County detective, as his top investigator. He
also indicated that he expected to call upon anyone else who
could be helpful to him, including the celebrated Ellis
Parker.

While Mott was preparing to take charge of the investigation, Frank Csister, a Bound Brook chauffeur, told reporters
that he had turned some information over to the authorities
shortly after the bodies had been discovered which had never
been acted upon. It seemed that he and a friend had been
driving to Red Bank on the evening of September 14 to attend a volunteer firemen's ball. Between eight thirty and
eight forty-five they had noticed a small Ford or Dodge
parked on the side of Easton Avenue, a half mile west of
the entrance to De Russey's Lane. The car, which bore no
license plates, was unlit, except for a taillight.

As Csister drove by, someone had thrown a tire out of the parked automobile. Then three Negroes had leaped out and begun shouting and waving their arms. Afraid of a holdup, Csister had not stopped his vehicle.

About two hundred feet farther down the road he had seen a "highly polished" touring car parked on Smalley's Lane, a little-used thoroughfare that led to Middlebush. Like the first car, it was illuminated only by a taillight and did not have any license plates.

On September 16, the day the bodies were found, Csister had reported what he had seen to the Bound Brook police, who had relayed the information to Detective Totten. Csister said that he had never been questioned by either Beekman or Stricker.

Totten told the curious reporters that Csister's story had been checked with those of other persons who had attended the same firemen's ball. Although they, too, had seen the carload of Negroes on Easton Avenue, they had assured the detective that the incident had taken place at approximately 1 A.M. on September 15. Since Totten was convinced that the murders had occurred several hours before midnight on the fourteenth, he had not bothered to question Csister further.

The possibility that the Negroes might have been white men who had blackened their faces revived earlier rumors that the Ku Klux Klan was involved in the murders. Florence North added to the speculation by the revelation that she had recently received two anonymous letters referring to the Klan. The first, which bore a Florida postmark, urged her to "find out who belongs to the Ku Klux Klan in the church. In this you will find the answer to the mystery." The second warned the lawyer that if she continued to meddle in the case, "the Ku Klux Klan will give you a taste of the same medicine we gave to Mrs. Mills, so beware or you will see the fiery cross some night and get your due reward." In addition, a cross which had been found carved into the trunk of the crab apple tree was attributed by many to the Klan.

The day after their respective appointments, Tuesday, October 24, Mott and Mason set up their headquarters in Somerville. At the same time it was revealed that the anonymous eyewitness to the murders whose story had raised such high hopes of an indictment four days earlier was a fifty-year-old widow by the name of Jane Gibson. Mrs. Gibson lived with her weak-minded son, William, in a converted barn near the Hamilton Avenue end of De Russey's Lane.

The swarthy widow, who was quickly dubbed "the Pig Woman" by newsmen because she raised hogs on her sixty-acre farm, had told the police that she had been alarmed by the barking of one of her five dogs shortly before 9 P.M. on September 14. When she went to the front door, she had seen the shadowy figure of a man leaving her cornfield. Thinking that the intruder had been stealing her corn, she had decided to find out where he hid his loot. She had mounted a mule and followed her quarry, who had driven off in a horse-drawn wagon, along Hamilton Avenue and into De Russey's Lane. After riding for almost a mile toward Easton Avenue, Mrs. Gibson had tried to head off the suspected corn thief by cutting across a field.

Suddenly she had brought her mule up short. In the dark she had noticed what looked like two men and two women standing near a crab apple tree. Although it was a moonless night, she had been able to see the quartet clearly because they were "silhouetted" against the sky. Seconds later there was a sharp report and one of the figures fell to the ground. Then she had heard a woman scream, "Don't! Don't! Don't!"

Thoroughly frightened, Mrs. Gibson had pressed her heels into her mule's sides. As the animal backed away, she had heard a volley of shots, after which another person had slumped to the earth. A few seconds later one of the remaining figures—she was sure it was a woman—had placed her hands on her companion's shoulders and shouted the name

"Henry." All of this had taken place "a little before ten o'clock."

Although Mrs. Gibson's story conflicted with the autopsy report, which indicated that Hall had been shot by someone who was standing above him, Stricker had thought enough of it to request Justice Parker to delay naming a new prosecutor until it could be checked out. The justice, of course, had not done so.

Beekman, on the other hand, was of the opinion that her descriptions of the people she had seen in the crab apple orchard were so vague that it would be useless to make a grand jury presentment without some more definite identification of the murderers.

When reporters attempted to question Mrs. Gibson, she was extremely hostile. "I don't know anything about the case," she insisted, "except what I read in the newspapers. I was not even out of my house on the night of the murder." But she made no secret of where her sympathies lay as far as Mrs. Mills and Mrs. Hall were concerned. "I'm a widow," she shouted, "but if I had a husband and anybody stole him, I would go to the end of the earth to kill her."

While the Pig Woman was refusing to discuss the case with the reporters who had invaded her converted barn, Nicholas Bahmer and his daughter were being arraigned in Judge Daly's court on the charges they had filed against each other. Pearl, who had signed a statement in which she recanted her incest accusations, was committed to Newark's House of the Good Shepherd as a wayward minor.

Judge Daly, who stated that he now believed the girl had lied about her father, reduced the latter's bail to two thousand dollars. After a bond in this amount had been posted, Bahmer, looking none the worse for his two-week imprisonment, walked jauntily out of the courthouse. Ten minutes later he was back behind the bar of his George Street tavern.

Pearl's commitment and her father's release were hardly noticed, however, because of Mrs. Gibson's sudden change of heart. She was now ready, she declared on Wednesday morning, to talk to the press. She said that after conferring with Mott she felt free to divulge the contents of the affidavit she had signed for the special prosecutor.

First of all, she wanted it clearly understood that she had always been ready to talk to the police about the murders. "I wanted to tell my story to the authorities long before they listened to me, long before the arrests of Clifford Hayes and Raymond Schneider, but every time I tried to talk to them they told me that they were too busy to see me."

After Hayes' arrest she was determined to see that her story got to the right people. "I couldn't stand by," she said fervently, "and see an innocent person punished for such an awful crime. I am sorry that I had to be mixed up in such a terrible affair, but it seems to me as if I was sent out there that night on purpose." She had finally managed to see Detective Totten and forced him to listen to her.

After she had signed a statement incorporating her account of what she had seen near the crab apple tree on the Phillips farm, Totten and Middlesex Detective David accompanied her to her home, where they made her reconstruct the strangest ride since Ichabod Crane's midnight excursion on the Albany Post Road.

Although the crowd of reporters who overflowed her ramshackle living room were eager to hear her version of the murders, Mrs. Gibson was not a lady to be hurried. First, she insisted that they take a look at the barn behind her house where she stored her crops. She complained bitterly that greedy land speculators were selling the lots around her farm to "foreigners" who regularly stole her corn and pigs.

If it had not been for one of her light-fingered neighbors, she would never have become involved in the Hall-Mills case in the first place. After one of her dogs had alerted her to the fact that there was a prowler near her house on the evening of September 14, she had gone to the front door.

"I suspected that a man I saw slinking across the cornfield was one of the foreigners who lives near me."

She had rushed to the barn, saddled up Jenny, one of her smartest mules, whose lack of shoes added to her value as a stalker, and started after the intruder. "I had made up my mind long before that," she told her spellbound audience, "that I would catch one of those thieves some night and empty a shotgun into him."

She had trailed the suspected thief into De Russey's Lane. "Before we reached the Phillips farm that night, the man I had been following eluded me. Having a suspicion that I knew the man, I took a roundabout course so as to come onto the little lane which runs in from De Russey's Lane past the old Phillips farmhouse." It was then that she had heard loud voices coming from the crab apple orchard on her right.

Suddenly she had been able to distinguish two men and two women arguing bitterly near one of the crab apple trees. "The quarrel was terrible," she recalled. "The mule kept going toward the four people, but they were in such a state, the quarrel was so bitter, that they didn't notice our approach and we got almost on top of them. They were yelling at each other in extremely loud tones."

At first Mrs. Gibson had thought that a girl was being attacked, but as her eyes became accustomed to the darkness she saw that the members of the quartet were only shouting at each other. "After they had been quarreling for some time," she said, "all four of them began to fight. Suddenly there were shots, four of them. I saw a man fall, and then I saw a woman fall."

It was only when she had read of the discovery of the bodies of the rector and Mrs. Mills that she realized what she had witnessed. But she had not gone to the police until Hayes' arrest. "I didn't want to get mixed up in a murder," she protested, "but I couldn't let an innocent boy take the rap."

It was she who had been the mysterious "peeper" in the Middlesex County Court House when Mrs. Hall was taken there on October 17 and forced to don the light gray coat the widow said she had been wearing on the night of the murders.

"When I saw that woman face to face in the prosecutor's office last week," Mrs. Gibson said, "I felt sorry for her, but the dying shrieks of Mrs. Mills came to my ears and I felt that justice must be done. I believe that Hall and Mrs. Mills got their just desserts, but the Bible says 'Thou shalt not kill,' and when one takes vengeance in his own hands justice must be done."

The Pig Woman's only regret was that she had not tried to prevent the crime. "If I had only called out," she said sadly, "I might have prevented the murders. But I was stunned and seemed to be powerless and I did not know what to do." When one reporter suggested that she might have been paid to forget what she had seen, Mrs. Gibson became furious. "No money would buy my silence," she retorted.

Although the Pig Woman's tale seemed incredible to some listeners, it was clear that it was being taken seriously by the authorities. By Thursday, Mott was calling it his "most valuable evidence." And it was on that same day that Mrs. Gibson elaborated even further. The Pig Woman now claimed that she would be able to identify the man and woman who had killed Hall and Mrs. Mills because she had seen them clearly in the glare of an automobile's headlights before they reached the crab apple orchard.

It seemed that she had ridden all the way to Easton Avenue before cutting across the Phillips farm. As she reached the turnpike, she had noticed an open touring car, which appeared to be empty, parked on the right-hand side of the road. She had then turned Jenny around and started back down De Russey's Lane.

At that moment a closed car had pulled into the lane from Easton Avenue. As it passed her, its headlights had picked up the figures of a woman in a light gray knee-length coat and a man with a dark mustache and bushy hair walking toward the little path that led to the Phillips farm. A few yards beyond the couple the automobile had stopped suddenly and then backed up toward Easton Avenue. The walking couple had again been illuminated by the headlights of the car as it proceeded slowly in reverse.

But the next morning, despite Mrs. Gibson's startling disclosures, New Brunswick and the rest of the nation were buzzing about a different murder. In Havre, Montana, Reverend Leonard Jacob Christier, the rector of St. Mark's Church of the Incarnation, who was known as "the bishop of all outdoors," had been shot to death in his home by a female parishioner who had pumped one shot into his right side and then turned the pistol on herself. But unlike the Hall-Mills tragedy, there was no mystery for the Havre officials to solve, so national interest soon subsided.

Mrs. Gibson, however, who apparently refused to be forced off the front pages even for a day, came up with a new surprise. Just before Hall had been shot, she revealed, she had heard a woman's voice ask, "How do you explain these notes?"

After the minister's murder Mrs. Mills had run away and hidden in some sumac bushes between the crab apple tree and the abandoned Phillips farmhouse. When the killers located her with the aid of a flashlight, they had dragged the screaming woman back to where the dead minister was lying. Three quick shots had ended her cries.

The Pig Woman had lost a moccasin during her cross-country ride, and at 1 A.M. she had decided to go back and look for it. She had saddled up Jenny once more and returned to the Phillips farm. As she approached the crab apple tree, she had heard a woman crying. After dismounting

and tying Jenny's reins to a stump she had crept to within
a few feet of where, three hours earlier, she had witnessed
the double shooting. As she peered through the sumac and
goldenrod that characterized the region, she was surprised to
find Mrs. Hall kneeling beside the minister's body and sobbing loudly.

Although Mott was satisfied that Mrs. Gibson's story
would "stand up before any jury," the Henry Stevenses
didn't share the special prosecutor's confidence. "It sounds
at present like a lot of rubbish," Mrs. Stevens told reporters.
"Exactly, exactly," her husband echoed. And if anyone believed that he had been the "Henry" in the crab apple orchard on the night of September 14, he could call upon ten
Lavallette residents who had seen him around town at various times that very night.

Chapter 10

MR. MOTT BUILDS HIS CASE

(Saturday, October 28, through Sunday, November 5, 1922)

Although Special Prosecutor Mott appeared satisfied as to the truth of Mrs. Gibson's story, there were many people, in addition to the Stevenses, who didn't share his opinion. Some indicated that Beekman and Totten had thought so little of it that they hadn't even bothered to have the Pig Woman sign her original two-page statement. It was only when Stricker had heard of the document and sent Middlesex Detective David to interview her that Mrs. Gibson's statement (now expanded sixfold) was put in the form of an affidavit.

Mrs. A. C. Fraley, who lived across De Russey's Lane from the Phillips farm, pointed out, "Neither I nor anyone in my family heard shots or screams that night although we were awake after the shooting is supposed to have taken place." Furthermore, none of her boarders, who were always coming and going, had said anything about seeing automobile headlights or a woman on muleback in De Russey's Lane that evening.

"I saw Mrs. Gibson a short time after the murders," Mrs. Fraley added, "and she never said a word about the matter."

As for Mrs. Hall, she was aghast at even a suggestion that she was the woman in the gray coat whom Mrs. Gibson claimed to have seen on the Phillips farm. But she had begun to sense that incredible as the story seemed to some, it might well be given credence by others.

"What can I say?" she asked helplessly. "I wasn't there. I know I wasn't there, but they probably won't believe me. Doesn't a person's past count for anything? I have been something of a figure in this community. I have been honest and honorable. Why should I not be believed?"

On Sunday morning the fact that Benito Mussolini, the leader of the Fascisti, had just been asked by King Victor Emmanuel to form a new Italian government barely caused a ripple in Middlesex County. What was of infinitely more importance was the news that reporters were now prevented from seeing Mrs. Gibson by a cordon of state police around her house. The best the newshawks could do was to talk to her son, who assured them that he was nobody's fool.

"They call me Dumb Willie," the youth said, "but maybe I'm not so dumb." He made no converts.

Hitting upon a simple but ingenious plan to penetrate the quarantine, the newsmen delegated one of their number to telephone the Pig Woman, who was listed in the New Brunswick Directory as *Miss* Jane Gibson. The call went through, and when Mrs. Gibson learned of Mrs. Hall's denial she flew into a rage.

"I'm willing to confront Mrs. Hall face to face," she snapped into the receiver. "I am willing to challenge her, face to face, to deny my charge that she witnessed the murder. I am willing to defy her, face to face, to deny that she was at the Phillips farm at one o'clock in the morning after the murders, sobbing over the bodies."

Then her tone softened. "I am sorry for Mrs. Hall," she said. "I am sorry she says she was not there. If she had fully admitted she was there and said that she was there to defend a wife's honor, I would have felt a deep sympathy for her. But the hand of Providence and destiny has guided me, and I will tell the truth. I sympathize with Mrs. Hall, but I will tell on the stand what I know. I have not disclosed all. Wait and see. Murder will out."

When the reporter reminded her that a great many people doubted her story because she had embellished it at every telling, she had a ready, if somewhat cryptic, explanation. She hadn't revealed all she knew at once because "I was afraid that when I got on the witness stand counsel for the defense would demand to know how I knew the woman I saw was Mrs. Hall." Besides, the authorities had not asked for any details when she was first questioned. "If I had been pressed," she declared, "I would not have withheld the details of my second trip."

At five thirty that afternoon, as the usual Sunday crowd at the Phillips farm began to wend its way home, two Clifton women made a startling discovery. They found two unexploded cartridges within a hundred feet of the crab apple tree. When the bullets were turned over to Mason, he ordered the entire area closed to the public for the first time since the bodies of the murdered couple had been found forty-three days earlier. He also instructed the state troopers to make a thorough search of the farm on Monday morning.

Over the weekend some reporters, who from the start had had grave doubts about Mrs. Gibson's credibility, had uncovered some interesting information about her. Although she maintained that her husband, supposedly a Kentucky minister, had died seventeen years previously, her neighbors revealed that Mrs. Gibson was known locally as the wife of William H. Easton, a toolmaker for the Mack Truck Company, who often stayed overnight at her farm.

According to his employer, Easton had given his address as Rural Free Delivery, Route 6, Box 15, which was the same as Mrs. Gibson's. In addition, he had listed Mrs. J. M. Easton, his wife, as his next of kin on his company record card.

Easton, a small, middle-aged man, refused to admit or

deny that he was the Pig Woman's husband. "I've nothing to say about that," he told newsmen who interviewed him at the Mack plant. He was less reticent about the information Mrs. Gibson had given to the authorities. "It's an amazing story," he commented. "She has a brilliant mind."

When the reporters asked him to explain why the New Brunswick City Directory listed the names of an Arthur, a May, a William, and a Mary H. Easton, as well as a Jane Gibson at the same Hamilton Avenue address, he shrugged his shoulders and returned to work.

Was the Pig Woman really Mrs. Easton? And if so, why did she persist in calling herself Mrs. Gibson? Matters became further complicated when the head teacher at the Franklin Township Public School said that nine years earlier Mrs. Gibson had enrolled her son, Willie, under the name of William Easton.

In another telephone interview Mrs. Gibson denied that Willie was her son although he had always been considered so by neighbors. "He is the son of my sister, Mrs. Jennie May Easton," she insisted. "My sister is a trained nurse, and she makes her home here when she has no case to go on, and her husband usually stays here."

She also insisted that the older Easton was not her husband. "He did not say he was," she pointed out. "My husband died in 1904." As for her listing in the telephone directory as *Miss* Jane Gibson, "that's the telephone company's mistake, not mine."[1]

She appeared upset at the attempts to check into her past life. "I know I am here in New Brunswick," she declared with the air of a woman much put upon, "and I witnessed the murder of Dr. Hall and Mrs. Mills. What difference does it make whether I have a past or not? My past is my own business."

Although Mrs. Gibson had said that young Willie could

[1] To this day it is still not clear whether the Pig Woman's last name was Gibson or Easton.

verify her departures on the night of the murders, the reporters could find no evidence that even this was so. One of
Willie's chums said that he had spoken to him on the day
that the Pig Woman's story broke in the newspapers, and
that Willie had told him he didn't know why all the newspapermen had flocked to his house. His mother, he said,
had told him nothing.

A neighbor reported that when he chided the boy for
letting his mother ride out alone on the night of the murders Willie protested vigorously. "I didn't know my mother
had gone out on the mule that night until a bunch of reporters came out to the farm the other day."

It became increasingly obvious that Prosecutor Mott's
faith in his star witness had been badly shaken by the investigation into her past life. But the Pig Woman's stock
suddenly soared when he received the meteorological report
for September 14. Mrs. Gibson had claimed that when she
went back to the Phillips farm for the second time that night
the moon had just risen and that she had had no difficulty
in seeing the woman in gray kneeling beside the rector's
body. According to the chief of the United States Weather
Observatory at Trenton, the moon had risen at 12:26 A.M.,
and an hour later its beam would have been bright enough
to detect moving figures at sixty feet. Mrs. Gibson had, at
least, established one point.

However, on Tuesday, October 31, Mrs. Gibson found
that she was compelled to defend herself on another front.
A group of frustrated cameramen had driven out to her
farm, and when one intrepid photographer leaped out of his
car and started to crawl under the rope which she had
stretched across the lane leading to her house, the Pig
Woman emerged and shouted, "Stay back there!" The man
refused to obey, and Mrs. Gibson reached behind her door
and picked up a double-barreled shotgun. One blast of bird
shot was enough to scatter the photographers.

Mrs. Hall was having her own trouble with the camera-men. Since the discovery of her husband's body she had been kept virtually a prisoner in her home by photographers who picketed her front gate from morning to night. In fact, since September 16 she had left her house only three times—twice to go to Stricker's office and once to visit her bank.

On Wednesday morning, November 1, Pfeiffer announced that his publicity-shy client was prepared to make two con-cessions as far as the press was concerned. At noon four photographers would be permitted to take all the pictures of her they desired in her rear garden. An hour and a half later she would be willing to answer any questions the reporters wanted to ask her, provided only that one of their number conducted the interview.

Promptly at twelve o'clock Mrs. Hall, who was dressed in a long black cloak as protection against the brisk wind, ap-peared at her rear door. She walked slowly across the garden and sat down on a cement bench which was shielded from the street by a white lattice fence. As the photographers shouted instructions at her, she demurred. "I can't look in all directions," she protested.

After five minutes of posing she rose and walked back to her house. She paused for a moment before entering. "I hope that you men are satisfied, and I hope you won't bother me any more for photographs," she said. "I haven't been able to leave my house because of you."

Mrs. Hall's press conference was held in the first-floor re-ception room. The twenty-five invited correspondents, to-gether with two stenographers, two typists, and a crew of mimeograph men, arrived promptly at one fifteen. As the re-porters filed into the reception room, Pfeiffer directed the mimeographists into the parlor, where the furniture had been covered with heavy casings of newspapers to protect it against ink stains. In one corner of the room two tables had been set up for the typists.

At precisely one thirty Mrs. Hall entered the reception room and sat down in a low rocking chair, facing the waiting journalists. "She has a face to look at twice," *Times* man Bruce Rae observed. "A long, narrow face, a firm tight-lipped mouth, a suggestion of hair on the upper lip, a broad chin. On her right temple, at the fringe of her hair, is a tiny crescent-shaped scar. Although her hair has turned gray, her eyebrows, unusually prominent, remain black and thin, and coupled with her pince-nez, give her quick-turning eyes rather a set-in look."

As she waited for her first question, she nervously moved her feet, which were encased in black oxfords, back and forth over the polished hardwood floor. A reporter in the front row noticed that she was still wearing the rector's three-diamond engagement ring, as well as her plain gold wedding band. The knuckles of her thin pale hands, which she kept in her lap during the entire interview, were white with strain.

The spokesman for the reporters read his questions from a typewritten sheet of paper.

Was there any truth to Mrs. Gibson's story?

None whatsoever.

When had she gone to the church on the night of her husband's disappearance?

"It was about half past two when I dressed and got up," she replied. "I was back here about half past three."

When had she called the police to inquire about any accidents?

About seven o'clock on Friday morning.

Did she think that the rector had written any love letters to Mrs. Mills?

It was "very unlikely."

No, she had never heard any gossip about her husband's relations with the choir singer. Yes, the minister had received two letters from Mrs. Mills when he was at Islesford, but they had only contained descriptions of Sunday services

at the church. She had never been jealous of Mrs. Mills because there simply was nothing to be jealous about.

Q. Did you immediately attach significance to the fact
that they were both missing?

A. I thought it was strange, yes.

Did she know why Mrs. Gibson was accusing her of being
a witness to her husband's murder?

She didn't have "the most remote idea."

Q. Do you know her?

A. I have never seen her.

Q. Would you be willing to confront her if it became
necessary?

A. I would do whatever the prosecutors wish me to do.

Was it true that Mr. Hall's estate was valued at forty thousand dollars?

Absolutely not. He had only half that amount in securities, a good part of which had been left to him by her
mother.

How did she feel now?

"As if I were up against a blank wall," she answered. "I
have no idea what to think." She hadn't made a complete
statement to the reporters before "because it seemed wiser
not to do it."

Q. Wiser to you or your advisers?

A. Well, in talking it over with my family.

No, she hadn't offered any reward for the capture of the
murderer.

Q. Do you want to see the murderer punished?

A. I don't want to see anyone punished. I want to get the
solution. I haven't a vindictive feeling to see anyone punished.

She had retained Pfeiffer instead of Senator Florence because "it seemed wiser to have someone not so connected
with New Brunswick." No, there was no insanity in her immediate family, only "in collateral branches."

As the interview, which had been limited to one hour,

drew to a close, Mrs. Hall's interrogator returned to the subject of the rector's relationship with Mrs. Mills. If her husband's diary and letters were authentic, would she be willing to admit that the murdered couple might have been in love?

She would.

What was her opinion of Mrs. Mills' character?

She would rather not say.

Q. Do you think she deliberately set her cap for Mr. Hall?

A. I never saw any indication of it.

No, Mrs. Hall had never asked anyone to spy on the minister. "I had such faith in my husband," she concluded. "If he were here he could explain."

Although Mott and Mason had seemed so confident when they first came into the case two weeks earlier, they now, it seemed, had lost most of their steam. Jim Mills probably echoed the sentiments of most of his fellow townsmen concerning the investigation when he said glumly, "Shucks, they've been talking about arrests, why don't they do something?"

Something was exactly what Mott was preparing to do, but he was not yet ready to reveal his plans other than to point out that he still believed Mrs. Gibson's story. As he put it, "Why should any woman tell a story like that unless she had some real foundation for it?"

But what Mrs. Gibson's story would be if she ever got to the stand was not exactly clear either. Now she had adopted a new line with reporters.

"The story I told the authorities and the story I told you reporters are two different things. And when I get on the stand, I will give you a better story than you have had yet."

A strange case gave every indication of becoming stranger yet.

Chapter 11

MR. PFEIFFER STRIKES BACK

(Tuesday, November 7, through Sunday, November 19, 1922)

Election day in 1922 fell on November 7. While Al Smith was piling up a plurality of 390,000 votes over his Republican opponent in New York, New Jersey's voters were also flocking to the polls in record numbers. Both Mason and Mott were wise enough to realize that any announcement they might have concerning the hyphenated murder case would be lost in the election news. So for several days preceding the election and on that day itself the special prosecutor and his assistant remained firmly silent.

The only result of the election, as far as the Hall-Mills case was concerned was to show that it had had little effect upon the politics of the State of New Jersey. Governor Edwards easily defeated Joseph S. Frelinghuysen, a personal friend of President Harding, for a seat in the United States Senate. George S. Silzer, also a Democrat, experienced little difficulty in beating out William N. Runyon for the governorship.

With the election out of the way, it was assumed that Mott would waste no time in seeking indictments. In fact, on Wednesday he boasted, "Our case is complete. We have enough evidence to go before the grand jury immediately."

But this was not to happen quite so soon. The Somerset County Grand Jury could not be convened except by order of Justice Parker, and it turned out that the justice, who had just finished presiding over a long murder trial, had taken a Cuban vacation. He had even left a letter with Mott so that the special prosecutor could prove to newspapermen that this was the sole cause of the unexpected delay.

By Friday it had become clear that there was little likelihood of any grand jury action until Parker's return on November 19. Mott was incensed at a rumor that the panel, in executive session, had rejected his evidence. "That report is untrue," he declared. He refused to indicate what evidence he had, but insisted, "The only question now is one of procedure. I will probably know by Monday what steps I shall take."

At noon Mrs. Hall, accompanied by Sally Peters, went out for a drive. As the two women passed the courthouse, they saw Pearl Bahmer being escorted into the building. The girl had been brought from Newark's House of the Good Shepherd to testify against Raymond Schneider before the Middlesex County Grand Jury on her statutory rape charge. Five minutes after she left the stand, the jurors voted an indictment. However, in view of Pearl's reluctance to accuse her father of incest, the panel took no action in his case, and his bail of two thousand dollars was continued indefinitely.

On Saturday morning Mott revealed that Mrs. Gibson had finally identified the actual murderer. Three days earlier Detective Ferd David had taken her to the Pennsylvania Railroad station and instructed her to scrutinize the faces of the commuters who were rushing to board the New York train. The thirteenth man to pass her vantage point was, she excitedly told David, the person whom she had seen shoot Hall and Mrs. Mills. The special prosecutor refused to comment on the new suspect except to state that he wore glasses and was one of New Brunswick's most prominent citizens.

Henry Carpender, one of Mrs. Hall's cousins, apparently thought enough of Mott's sketchy description to make public his alibi for the night of September 14. Carpender, whose full name was Henry de la Bruyère, lived only two doors away from the Halls. A member of the New York stock brokerage firm of McClave & Company, he was a tall, well-built man of forty with thinning hair and a closely trimmed mustache. Despite his close relationship to Mrs. Hall and his proximity to her house, he had managed thus far to avoid much publicity. Now, however, the situation had changed.

Carpender revealed that at seven on the evening of September 14 he and his wife had arrived at the home of his friend J. Kearny Rice, Jr., for supper. Rice, a dealer in unlisted securities, lived in a cottage in Highland Park, a suburb across the Raritan River from New Brunswick, and more than a mile from the Phillips farm. Because he had had an early morning engagement in New York, Carpender had left around ten thirty.

While Mott waited impatiently for Justice Parker's return, Pfeiffer decided to use the delay to his client's advantage. At noon on Sunday, November 12, he showed up at the special prosecutor's home with an affidavit signed by a Mrs. Nellie Lo Russell, one of Mrs. Gibson's neighbors, which completely contradicted the Pig Woman's claim that she had been at the Phillips farm at 10:20 P.M. on September 14. According to Pfeiffer, Mrs. Hall had recently received a startling letter from Mrs. Russell.

"Dear Madam," it read. "In regard to September 14, Mrs. Jane Gibson was not at the Phillips farm at ten o'clock as I live back of her. She came over at ten o'clock or a little before to tell me that she had took my dog from a man on Hamilton Road. She set on the steps of my little shanty awhile and I gave her a dollar for bringing my dog. Then I went with her to get the dog. We talked awhile, and I came home about eleven o'clock. She has told me things that were not so. I don't think she can help it."

The day after Mrs. Hall received this letter, Pfeiffer and Felix De Martini, a New York private detective who had just been hired by Mrs. Hall, had visited Mrs. Russell's one-room shanty on Churchill Avenue, only to find that she worked days for a dressmaker in New York. The two men had returned that evening and talked to the twenty-eight-year-old seamstress for an hour and a half. On Friday, Mrs. Russell had gone to Pfeiffer's Manhattan law office and signed the lengthy affidavit which the attorney was now waving under Mott's nose.

The newspapermen at once flocked to Mrs. Russell's drafty shack, where they noticed three horseshoes hanging on one wall. It was because she was so superstitious, she said, that she was positive that it had been September 14 when she had recovered her dog. "The animal was first missing the day before, on the thirteenth," she explained, "and I remember thinking to myself that it was an unlucky day."

But if Mott was to have his way, Mrs. Russell would not appear before the grand jury. "I'm not in the least interested in Mrs. Russell," the special prosecutor said. "I do not think much of her story."

Totten chimed in that there had been bad blood between Mrs. Russell and Mrs. Gibson since last spring, when the Pig Woman had been accused by her neighbor of reporting her to the county detective for neglecting her livestock. As recently as last Sunday, the two women had had words over a pig, and at Mrs. Gibson's request, the state troopers had ejected Mrs. Russell from the Gibson farm.

There were attacks on Mrs. Russell's credibility from other sources. For more than a year the Pennsylvania Railroad had refused to sell her a commutation ticket from nearby Voorhees Station to New York because of some trouble over her use of this type of ticket. Furthermore, a poultry farmer who lived in the vicinity denied her statement that she had told her story to him three weeks ago. "It was only a week ago," he said. "We didn't pay any attention to her because she talks in bunches. I don't think she's reliable."

On Tuesday, November 14, the Pig Woman, who had obviously been nettled by Mrs. Russell's affidavit, invited reporters into her house for the first time in three weeks. She showed them a calendar diary on which she entered such information as the number of eggs collected, the birth of pig litters, and neighbors' visits to her farm. As the newsmen flocked around the calendar,[1] which hung on her living room wall, Mrs. Gibson pointed triumphantly at the entry for September 9. The penciled notation indicated that the ninth and not the fourteenth was the day when she had rescued Mrs. Russell's dog, Prince, from a "Polack."

Pfeiffer was not overly impressed by the wall calendar. "It seems strange," he observed dryly, "that this calendar diary of Mrs. Gibson's was not mentioned before, when it might have given the authorities such valuable information as to just what did happen on the night of September 14."

He still had high hopes that the grand jury would call Mrs. Russell, even if Mott did not. "With respect to the attemps to discredit Mrs. Russell's affidavit, I can only say that the grand jury will determine who is telling the truth," he added.

As the grand jury hearing approached, Mott, Mason & Company began to exhibit an optimism that had been conspicuously absent in their camp for more than a week. One of the reasons for their renewed confidence became clear when Mason announced the results of a test his men had conducted at the Phillips farm when the moon was in the same quarter as it had been on September 14. His detectives had followed the route of Mrs. Gibson's second trip to the scene of the murders, arriving there at the identical time she said she had seen a woman kneeling beside the dead rector's body. Even though the stars had been partially obscured by some light clouds, the policemen had been able to see quite clearly the area where the corpses had been found. At least the moon and the stars still seemed to be on the prosecutor's side.

But Pfeiffer and De Martini were also busy accumulating

[1] This calendar later mysteriously disappeared.

evidence. The two men visited Mrs. Russell again and obtained a new statement from her.

"On a visit to Mrs. Gibson's home," she said, "I have seen the calendar diary on her wall, but I have never noticed any writing on it. Mrs. Gibson is wrong in saying she went to my house on September 9 about my dog that had been stolen. I remember the night of September 9. I was home that night, all night, and Mrs. Gibson did not come to see me. The dog was stolen on the night of September 13. I remember that because the thirteenth of the month is an unlucky day. It was the next night that Mrs. Gibson came over at ten o'clock and told me she had my dog and I walked over to her house with her and brought the dog back home."

On Wednesday, as New Brunswick seethed with rumors about surprise witnesses who would clinch Mott's case, George Kuhn, the owner of a cigar store near St. John's, disclosed that an extremely agitated Willie Stevens had entered his shop on September 19. When Kuhn expressed the hope that the murderer would be caught and severely punished, Willie had leaned over the counter and said, "My heart is almost coming through my clothes, George. I don't know how I can stand it."

Before he left the store, Mrs. Hall's brother had asked Kuhn to do him a favor. "I want you to deny any rumors you hear about the Hall-Stevens-Carpender family having anything to do with these murders," he had pleaded.

A slight flurry of excitement was generated on Friday, November 17, by Paul F. B. Hamforszky, a New York automobile parts dealer, who had resigned under fire in April as the pastor of New Brunswick's Hungarian Reformed Church. In a story which was originally published in a Hungarian newspaper, Hamforszky claimed that Hall had once confided in him that his wife knew all about his affair with Mrs. Mills and that one of her relatives had threatened to kill him unless he stopped seeing the choir singer. The rector had said that he had no intention of giving up Mrs. Mills and that he was going to leave New Brunswick with her after his summer vacation.

In his statement Hamforszky said that he had known Hall for more than ten years. In February 1922, while both men were traveling together to an Episcopal conclave at Rahway, New Jersey, the rector had complained that his wife was "very jealous of Mrs. Mills." Four months later, when they met on a train to New York, Hall had revealed that he intended to run away. "I am leaving on account of Mrs. Mills, I am sorry to say, and cannot get over it. I am planning to do something, to go away."

Not only had one of his wife's relatives threatened to kill him, but he was afraid to stay in his own house. "Mrs. Hall was a very cool woman," he had said. "She has changed very much lately, and I am very much afraid that she will do me some bodily harm. We very often have quarrels on account of Mrs. Mills. I will have to leave New Brunswick."

But he could not throw Mrs. Mills aside. "I love her, and I won't give her up," he insisted. "I am going to get out of New Brunswick as soon as I come back from my summer vacation." He had mentioned going to Mexico or Europe for a divorce.

Hamforszky, a youthful-looking man in his late forties, said he had told his story to some of his employees two days after the bodies had been found. On September 19 he had cashed a check in a New Brunswick poolroom. When he mentioned his conversations with the dead rector, a "minor politician" had warned him to keep his mouth shut or he might find himself in serious trouble. The pool hall owner remembered that the ex-minister had cashed a check on the nineteenth, but couldn't recall whether he had said anything about the murdered rector.

Hamforszky, who admitted that he had been motivated by the various rewards offered for information leading to a solution of the crimes, had recently been interviewed by Mott's law partner. Although the latter had assured him that his story would be of interest to the special prosecutor, he had never been contacted again. "His story had little evidential value," Mott explained, "and would not justify presentation to the grand jury."

By Saturday evening all of Mott's more than fifty subpoenas had been served. Orders had also been issued to bring Pearl Bahmer and Raymond Schneider from Newark's House of the Good Shepherd and the Middlesex County Jail respectively to Somerville on Monday morning. "Everything is now ready," Mott said, "to present to the grand jury." But he was wary about predicting an indictment. "I do not say now," he continued, "and I have never said, that I am confident of getting an indictment. I shall comply with my duty by presenting the case to the grand jury. It is up to them to decide whether there will be an indictment."

Sunday, November 19, passed slowly for everyone. Out at the Phillips farm hundreds of curious people waited in line for hours to enter the ancient farmhouse, which had been converted into a makeshift "Murder Museum" by an enterprising New Brunswicker. The only activity at the Hall house was the release of a brief statement by Pfeiffer that Hamforszky's story was "preposterous." Jim Mills had nothing to say to the press, but his daughter, who was patently disgruntled about Mott's failure to have her subpoenaed to appear before the grand jury, told one reporter that if she were called she could tell how the letters from her mother to Hall, which had been found near the bodies, had gotten there.

"Humbug!" snorted the special prosecutor.

Chapter 12

THE GRAND JURY

*(Monday, November 20, through
Tuesday, November 28, 1922)*

At nine thirty on Monday morning, November 20, the grand jurors filed into the hearing room on the first floor of the Somerset County Court House. Fifteen minutes later Beekman drove into town from Bound Brook, parked his car in front of his office in the Second National Bank Building, and walked the two blocks to the courthouse. Mott, who had taken the train from East Orange, arrived at nine fifty. As the two prosecutors conferred briefly in the rotunda, a squad of seven state troopers, dressed smartly in blue coats, whipcord trousers, and leggings, took up stations around the building.

It was precisely ten o'clock when Mott and Beekman entered the grand jury room. Reporters who were able to get a quick glimpse inside when the door was opened to admit the two men saw that an easel, on which a detailed map of the Phillips farm area had been placed, stood at one end of the room. The map, they were informed, had been prepared by a former Somerset County engineer, and would be used to clarify the witnesses' testimony.

The crowd, which had ringed the white stone courthouse since early morning, soon found that it was possible to peer into the grand jury room from the park on the west side of the building. Sergeant John J. Lamb, who was in command of the state troopers, promptly ordered two of his men to keep the spectators behind a row of hedges some twenty feet away. At the same time one of the grand jurors hurriedly drew the shades on the window facing the park.

Inside the courthouse a group of enterprising reporters had discovered that by kneeling on the mezzanine floor directly opposite the grand jury room they could get a limited view of the hearing through the transom. "All we could see," one of them wrote that evening, "was Mr. Mott in a swivel chair beside the bald head of one juror and the man-sized foot of another."

When Totten, who was waiting to be called as a witness, noticed the kneeling newsmen, he obtained a ladder and dropped a piece of black muslin over the transom.

Al Cardinal, the former reporter for the New Brunswick *Daily Home News* who had trailed Officers Garrigan and Curran to the Phillips farm on September 16, was the first witness to appear before the jury. It was he who had called Mrs. Hall, after her husband's body had been tentatively identified, to inquire if the rector was at home. The ex-reporter took the stand at eleven o'clock and was excused fifty minutes later.

He was followed by Dr. E. Leon Loblein, the veterinarian who had been stopped on Easton Avenue by Officer Curran and asked to identify Hall's body. During Loblein's fifteen-minute stint Mott left the grand jury room, returning several minutes later with two boxes containing the dead couple's clothing. The veterinarian's place in the witness chair was taken by Totten. The detective was still on the stand when the jury adjourned for lunch at twelve forty-five.

Daniel J. Wray, the city editor of the *Daily Home News*, and Frank M. Deiner, one of his reporters, were the first witnesses of the afternoon session. The two newspapermen, who had rushed to the Phillips farm after Cardinal had called in his flash on September 16, were in the jury room less than fifteen minutes. They were succeeded by former Somerset County Sheriff Bogart F. Conkling, who had gone to the scene of the murders with Totten and Dr. Long shortly after the discovery of the bodies.

Pearl Bahmer was next. The girl, who appeared extremely nervous, was escorted into the jury room by one of the nuns from Newark's House of the Good Shepherd. After listening to the fifteen-year-old for almost an hour the jurors called it a day with the brief testimony of Mrs. Grace Edwards, Edward Stryker's niece, who had telephoned the news of Pearl's grisly discovery to the New Brunswick police.

Although it was impossible for the reporters to learn what was transpiring in the courthouse, a letter in the *Daily Home News* by a Mrs. George Sipel provided them with enough copy to satisfy their editors. Mrs. Sipel's plaintive letter implored the authorities of Middlesex and Somerset counties "to take notice that if Mrs. Jane Gibson should at any time offer new evidence supposedly from my husband, George Sipel, regarding the case, I want them absolutely to ignore same, as it is untrue."

According to Mason, Sipel, a Middlebush farmer, might be the owner of the mysterious car whose headlights had illuminated the man and woman Mrs. Gibson said she had seen walking down De Russey's Lane on the night of the murders. The reporters were immediately all ears.

Would Mr. Sipel be a witness?

"I hope to tell you he will be," the detective replied.

Was he one of the surprise witnesses that the prosecution had intimated would corroborate Mrs. Gibson's story?

Mason smiled. "Now you are getting too close," he said pointedly.

Sipel was still very much in the news on Tuesday. Not only was the Middlebush farmer served with a grand jury subpoena, but Totten and Mason revealed that he, too, had had a recent altercation with Mrs. Russell. Two weeks before the murder Sipel had sold a horse to her. On September 13, Mrs. Russell had returned the animal, claiming that it was much older than she had been led to believe. The next morning Sipel had found the horse dead in its stall, and immediately filed a complaint against Mrs. Russell with the New Brunswick Society for the Prevention of Cruelty to Animals.

At eight that evening, the night of the murders, Sipel and an SPCA agent had gone to Mrs. Russell's shanty, but she had not yet returned from New York. The two men had then started out in Sipel's Ford for Bound Brook, where they hoped to obtain a warrant for Mrs. Russell's arrest from Recorder H. D. Flammer. They had gone only a few hundred yards when a flat tire forced them to abandon the trip. The SPCA agent had returned to New Brunswick by trolley while Sipel was changing tires.

It was 9 P.M. when the farmer reached home. A laborer he had hired to bury the dead horse was hard at work, so Sipel decided to see if Mrs. Russell had returned from New York. The shanty was still empty, and he waited until 10 P.M. before going back to Middlebush. He had then driven the laborer to New Brunswick. After dropping him at his home, Sipel had left town via Easton Avenue.

The SPCA agent, who had also been summoned by the grand jury, was hazy as to what day he and Sipel had started out for Bound Brook. As he recalled it, they had reached the town only to discover that the local judge was in New York for the Police Department Field Day games. The games had been held on September 9 and September 16, successive Saturdays, and the agent was fairly certain that the incident had taken place on the ninth. After returning from Bound Brook he and Sipel had driven to Mrs. Russell's place, arriving there "between seven and nine o'clock," but she had not been at home.

Seventeen witnesses appeared before the grand jury be-

fore it adjourned at 3:20 P.M. The doctors who had performed the autopsies, Officers Garrigan and Curran, under-
takers Sutphen and Hubbard, and a number of people who
had seen Hall and Mrs. Mills on the last night of their lives
were heard in the morning. After lunch a red-faced Raymond Schneider testified for almost two hours. The last witness of the day was Dr. John F. Anderson, the director of the
Squibb laboratory, whose analysis of the soil under the
bodies had convinced him that the dead couple had been
killed where they were found.

A letter signed by seventy-six New Brunswick women,
none of whom was a member of St. John's, appeared on the
editorial page of the *Daily Home News*. "A few of the
friends of Mrs. Frances Stevens Hall," it began, "desire to
express their unswerving faith in her absolute and unswerving devotion to truth and integrity and to all the highest
ideals of Christian character. . . . To them, she is now and
always has been a woman of the highest type, above suspicion and above reproach, incapable of thinking, much less
of doing, evil."

Its sponsors denied that its publication had been timed
to coincide with the grand jury hearing. "The idea was con-
ceived the week following the finding of the bodies," one of
them explained. "All the signers felt we should do something
to show our confidence in Mrs. Hall." It had been their intention to issue the statement long before the convening of
the grand jury, but publication had been delayed because
many of the women who had been solicited had at first been
afraid to sign.

On Wednesday morning Mrs. A. C. Fraley and her daughter, Catherine, took the witness stand. Both women claimed
that they had heard shots shortly before 10 P.M. on September 14. "The Italians are at it again on the Phillips place,"
Catherine had remarked at the time.

After testifying the cantankerous Mrs. Fraley kept both

hands over her face to foil the photographers, whose exploding flash powder signified the exit of each successive witness from the jury room. When a cameraman got too close, she dropped one hand and punched him in the jaw, which, one amused reporter noted, "she did very neatly."

Captain Michael Regan of New Brunswick's Fire Company No. 3 inaugurated the afternoon session. According to the fireman, Willie Stevens, who was one of the most devoted buffs in town, had told him on Friday, September 15, the day before the bodies were discovered, "There's been trouble at our house." When Regan pressed him for details, Willie had refused to elaborate. "Something is going to happen," he had prophesied gloomily. "You'll hear about it later."

Mrs. Russell, the woman whose letter to Mrs. Hall had caused a sensation ten days earlier, took Regan's place in the witness chair. Since her testimony would tend to cast doubt on Mrs. Gibson's veracity, Mott had not ordered the sheriff to issue a subpoena in her name. The grand jury, however, had insisted on hearing her, to Tim Pfeiffer's delight. At the conclusion of her twenty-five-minute examination Mrs. Russell told the reporters that she had not deviated from the story she had told Pfeiffer.

The afternoon ended with the appearance of Jim Mills. The sexton, who was dressed in a well-worn brown overcoat, testified for more than an hour. One reporter, who watched him shuffle into the jury room, described him as "a thin, emaciated, drooping man with a perpetually apologetic expression on his face."

As soon as his stint was over, he rushed over to Totten to inquire when he could collect his witness fee. While the detective was certifying Mills' subpoena, the foreman of the grand jury announced that in order to give the jurors time to take care of their personal affairs, they would adjourn until 10 A.M. on Monday, November 27.

Amid these grim proceedings a press release from St.

John's indicated that the church had finally hired a new rector. Thirty-five-year-old J. Mervin Pettit, a former resident of Camden, whose present preserve was St. Mark's Protestant Episcopal Church in Bay City, Texas, had accepted a call to the New Brunswick pulpit, effective January 1, 1923. Pettit, who had learned his theology as a lay reader at St. Stephen's in Camden while employed by the Victor Talking Machine Company, had attracted the vestrymen's interest by a guest sermon which he had preached on the Sunday before the grand jury convened.

Despite the season's first snow on Monday, November 27, the jury, many of whose members lived more than ten miles from Somerville, met promptly at 10 A.M. Mrs. Anna K. Bearman, who had sent Mrs. Hall's brown coat to Philadelphia to be dyed on September 19, was the first of the day's nineteen witnesses. She was followed by Cedric Paulus, who had noticed a light in St. John's at 1:30 A.M. on September 15, and Russ Gildersleeve, one of the church's lay readers, who had seen Hall and Mrs. Mills walking "arm in arm" in front of New York's Rivoli Theatre in the summer of 1921.

Mrs. Hall's servants were next. Louise Geist said that she had served dinner to the Halls, Willie Stevens, and Frances Voorhees at 7 P.M. on September 14. She had seen Mrs. Hall several times between the end of the meal and 9:30 P.M. At the latter time the rector's wife had asked her to make sure that all the shutters were closed before she went to bed. After complying with this request Miss Geist had retired to her room, where she had been able to hear Mrs. Hall moving about in the house until well after ten o'clock. Barbara Tough added that she had never heard any quarrels in the Hall household since her arrival from Scotland in February 1916.

Ralph Gorsline, a St. John vestryman and a member of its choir, was asked only about church gossip concerning the dead couple. He told reporters that he had testified about some "catty" remarks he had heard bandied about during choir practice. A shrewish alto, he remembered, had once said, "I saw the rector and the choir leader downtown again tonight."

At 5 P.M. after hearing the testimony of eleven other witnesses, including Clifford Hayes, Millie Opie, William Phillips, Elizabeth E. Kelly, and two delivery boys who worked for a dry cleaner patronized by Willie Stevens, the grand jury closed its longest session.

The next day promised to mark the highlight of the hearings. It was to be the day that Mrs. Gibson finally testified. But the unexpected arrival in Somerville that morning of Mrs. Hall, who was, according to most people, the grand jury's chief target, made the Pig Woman's appearance anticlimactic.

The widow, accompanied by Timothy Pfeiffer and Sally Peters, entered the courthouse shortly before ten o'clock and stationed herself on a straight-backed wooden chair against one wall of the building's octagonal rotunda. While her lawyer tried unsuccessfully to persuade Beekman to call her as a witness, she sat staring fixedly at the door to the jury room. She was destined to sit there for almost seven hours.

Meanwhile Mrs. Gibson, who was one of the eight witnesses on the day's schedule, walked into the rotunda on her way to the jury room. Although she passed close enough to the rector's widow to touch her, it was obvious to the crowd on the mezzanine that the Pig Woman had not noticed Mrs. Hall. But when she emerged, after almost two hours of questioning, she immediately recognized the seated woman. Her face flushed a deep red and she hurried out of the courthouse.

At 3:30 P.M., Mott and Beekman left the grand jury room.

"This is a dramatic moment," said Pfeiffer, who, with Sally Peters, had spent the day by Mrs. Hall's side.

As the jurors began their deliberations, County Judge Frank L. Cleary, who would be required in the event of any indictments, arrived in his chambers and ordered the court crier to take up his station in the courtroom.

The tension mounted as state troopers and county detectives were sent to guard every door leading out of the building. On the street side the police were hard-pressed to control the crowds of curious spectators who had begun to assemble as soon as news that the jury had begun its deliberations spread through Somerville.

As the long minutes dragged by, Mrs. Hall looked supremely confident, although both Pfeiffer and Miss Peters were visibly nervous and ill at ease. Suddenly, at four twenty-three, the door opened and the jurors filed out. Their foreman finally managed to make himself heard above the din of the reporters who surrounded him. "Are you ready, ladies and gentlemen?" he shouted. A chorus of impatient yeses answered his question.

"For reasons which seem sufficient and controlling," he intoned sonorously, "the grand jury took no action on the Hall-Mills murder case and laid the matter over. This does not necessarily mean that the matter cannot be taken up by this or a subsequent grand jury."

After five days and sixty-seven witnesses the verdict was in. Although it seemed a popular one in Somerset County, there were many in New Brunswick who hoped that the investigation would go on. The *Daily Home News* thundered, "No matter what the cost and no matter what the length of time that may be involved in the effort, there would be no place in public office for any official who would be willing to let the inquiry simply die."

Jim Mills was philosophical about the whole thing. "I suppose they will never do anything now," he sighed, "but there is a higher judge."

As for Mrs. Hall, she had received the news of the grand

jury's action with her usual stoicism. When one of the reporters informed her of the foreman's announcement, she
immediately rose and followed by Pfeiffer and Miss Peters,
walked to her Dodge, which was parked in front of the
courthouse.

"She displayed no emotion," the reporter later recalled.
"She just walked away, a silent, black-clad figure, with her
head held high."

Chapter 13

THE AFTERMATH

*(Wednesday, November 29, 1922, through
Tuesday, January 2, 1923)*

With the grand jury's refusal to indict anyone for the double slaying, national interest in the Hall-Mills case faded abruptly. For the next month, however, the few out-of-town reporters whose hopeful editors had ordered them to remain in the area fed regular but hardly startling stories back to their papers. In fact, it was a rare day that some reference to the case did not see print.

On Friday, December 1, for example, the New York *Times* revealed that Jim Mills had just sent a letter to New Jersey's United States Senator Walter E. Edge, who had recently promised his colleagues that the Hall-Mills case would eventually be solved. "As I saw in the paper the discussion on the Senate floor about the crime," Mills had written, "will you please continue the investigation of the case? Mr. Edge, it has been a lonesome Thanksgiving Day for me and my children, but it might have been a brighter holiday if the grand jury had brought the guilty ones to justice."

The next day Charlotte Mills made her first statement since the grand jury's action. The young girl declared that she was "disgusted" with the turn of events and that, influenced by Sir Arthur Conan Doyle's *The New Revelation*, she was turning to spiritualism. "If what I read is true," she said brightly, "I shall certainly be able to communicate with my mother and learn the truth."

She hinted darkly at mysterious plans to put her in a home for wayward girls, but served notice that she would resist any such attempt. "I'll not be put away!" she exclaimed. "I'm going to keep up my fight for a real investigation!"

But it was obvious to everyone that the investigation was all but over. Although Colonel H. Norman Schwartzkopf, the superintendent of the state police constabulary, had ordered his men to remain in New Brunswick until Attorney General McCran decided whether the state would withdraw from the case or not, it was clear that it was only a matter of time before the investigation was officially abandoned. Even Mott's year-end insistence that he would push the case vigorously in 1923 was greeted with derision by everyone who read his words.

On December 8, after a two-day trial, Raymond Schneider was convicted of perjury by a jury that deliberated for only twenty-five minutes. As the verdict was announced, the defendant's mother and father collapsed and had to be carried from the courtroom. A week later Schneider was sentenced to two years in the Rahway Reformatory. At the same time Pearl Bahmer's statutory rape charges against him were dismissed because of her unreliability as a witness.

Three days earlier Justice Parker had discharged the grand jury. "It is unusual for a Supreme Court judge to attend the discharge of the jury," he explained, "but I felt that it was due to the grand jury to attend, so as to indicate my appreciation of the painstaking care with which you have performed your duties at this time." He was happy that the panel had not been stampeded by public pressure into voting indictments that were not justified by the evidence. "You may now go to your homes," he concluded, "with satisfaction and with the appreciation of the court and your neighbors, feeling that you have done your duty."

As the year drew to a close, Mrs. Hall and her brothers

disclosed that they intended to leave the state shortly after the new grand jury adjourned in early January. The widow planned to travel to Italy with Sally Peters, while Willie Stevens prepared to make his annual winter pilgrimage to Florida. Mr. and Mrs. Henry Stevens, whose contemplated European trip had been canceled because of the murders, now hoped to complete a South American tour.

Mott voiced no objection to the proposed departures of his principle suspects. "We can always get them if we have to," he added quickly.

On January 3, 1923, the new Somerset Grand Jury adjourned without taking up the Hall-Mills case. That evening the county freeholders grudgingly approved an $8,500 bill submitted by Attorney General McCran. Included in the two-page itemized statement were $3,500 for Mott and $1,623 for Detective Mason.

"Good money after bad" was the general consensus of Somerville sentiment.

Chapter 14

HIATUS

(January 4, 1923, to July 3, 1926)

Although the next three and a half years passed quietly enough in New Brunswick, the world scene was anything but tranquil. In the middle of January, 1923, French and Belgian troops invaded and occupied the Ruhr because of Germany's default in its reparations payments. Eleven months later Munich police succeeded in thwarting Adolf Hitler's Beer Hall Putsch. Lenin's death early in 1924 marked the beginning of a power struggle between Stalin and Trotsky that was to last until Trotsky's compulsory exile, five years later.

In the summer of 1924, after the mark had skidded to more than four trillion to the dollar, the Dawes Reparation Plan was accepted by both the Allies and Germany, and foreign troops began to evacuate the Ruhr. In April 1925, four months after Hitler's release from the Landsberg fortress, Field Marshal von Hindenburg was elected President of a chaotic and divided Germany. The following fall an international conference which was hopefully designed "to insure world peace" began in Locarno, Switzerland.

In the United States events were hardly less tumultuous. Harding's death in the summer of 1923 had ushered in the Teapot Dome scandal, which resulted in the forced resignation of Attorney General Harry M. Daugherty the following spring. In July of that year Nathan Leopold and Richard Loeb, after pleading guilty to the thrill slaying of fourteen-year-old Bobby Franks, were sentenced to life imprisonment. In the summer of 1925 a country that was preoccupied with the Sacco-Vanzetti drama, prohibition, the boom in Wall Street, and the League of Nations controversy was convulsed by Clarence Darrow's antics in the Scope's "monkey trial" in Dayton, Tennessee.

Faced with such formidable competition, the Hall-Mills case rarely made the news columns. But many of its more prominent figures managed to break into print from time to time. Indeed, the first few months of 1923 were to feature a significant number of articles about those participants whose names had become, in a matter of months, household words the length and breadth of the United States.

At the beginning of February a band of newspaper photographers descended upon Manhattan's Pier 55, where the S.S. *Mauretania* was about to leave on a Mediterranean cruise. They had been tipped off, they told the ship's officers, that Mrs. Hall was about to sail for Europe. With the help of many of the liner's curious passengers, the cameramen searched the vessel from stem to stern without finding the elusive widow.

Forty blocks to the north the Italian liner *America* edged into the Hudson River, bound for Genoa and Naples. In one of its commodious cabins Mrs. Hall and Sally Peters sat huddled together until the boat cleared the harbor. In order to avoid reporters, they had asked that their names be left off the passenger list.

A week later Mrs. Gibson was found in a dead faint behind her barn. Dr. Long, who was summoned by one of her neighbors, reported that she had suffered a nervous collapse. When she recovered consciousness, she kept asking, "Where's that woman? Where's that woman?"

According to Long, the Pig Woman told him that she had been visited by an unidentified woman just before her collapse. In addition, she said that she was worried about people spying on her because of a lady's gray glove that had been found near her barn recently and that had been turned over to Detective Totten.

The officials of both Somerset and Middlesex counties responded to Mrs. Gibson's sudden public reappearance by declaring that they were convinced she had been thoroughly discredited. "We have for some time disregarded her story," one detective said. "It is probable that she was inspired by a desire to make some money out of the murders. We have checked her story thoroughly and found no evidence to support it. In fact, what we have heard pretty thoroughly discredits her story."

In July 1923, Sally Peters left Mrs. Hall in Venice and returned to New York to campaign for the Republican nomination for the Assembly in Manhattan's Ninth District. She refused to discuss the case. "What little I had to say," she explained, "I said at the time, and there is nothing I can or will say now." She did not know when Mrs. Hall expected to return to the United States nor when the house on Nichol Avenue, which had been closed for more than seven months, would be opened again.

On the first anniversary of the murders the New York *Times* titillated its readers by bringing them up to date on the goings and comings of many of the case's dramatis personae. Louise Geist was reportedly engaged to an employee of the Cunard Steam Ship Company, while Barbara Tough was now working for a New Brunswick housewife. Ray Schneider was approaching the end of his ninth month in the Rahway Reformatory, a period of time that roughly paralleled the length of Pearl Bahmer's sojourn in Newark's House of the Good Shepherd. An incest charge was still pending against her father, who had been free on bond since October.

In addition to his periodic complaints about official procrastination, Jim Mills, who had resigned as St. John's sexton shortly after the appointment of its new rector, was still going about his janitorial duties at the Lord Stirling School. He took great pride in explaining that despite his family's pressing need for money, he had refused to let Charlotte accept an offer of $750 a week from a New York theatre owner "just to show herself on the stage without singing or saying a word."

In Franklin Township, Mrs. Gibson and Mrs. Russell maintained an uneasy truce along the boundaries of their respective properties. Two miles to the north the Phillips farm had recovered its attraction as New Brunswick's favorite trysting place. The ghosts of the handsome rector and his amorous choir singer did not seem to dampen the ardor of its nocturnal visitors.

As the years slipped by, there were occasional halfhearted assurances by the authorities of the two New Jersey counties that the Hall-Mills investigation was still in the active stage.

"The case is not dead," said a Middlesex detective in September 1923. "We have not forgotten. Someday something may turn up."

One month later a Somerset official was hardly more hopeful. "We're pretty sure we know who killed them," he stated, "but we may never be able to make an arrest. Not enough legal evidence is in sight to justify an arrest, and we can't make an arrest unless we are reasonably certain of a conviction."

During 1924 and 1925 the authorities hinted sporadically at "new developments" in the case. In September 1925, for example, Middlesex Detective Ferd David announced that a solution might be close at hand. But several days later he recanted, blaming the bungling efforts of what he termed "amateur investigators" for the failure of the police to solve the crimes. He was quick to point out, however, that he did not intend to criticize the Ku Klux Klan, which, he understood, had recently taken an active interest in the case. "I can only say that I would welcome the assistance of the Klan," he emphasized.

In the spring of 1924, Mrs. Hall finally returned to the United States. After disembarking in New York she visited the Park Avenue apartment of her sister-in-law, Mrs. Theodora Bonner. Four days later she arrived unannounced in New Brunswick and went immediately to the home of Mrs. Anna K. Bearman. That evening she attended services at St. John's, and the many enthusiastic greeters who filed by her pew were surprised to see how well she looked.

After lunch the next day she drove around town, calling on friends. During her absence Mrs. Bearman revealed that Mrs. Hall would stay with relatives for several months, after which she intended to open the Nichol Avenue house, where only her brother Willie had been living since his return from Florida. It was expected that Henry Stevens would visit his sister in a few days.

Several months after Mrs. Hall's return to New Brunswick, Mrs. Gibson and Mrs. Russell finally came to blows. The Pig Woman claimed that her neighbor had assaulted her in a dispute over a horse. Mrs. Russell was promptly arrested by Detective Totten, charged with atrocious assault and battery, and lodged in the county jail when she was unable to raise twenty-five hundred dollars' bail.[1]

Just before Christmas 1924 a rumor that Mrs. Hall had married a Cornell professor swept New Brunswick. In New York, Sally Peters, whose political ambitions had foundered in the 1923 primaries, classified the rumor as "a pure falsehood." But Mrs. Hall was so unnerved by the revival of interest in her private life that she promptly sailed for Europe, returning in April 1925.

Two months later Mrs. Fanny Hall, the rector's mother, died of a heart attack at the home of her daughter, Mrs. Frank Voorhees, in Jersey City.

[1] Her bail was subsequently reduced to one thousand dollars, and she was released when a friend posted a bond in that amount.

As the summer of 1926 began, the Hall-Mills case had all but been forgotten, even in Somerville and New Brunswick. Then on July 3, 1926, Arthur S. Riehl, a Roselle Park piano tuner who ten months earlier had married Louise Geist, the Halls' ex-maid, filed a petition for an annulment in the Court of Chancery in Trenton.

The hiatus had ended.

PART II

Chapter 15

THE CASE COMES BACK TO LIFE

(Saturday, July 3, through Sunday, August 1, 1926)

Riehl's petition made startling reading. Following his marriage to Miss Geist in late 1924, he had unearthed some disturbing information about her. "Before marriage," his petition read, "the respondent carefully and deliberately withheld from your petitioner the fact that she had knowledge of the doings of certain of the principals in the well-known Hall-Mills case, and she told your petitioner the following facts regarding said case: Referring to detectives and reporters, she said, 'I was too smart for them; they couldn't get anything on me.' She was in the confidence of Dr. Hall and referred to him as 'my old buddy.'

"Respondent told Mrs. Hall on September 14, 1922, that she knew Dr. Hall intended to elope with Mrs. Mills. About ten o'clock that night respondent, Mrs. Hall, and Willie Stevens were driven to Phillips farm by Peter Tumulty, the chauffeur, in Dr. Hall's automobile. Respondent told your petitioner that she got five thousand dollars for her part in the matter and for keeping quiet about it. . . . Respondent told your petitioner Willie Stevens was a good shot and that there was always a pistol in the Hall library drawer."

Riehl's petition immediately became front page news when the New York *Daily Mirror*, William Randolph Hearst's newest journalistic venture, gave it full coverage. Impressed by the phenomenal success of Joseph Patterson's *Daily News*,

Hearst had entered the tabloid field with the *Mirror* in June 1924. For the next two years he resorted to every competitive trick learned in a lifetime of publishing to overtake the older paper. From the piracy of key *News* personnel to a daily dispensation of sin, sex, and sensation, he stopped at nothing in his frenzied attempt to wean away Patterson's readers.

By 1926, however, despite all of Hearst's efforts, his paper still lagged far behind its chief competitor. But to Phil Payne, its flamboyant editor who shared his boss's anti-*News* mania,[1] Riehl's accusations gave every promise of being the circulation booster he was so desperately seeking. With a fond remembrance of what the sinking of the battleship *Maine* in Havana harbor twenty-eight years earlier had done for its older sister, the *Journal*, the *Mirror* threw all restraint to the winds as it dared Governor A. Harry Moore to reopen the juicy murder case.

HALL-MILLS MYSTERY BARED, it headlined on July 16. The next day the paper implored Mrs. Hall: TELL US WHY. On July 19 it hinted at the machinations of MRS. HALL'S SPIES. Two days later it proclaimed, HALL'S BRIBERY IS REVEALED. On successive days, starting with July 22, the tabloid blared: HALL-MILLS STATEMENTS GONE; MRS. HALL'S SPIES HELD TOWN IN TERROR FOR WEEKS; HOW HIDDEN HAND BALKED HALL MURDER JUSTICE, and MILLS TELLS OF HOUNDING AFTER DR. HALL'S MURDER.

Impressed by the *Mirror's* burgeoning circulation figures, other New York and New Jersey newspapers soon added their strident calls for action.

Finally Moore could resist the mounting pressure no longer. On Wednesday, July 14, he summoned Attorney General Edward L. Katzenbach and John Toolan, who had

[1] Payne had never forgiven the *News*, which had discharged him as its editor because of his well-publicized attentions to divorcée Peggy Hopkins Joyce.

succeeded Stricker as Middlesex County prosecutor, to a conference at his office in Trenton. Upon his return to New Brunswick, Toolan spent a day poring over the old Hall-Mills files and then questioned Mrs. Riehl for several hours. "I want it clearly understood," he later told reporters, "that I am conducting this investigation through personal interest and on my own hook, not officially."

In New York, Timothy Pfeiffer revealed that after the publication of Riehl's petition by the *Mirror*, Mrs. Hall had visited him in his office. He had assured her that this latest development was only a publicity stunt. "The petition has evidently been written by a newspaperman to produce a summer sensation," he said. "The statements in the petition are so ridiculous it is useless to say anything about them."

Mrs. Riehl, who was now living near New Brunswick, said that her husband's allegations were "a pack of lies." He had visited her in May "and threatened to drag me into an investigation of the Hall-Mills murders if I did not go back to him." Her brother said that nobody in his family had learned of Louise's marriage to Riehl until last Christmas, and that as far as he knew, the couple had never lived together. The annulment action was, in his opinion, nothing more than "a spite action."

On Friday, July 16, the clerk of the Chancery Court said that three days after the filing of Riehl's petition Reinhold Hebeler, Riehl's attorney, had attempted to withdraw it. He had been informed that this could not be done without a formal application to the court. The lawyer promptly denied that he had authorized anyone to terminate the suit. "The petition was filed in good faith," he insisted, "and will not be withdrawn voluntarily."

Despite the announcement by Moore's executive secretary that the governor was "prepared to take prompt action" if the attorney general and Prosecutor Toolan recommended opening the case, it did not appear that any immediate decision would be forthcoming. Big, rangy Francis L. Bergen,

who had succeeded Beekman[2] as Somerset County prosecutor, shared Toolan's opinion that there was little probability of a new investigation. Returning to Somerville on
Monday, July 19, from a fishing trip in Canada, he stated
emphatically that the information in the Riehl petition did
not warrant further action.

The following day, however, while New Jersey sweltered
under a heat wave that was breaking all modern records, Mr.
and Mrs. George Sipel[3] were brought to Toolan's office. For
more than four hours the hapless couple were questioned by
the Middlesex prosecutor and several Jersey City police
officers who had been brought into the case at the governor's
insistence. When the bewildered Sipels were finally ushered
out of Toolan's humid office, the prosecutor announced
that the investigation was being shifted to Somerset County
and that Bergen was now in command.

For the next eight days, despite the *Mirror's* frenzied pleas
for immediate action, no official news whatever emanated
from Somerville. Then suddenly, at 10 A.M. on Wednesday,
July 28, the telephone rang in the home of Justice of the
Peace William R. Sutphen. The justice's caller was Prosecutor Bergen, who asked him to come to the county courthouse
as soon as possible. When Sutphen arrived at Bergen's office,
he was informed that certain evidence had been found which
clearly pointed to Mrs. Hall as one of the murderers of her
husband and Eleanor Mills.

Sutphen was easily convinced. Fifteen minutes after entering the prosecutor's office he was busy dictating two warrants
for the widow's arrest.

"Frances Hall," the first one read, "stands charged that on
or about the fourteenth day of September, 1922, at the

2 Beekman had died during the winter, after being named a judge of the
Court of Common Pleas.

3 In 1922, Sipel, a Middlebush farmer, claimed that Mrs. Gibson had tried
to bribe him to confirm her version of what she had seen in De Russey's
Lane on the night of the murders.

Township of Franklin, county aforesaid, she did willfully and feloniously and of malice aforethought, kill and murder Edward Wheeler Hall against the peace of the state."

The second warrant was identical except that it substituted Mrs. Mills' name for that of the rector.

For some reason no attempt to apprehend the suspect was made until more than thirteen hours after Sutphen had issued the warrants. A few minutes before midnight a car containing State Police Captain John Lamb and five officers drove into Mrs. Hall's circular driveway. After Lamb rang the front bell, a servant opened the door. "Tell Mrs. Hall that I want to see her," the officer ordered the wide-eyed girl.

Willie Stevens was the first member of the family to come downstairs. "Hello, Willie," Lamb said. "I came here to see Mrs. Hall right away. I have important business of an official character to transact with her." Willie, who seemed to be only half awake, shouted up the stairwell, "Frances, they want you."

Several minutes later Mrs. Hall descended the stairs. "Good evening, gentlemen," she said. "Your visit is a rather late one. I suppose you want to question me again."

Lamb came right to the point. "I have a warrant calling for your arrest," he explained. "I have been instructed to take you to Somerville at once." When Mrs. Hall asked to see the warrant, the big trooper handed it to her.

As soon as she had read it, she asked quietly, "May I telephone my attorney?" Lamb nodded, and she went to the study and called Russell E. Watson, a New Brunswick lawyer, who arrived ten minutes later. After scanning the warrant Watson told Mrs. Hall that the document was authentic and advised her to accompany the officers.

Before being driven to Somerville in Lamb's car the widow called Elovine Carpender, Henry's wife, and asked her to come with her. The two women were then taken to the Somerset County seat, where Mrs. Hall was arraigned before Justice Sutphen. By 3 A.M. the formalities were com-

pleted, and Warden James P. Major escorted Mrs. Hall to a
detention cell on the second floor of the county jail, a grim
little building of yellow brick behind the courthouse.

New Brunswick was alive with rumors early on Thursday,
July 29. One of the most persistent was that Louise Geist
Riehl had changed her 1922 story and admitted that Mrs.
Hall had received a telephone call from Barbara Tough on
the evening of the murders, informing her that the rector
and Mrs. Mills were sitting on a bench in Buccleuch Park.
But Louise quickly threw cold water on the story. "I never
said Barbara telephoned about seeing the rector," she said
angrily. Barbara Tough characterized the report as "one big
lie."

Peter Tumulty indignantly denied that he had driven
Mrs. Hall, Willie Stevens, and Louise Geist to the Phillips
farm on the night of September 14, 1922. "I didn't drive for
anyone that day," he stated. "I did very little driving at all
for the Halls, working mostly in the garden, and on that day
I worked steadily up until five o'clock and then went home.
When I got home, I stayed there."

So far there had been no public corroboration of Riehl's
amazing story. But if Prosecutor Bergen had any new evidence to support the piano tuner's annulment petition, he
obviously did not intend to reveal it.

"The previous investigation of the case was hampered by
premature publication of evidence," he said. "We are not
going to give out anything that would disclose the nature of
our new evidence. We will make public nothing. After going
over some new evidence, however, I can say that it is of
sufficient importance to be taken to the grand jury."

In the meantime Mrs. Hall languished in her cell. The
15′ x 15′ gray-painted room contained two chairs, two cot-
like wooden beds, a small rickety table, and a strip of worn
carpet. Its barred windows looked out on a short stretch
of lawn at the rear of the courthouse, where a group of

small boys, in open defiance of Warden Major's orders to move on, were busy pointing out the location of the widow's cell to curious passers-by who were willing to pay for the information.

At noon it was announced that Mrs. Hall had just retained Robert McCarter of Rumsen as her chief defense counsel. A lifelong Republican, the sixty-seven-year-old McCarter, who was one of New Jersey's best-known trial lawyers, was a former attorney general and state senator, and at present served as counsel to the Public Service Commission. Despite his age, he was a man of extraordinary vigor, an attribute that was immediately apparent to the reporters who met his car when he drove into Somerville that afternoon.

McCarter's first step was to ask Bergen for a summary of the new evidence that had led to the widow's apprehension. When the young prosecutor refused to discuss this phase of the case with him, McCarter berated him for arresting his new client in the middle of the night. "After all," he complained, "the warrant was issued at 11 A.M. and she could have been arrested at any time during the day."

Bergen pointed out that William Phillips, a watchman at the New Jersey State College for Women, had been arrested at the same time as Mrs. Hall. Phillips, who had previously identified the widow as the woman he had seen entering the Hall residence after midnight on the night of the murders, was being held in the Somerset County Jail as a material witness. "We have not treated your client any different than anyone else," the young prosecutor assured McCarter.

The next morning McCarter submitted a petition to Chief Justice William S. Gummere, asking him to schedule a bail hearing for his client. Included in his papers was an affidavit from Mrs. Hall in which she asserted that she was "absolutely innocent." Gummere immediately informed Bergen and McCarter that he would hold a hearing at his summer home in Point Pleasant at three that afternoon.

The hearing began promptly at three in the study of the tall, white-haired justice. McCarter's brief argument stressed the fact that Mrs. Hall was entitled to bail as a constitutional right. "Bail is admissible in capital cases," he said, "except when the proof is evident and the presumption is great. In this case every presumption is in her favor. They have thoroughly investigated every proof against her and they have nothing. So far as the evidence is concerned, it is purely the affidavit of the prosecutor, a young man, newly appointed—"

Gummere cut him off abruptly. "That's not against him, is it?" he asked. McCarter was all apologies. "No, no," he said quickly. "I have the greatest admiration for Francis. I knew his father well, and I am only sorry that he did not live to see his son appointed prosecutor."

With the amenities out of the way, McCarter resumed his argument. "Mrs. Hall is a responsible person," he explained earnestly. "We therefore respectfully urge that she be released, in whatever bail you see fit to fix, to await the action of the grand jury."

For a long moment Bergen seemed at a loss for words. Then speaking in a soft, hesitant voice, he agreed with most of what his elder adversary had said. When Gummere broke in to ask if the prosecutor had any new evidence, Bergen demurred. "I am not in a position to give the evidence now," he replied.

"Unless you can lay before me facts which would warrant my acting otherwise," Gummere said, "I shall be inclined to grant the application for bail." There was little argument about the amount. After McCarter pointed out that Mrs. Hall was "a person of standing in the community, but is not a Croesus," Gummere fixed bail at seventy-five hundred dollars for each murder charge.

It was 3:35 P.M. when Warden Major broke the good news to his impassive prisoner. By four every street around the jail was jammed with cars, and it took the joint efforts of several Somerville policemen to keep traffic moving. Shortly after seven o'clock a copy of Justice Gummere's bail order and two bonds in the amount of seventy-five hundred dollars each were served on the warden. Fifteen minutes later Mrs. Hall appeared at the entrance to the jail.

For an instant her composure left her as she caught sight of the tremendous throng which filled the sidewalk in front of the building. Recovering herself quickly, she agreed to pose for the score of photographers who had been waiting for almost three hours. When the cameramen were finally satiated, Mrs. Hall, accompanied by Elovine Carpender, walked to the latter's car, which was parked behind the jail.

Arriving home thirty minutes later, she ordered a light supper and retired as soon as she had finished it. One of her attorneys informed the waiting reporters that she would not issue a statement. "She made an affidavit denying all knowledge of the crime," he explained. "What more can she say?"

While Mrs. Hall's bail hearing had been in progress, Governor Moore announced that he had just spoken to Attorney General Katzenbach, and suggested that Bergen be superseded by State Senator Alexander Simpson of Hudson County.

"I had two reasons," Moore told reporters at his Sea Girt summer home. "In the first place, this case is peculiar in that while the crime was committed in Somerset County the people concerned in it all live in the adjoining county of Middlesex. For that reason there is a sort of divided authority. But in addition to that, it is quite clear that the defendant is to be represented by very eminent counsel, and I think the state should be similarly represented."

Simpson, an experienced trial attorney who was a close political ally of the governor, had already wired him that he was willing to accept the assignment. Moore indicated that the next step was up to Justice Parker. "He doubtless will make the request, and the attorney general will make the appointment," he predicted. "I feel there will be neither any hitch nor any delay."

The governor refused to answer any questions about Gummere's fixing of bail for Mrs. Hall. "Far be it from me to make any comment on the action of the Chief Justice," he said with a smile.

In Jersey City, Simpson, who expected speedy confirmation of his appointment as special prosecutor, was busy organizing his staff. Patrick Hayes, who had been the head of the Hoboken Police Department for more than twenty years, would be in charge of the investigation. In addition, Simpson had arranged with Mayor Frank Hague of Jersey City to use some of the latter's best detectives.

The Hudson County senator said that he intended to "go over the evidence with a fine-tooth comb, without fear or favor." Above all, he wanted to knqw if any influence had been used to sidetrack the first investigation. "I consider this a necessary preliminary step to a proper and comprehensive investigation," he explained. He was also particularly interested in whether fingerprints had been obtained from the love letters that had been scattered around the bodies of the murdered couple.

In the red brick and stucco house on Nichol Avenue, Mrs. Hall promptly resumed her normal routine as if nothing had happened. Callers who rang her front bell that day were met by a clerk from Russell B. Watson's law office who said that Mrs. Hall did not plan to leave the house for some time. He also reported that Willie Stevens, who had taken refuge with friends after his sister's arrest, had returned home early that morning but would not be available for interviews.

In New York all callers were referred by Tim Pfeiffer to McCarter's Newark law office, but McCarter had little to report. "There is nothing we can do to fight the case," he explained patiently, "until we see whether Mrs. Hall is indicted. We have to follow a policy of watchful waiting."

At his office in Somerville, Bergen was being plagued by a roomful of curious reporters.

Did he intend to work with Senator Simpson when the latter's appointment became official?

"I will assist him for some time," he replied, "and then, perhaps, withdraw."

Did he know anything about the rumors that State Trooper Henry L. Dickman, who had mysteriously disappeared in June 1923 after independently investigating the crimes, had been paid to vanish from the scene?

"That question I do not want to answer," the prosecutor said.

On Saturday a Somerville attorney applied to Justice of the Peace Sutphen for a reduction of William Phillips' bail from five thousand dollars to twenty-five hundred. Although the request was granted, the watchman's family was unable to post the lowered sum. "I couldn't raise fifty dollars, let alone twenty-five hundred," his wife said bitterly. "We have no money, and the landlord has been here twice today. I don't know what we are going to do."

Mrs. Phillips said that her husband had been listening to the radio on Thursday night when several state troopers entered their tiny apartment. "They told my husband that the court officers wanted to talk to him. They did not tell him he was being arrested as a material witness. He got up and put on his coat and went with them." In fact, it hadn't been until the next evening that Mrs. Phillips had learned from the newspapers why her husband had been arrested.

As the weekend drew to a close, Phillips seemed headed for a long sojourn in the Somerset County Jail. His wife, who had gone to Somerville on Sunday morning, had not been permitted to see him. She was in tears when she returned to New Brunswick after dark. "He didn't fire any shots," she sobbed, "he didn't commit the murders. Why do they hold him this way? I don't understand it."

Nobody had any answers for her.

Chapter 16

SIMPSON IN COMMAND

(Monday, August 2, through Wednesday, August 11, 1926)

Francis Bergen was working late on Monday, August 2, when the door to his Somerville office suddenly swung open. A jockey-sized man, with a striking resemblance to William Jennings Bryan, burst into the room. "Mr. Bergen," he said in a high-pitched voice, "I'm Simpson. I received a telephone call from the attorney general and I am here to discuss the situation."

This was the youthful prosecutor's first introduction to the man who was replacing him.

After conferring briefly with Bergen the Hudson County senator had a statement to make. First of all, he was "horrified" at the amount of evidence which had disappeared since 1922. "Among it is the pistol of Willie Stevens," he declared. "This, I am told, was returned to him after it had been kept some time in the safe of the warden of the Somerset County Jail. There are also many important statements by witnesses which were placed in the warden's safe that are missing."

He refused to reveal whether any other arrests were contemplated. "It is sometimes wise to leave people at large," he explained, "even when they are under suspicion." The only witness he intended to question at this time was Mrs. Gibson. "If I find there is not sufficient evidence to make a case, I will interview all the witnesses."

After concluding his statement Simpson walked rapidly to his automobile, and followed by five carloads of reporters, drove to Mrs. Gibson's farm. Mrs. Gibson, who was feeding her pigs, became so alarmed at the sight of the motor caravan which came to a halt in her driveway that she ran into her house and bolted the door. Simpson finally persuaded her to open it, and conferred with her in her cluttered living room for half an hour. That he was satisfied with her story was obvious when he said after the interview that he expected to tell the governor there was "ample evidence" to support a murder indictment.

Before returning to Jersey City, Simpson elaborated on his earlier statement that much of the evidence had unaccountably disappeared. Not only were the autopsy reports missing, but Hall's eyeglasses had been "wiped clean" of fingerprints. In addition, he had learned that private detectives employed by the defense had visited state witnesses and forced them to change their stories. "A case in point," he said, "is that of William Phillips. Phillips was badgered by private detectives and was even threatened with perjury proceedings if he did not change his story." That was why the night watchman had been arrested this time.

Simpson's blunt statements evoked immediate reactions. In New Brunswick, Prosecutor Toolan was extremely upset about the implication that the failure of the original investigation had been caused by political influence. "There has been a lot of accusing, directly or by inference, not only of the murderer or murderers, but of everybody concerned with the case," he declared. "What we all should have is a clean bill of health, and I expect that we'll get it from the investigation."

Bergen promptly released the results of his private investigation of what had happened to the Hall-Mills papers. He had begun by searching through his own official files without success. Then he had consulted Judge James L. Bowers, his immediate predecessor as prosecutor, who had succeeded Beekman when the latter ascended the bench. Bowers said that Beekman had told him that all documents in the case had been forwarded to the attorney general's office in Trenton while the other exhibits were put in the Somerset County Jail safe.

After Beekman's death in March, County Judge Frank L. Cleary, whose chambers adjoined those of the dead man, had been asked by Beekman's family to go through the files. In doing so Cleary had found a sheaf of papers marked *Hall-Mills*. "I did not go through these papers," he explained, "but I turned them over to County Detective George D. Totten to take to Prosecutor Bergen."

Totten, who was now a private detective, said that the packet had been placed in the county clerk's safe, but that worthy claimed he knew nothing about them. Bergen insisted that he had never seen any of the documents and that the jailhouse safe had been opened only once since 1922, and then only to extract an insignificant statement about Jane Gibson's brother. The other exhibits in the case had been turned over to the state police several weeks ago.

In Troutsdale, Maine, Wilbur A. Mott made no bones about his resentment of Simpson's criticism of the first investigation. Mr. Mott interrupted his vacation to telegraph the New York *Times* that he had pulled no punches during his tenure as special prosecutor. "Remember the case was five weeks old when I took charge," he wired. "I can only speak for myself. Nothing was suppressed and nothing was retained by me or with my knowledge."

Before Monday ended, William Phillips was back home. When his obliging landlord posted the necessary bail, the watchman took the first trolley for New Brunswick. An hour later, after a fist fight with a photographer who tried to snap his picture as he walked up his street, he was back in his apartment.

His wife barred the door against the onrushing reporters.

"Why don't you go to the right people?" she cried. "We don't know anything about that murder. What do you want to bother us for?"

On Wednesday, August 4, Simpson's commission as an assistant attorney general was finally signed by Katzenbach. At the conclusion of a brief swearing-in ceremony in his Jersey City office, Simpson said that the governor had ordered him to "spare no person to get at the truth in the matter."

The special prosecutor, who seemed to thrive on hot weather, grew more energetic as the humid August day dragged on. In the early afternoon he called Frank Hague and prevailed upon the Jersey City mayor to lend him an inspector and five more detectives. The additional investigators were needed, he explained, to locate the missing evidence in the case. "We are still looking for some documents, the visiting card of the clergyman found in his shoes, his eyeglasses, shirt collar, and cuff buttons."

At nine that evening Simpson suddenly appeared before County Judge Frank L. Cleary and asked for warrants for the arrests of St. John's vestryman Ralph Gorsline as an accessory to murder and Mrs. Nellie Russell as a material witness. State troopers were sent at once to Gorsline's home, only to find that he was vacationing with his family at Wildwood, a beach resort some ten miles north of Cape May. The special prosecutor indicated that when Gorsline was taken into custody he would be held without bail.

When Simpson walked into his office the next morning, he found that he had been upstaged by a full-sized Indian leopard that had escaped from a nearby zoo. But he managed to bounce back into the headlines by withdrawing the arrest warrants as precipitously as he had asked for them. He had been advised by the state police, he explained, that there was no danger of Gorsline's departure from the state. The order for Mrs. Russell's arrest had been made under the mistaken impression that she was a witness for the prosecution.

But even Simpson, with all his flamboyance, could not compete with Friday's report that nineteen-year-old Gertrude Ederle had become the first woman to swim the English Channel. The New York girl, whose time was a new world record for the crossing, bucked rough seas and a stubborn tide during her ordeal. "I did it for Mummy," she said wearily to the reporters who met her on Deal's Kingsdown Beach.

Like millions of his countrymen, Simpson spent most of the day glued to his radio, listening to reports of the young swimmer's progress. Although he had arranged to interview six witnesses in Somerville, he didn't leave Jersey City until noon, when Miss Ederle was on the last lap of her swim. It was with the greatest reluctance that he removed the earphones of his crystal set and started the thirty-mile drive to the Somerset county seat.

Before returning to Jersey City, Simpson intimated that it would take at least a week to interview all the prospective witnesses for the prosecution. "It may seem queer to some people," he acknowledged, "why I should be chasing around Somerville and other places to interview witnesses when this ought to be done by the detectives assigned to the case. The reason is the case is four years old. I have laid the groundwork, and after the next day or two the statements can be taken by the detectives working on the investigation."

Neither Mrs. Hall nor her team of attorneys, which was already being referred to as "the million-dollar defense," had issued a public statement since her release on bail on July 30. On Saturday, however, their silence was suddenly broken. Since one of Simpson's investigators had expressed an interest in a transcript of the accused woman's accounts at the National Bank of New Jersey from September 1922 through 1924, McCarter announced that he had agreed to make such information available to Simpson, provided the transcript was not made public.

Simpson promptly—and angrily—denied that he had ever asked for any transcript. "I don't know how the story gained credence," he snapped. "I cannot make my denial of the transaction any too strong." Moreover, if anybody on his staff had asked for such a transcript, he would see that the man was relieved of his duties at once.

Sunday, August 8, was a day of quiet, broken only by Simpson's announcement that Governor Moore had offered the help of the FBI if the special prosecutor wished it. "He told me if I needed any more assistance he would be able to obtain some United States Department of Justice operatives," the assistant attorney general reported. "I told him that the investigators now working on the case were going over the ground pretty thoroughly and I did not think that we needed as yet assistance of the federal detectives."

He expected to visit the Phillips farm on Monday. "I shall go over the ground and get some idea of what it looks like. Of course, there have been many changes there in the four years that have passed, but I want to get a picture of it just the same." Before he shooed the reporters out of his house, he told them that he was more than satisfied with the progress of the investigation, although he refused to reveal whether any new information had been uncovered by his probers.

On Monday the investigation resumed in earnest. Before the long day ended, thirteen persons had been questioned at Somerville's Waldorf Hotel[1] by a battery of state troopers and detectives organized into smooth-functioning interrogation teams.

By all odds the most important witness of the day was Jimmy Mills. For the first time since the murder of his wife he admitted that he had known of her affair with the minis-

1 Headquarters for Simpson's investigative staff.

ter for some time. In fact, he had often complained to Eleanor about her romance and even threatened to divorce her. He had never done so "because I lacked the money and was a busy man."

Coming from any other major witness, such a change in testimony would have caused an immediate sensation. But apparently nothing Mills said could implicate him. After the janitor had left the hotel, one of his questioners told the reporters who filled the lobby that he and his fellow officers did not suspect him. "That man doesn't know what it is all about," he explained. "I am convinced that he knows nothing and never did know anything about this business."

Simpson appeared fully satisfied with the day's work, which he claimed had produced "two important breaks." He predicted that it would take only a few days more to finish his examination of the remaining witnesses. Then after studying the testimony, he intended to call a high-level strategy meeting. "At the conference we will hold," he said, "we shall decide the future course of the investigation."

On Tuesday, August 10, Charlotte Mills was questioned for two hours. Now twenty years old and a secretary for a New York firm, the girl swore that Beekman had coached her as to her testimony before the 1922 grand jury. By forcing her to answer either "Yes" or "No" to many questions, he had prevented her from testifying accurately. "There are certain places for girls of your kind when they don't know how to behave," he had warned her when she objected to his orders.

Charlotte told her inquisitors that her mother had often told her that Mrs. Hall was fully aware of her relationship with the rector. After the murders the minister's widow had asked Charlotte to come to her house, where she had urged the girl to apply for admission to an institutional home. When Charlotte refused, Mrs. Hall had dismissed her abruptly.

Chapter 17

THE PRELIMINARY HEARING

(Thursday, August 12, through Thursday, August 19, 1926)

At noon on Thursday the telephone rang shrilly in Simpson's Jersey City office. After listening to his caller for a few moments the diminutive prosecutor slammed down the receiver and rushed out of the building. Ten minutes later he was on his way to Somerville in a Jersey City police car. When he reached the Waldorf Hotel at 1 P.M., he was joined by his chief aides, who accompanied him to the chambers of County Judge Frank L. Cleary.

When Simpson emerged from the judge's office at three o'clock, he announced triumphantly that two arrest warrants had just been issued. State troopers were already out looking for the new suspects. Although he refused to name them, he said that their arrests had been ordered on the basis of information contained in the fifty-seven statements which had been taken during the week.

The identity of the additional defendants did not remain hidden for long. At 5:15 P.M. a large touring car drove up Nichol Avenue and into the driveway of the Hall residence. Because of an impending thunderstorm the street lights had already been turned on, and the reporters who lined the sidewalk saw that the vehicle contained Captain Lamb and three detectives.

When Lamb rang the front bell, Russell B. Watson's law

133

clerk opened the door. "We have come to get Willie Stevens," the state trooper said. At that moment the object of his search came downstairs in his shirt sleeves. Willie turned white when Lamb announced that he was under arrest. "My God, I didn't expect this," he stammered.

While Willie was standing bewildered in the foyer, the law clerk went to the downstairs telephone and called his office. Several minutes later one of Watson's partners bounded up the front steps. As the attorney entered the house, Mrs. Hall, who had been in her room when the officers arrived, descended the stairs. She had just started reading the warrant for her brother's arrest when the storm, which was expected to break the hot spell that had gripped New Brunswick for three days, broke with a torrential downpour.

When Lamb said that he also had a warrant for Henry de la Bruyère Carpender, the state trooper was told that the stockbroker was staying with his brother, Sidney, while his wife was on vacation. When Carpender was called, he said that he would come right over to the Hall house and accept the warrant there. Ten minutes later the tall, mustached broker, stylishly dressed in a gray suit and carrying an umbrella, entered the front door.

After a brief delay while Mrs. Hall packed a bag for her brother, the two prisoners were escorted to the waiting sedan and driven to Somerville. At seven the vehicle pulled up in front of the Waldorf Hotel. Willie, who was wearing an unpressed blue coat and a yellow felt hat, which he had pulled down to shield his face from the photographers, was immediately taken into the hotel. While he was being questioned, Carpender was driven around town in another car in order to split the cameramen, who were blocking all traffic on Main Street.

At seven thirty the accused men were taken across the street to Judge Cleary's chambers. Tim Pfeiffer, who had rushed to Somerville after learning of the new arrests, asked Cleary whether each of his clients was charged with a single murder.

"There are two complaints on each warrant," the judge replied. "The warrant charges each of the men with the murder of each of the deceased."

After assuring the lawyer that the documents were properly signed, Cleary called out Willie Stevens' name.

Mrs. Hall's brother, who had been sitting next to Carpender in the back of the room, struggled to his feet and walked awkwardly toward the judge's desk. He was perspiring freely, and behind his bifocals his eyes were blinking nervously. Reaching the front of the room, he stopped short, twisted his hands behind his back, and peered expectantly at Cleary.

"How do you plead?" the judge asked after reading the complaint aloud.

"He pleads not guilty," Pfeiffer responded.

After Willie had returned to his seat, Henry Carpender was arraigned in similar fashion. With the formalities out of the way, Pfeiffer asked for permission to say a few words. His Honor waved him on. "At the request of Senator Simpson," the defense attorney began, "we ask an adjournment until two o'clock tomorrow afternoon. A hearing will be had then at the courthouse, and Mr. Simpson will be there."

Cleary promptly granted the request and committed the defendants to the county keep without bail.

When Willie and his cousin reached the jailhouse, Warden Major checked them in. He didn't bother to take their fingerprints, as this chore had been performed earlier at the Waldorf Hotel. Stevens and Carpender were then assigned to the first-floor reception room, which had been Mrs. Hall's temporary domicile two weeks earlier.

Jim Mills was cautiously optimistic about the new arrests.

"Well, what do you think of that!" he exclaimed to the reporters who brought him the news after the arraignments. "These arrests must be on the strength of the Pig Woman's story. Well, that Pig Woman didn't say anything at all about the murder until several weeks after it happened and she'd had plenty of time to read the newspapers. I don't know whether her story is any good or not." Then he added, "I suppose they're through bothering me now."

The preliminary hearing for Carpender and Willie Stevens began at 2 P.M. on Friday the thirteenth before Judge Cleary in the white stone Somerset County Court House. The poorly ventilated courtroom was jammed to the doors with sweltering humanity when Simpson rose to his feet. "Your Honor," he said in his high-pitched voice, "I move the preliminary examination of Henry Carpender and William Stevens, for whom you have issued warrants."

Cleary nodded and turned to an expectant deputy sheriff. "You may bring in the prisoners," he said.

Five minutes later Willie Stevens entered the room. His bushy black hair, which had begun to show some traces of white, was carefully brushed back, and he was neatly dressed in a blue serge suit, a batwing collar, and a black tie. He was followed by Carpender, a well-built man in his fifties, whose florid complexion contrasted strongly with his dark gray suit. After they had seated themselves near Pfeiffer and McCarter, Carpender began to chat with the lawyers while Willie folded his arms over his chest and stared fixedly at the ceiling.

The hearing consumed the better part of four days. Before it ended on the morning of Thursday, August 19, Simpson had called more than fifty witnesses in his attempt to convince Cleary that there was enough evidence to warrant holding the two suspects for the action of the grand jury.

With few exceptions, there were no surprises. At its initial session Mrs. Gibson, in a sky-blue dress and a black satin hat, repeated her all too familiar accusation that it had been Mrs. Hall, Henry Carpender, and Willie Stevens she had seen murdering Mrs. Mills and her clerical lover four years earlier.

When Mrs. Gibson stepped down, Simpson called Charlotte Mills. Dressed simply in a beige dress, the pretty blonde fascinated the crowded courtroom with a graphic description of her mother's heated correspondence with Hall.

Two months before her death the choir singer had told her daughter that because of the precarious state of her health she was afraid that she did not have long to live. "If anything happened to her," Charlotte said, "there were some letters she wanted me to take care of."

Tears filled the girl's eyes as Simpson showed her a packet of letters. Yes, these were some of the notes her mother had written to the minister.

The name of one of the last witnesses of the first day caused a murmur in the courtroom. That morning Simpson's investigators had received a tip that someone had telephoned the *Daily Mirror* and tried to sell some of Azariah Beekman's papers to the tabloid. The call had been traced to a Plainfield drugstore.

The description of the caller which police officers received from the druggist's clerk fitted Marcus W. Beekman, the dead prosecutor's brother, who lived several blocks away, and Simpson had immediately subpoenaed him to appear at the preliminary hearing.

Beekman, a thin sallow man in a dark suit who spoke in a low-pitched voice, admitted that he had found a manila envelope containing the missing statements of the witnesses his brother had interviewed in the fall of 1922. "I took them from an office across the hall from my late brother two weeks after his death," he told Simpson.

Q. Why didn't you turn them over to us? You knew we have been looking for these papers.

A. I didn't know what they were until a week ago.

Although he denied that he had offered to sell them to the *Mirror,* he refused to elaborate on the telephone call he had made to the newspaper.

At Simpson's request Judge Cleary ordered the witness to turn the papers over to the state police. Ten minutes later Beekman walked into the Waldorf Hotel with a large manila envelope containing the elusive statements. He told reporters that he had not inspected the contents of the envelope until the previous week.

"I did not sleep much during the week since I opened the package until today," he said, "because they worried me and I did not know what was the right thing to do with them. I did not sell them, so I didn't commit any criminal act. As long as I didn't do that, I guess I have a right to telephone to whom I please."

It was after five when Cleary adjourned the hearing until Monday morning. The two defendants were taken back to the county jail, where they had been placed in separate cells on the top floor of the building. Warden Major insisted that he had not been coddling his notorious charges. "I always try to keep in mind," he explained, "that just because a man is accused of a crime does not mean that he is guilty of it, so I try to treat everybody as decently as I can."

The evening papers carried a report from San Francisco that one Albert Curtis, a prisoner in the Alcatraz Disciplinary Barracks, claimed that Mrs. Hall had given him a large sum of money to leave the United States. Curtis, who was a friend of former State Trooper Henry L. Dickman, said, "Mrs. Hall did not kill her husband and his girl. She only hired someone to do it. I know all about the affair."

According to Curtis, Dickman, who, it now appeared, was confined to Alcatraz on a desertion charge, had told him that he received five hundred dollars for dropping the investigation in early 1923. "I was surprised when Dickman told me that he only got five hundred dollars," Curtis said. "I got more than that."

On Saturday, Simpson revealed that after the preliminary hearing he intended to apply for a revocation of Mrs. Hall's bail. "As soon as the hearing is completed and Judge Cleary has made known his decision," he said, "it will be up to Judge

Gummere to rule on Mrs. Hall. He will be the sole arbiter of her fate."

Later that afternoon Simpson and Newark architect Harry I. Briscoe arrived at the Hall house. The special prosecutor wanted permission, he explained, to measure the entrance to the brick structure. After a hurried telephone call to Russell Watson the latter's law clerk informed the senator that the defense had no objection to the taking of the desired measurements. For the next thirty minutes Briscoe, armed with a tape measure and a notebook, performed his chores under Simpson's watchful eye.

The two men then drove to De Russey's Lane, which was a sea of mud from recent rainstorms. After Briscoe had measured the distances between the cedar grove where Mrs. Gibson said she had tied her mule, the vantage point from which she had watched the fatal quarrel, and the place where the crab apple tree had stood, he and the prosecutor drove the two miles to the Gibson farm.

Before returning to Jersey City, Simpson said that he was highly satisfied with the progress of the case. "Those who have sneered at this investigation," he chortled, "will soon see what we have been doing in a different light. I have made it appear ridiculous on purpose to throw certain people off the track so that we could get what we wanted. And now we have it."

On Sunday, Simpson announced that he intended to call fifty-four witnesses during the preliminary hearing. "Although we have already established a prima-facie case for the purpose of the record," he said, "I want to get most of my evidence in transcript form. I want this for two reasons, the first in the event of any attempt to have the defendants admitted to bail, and secondly, I want the testimony in written form under oath in court before the grand jury convenes."

Monday's most important witness was Robert Erling, a local millwright, whose name had been given to the police by

Nellie Russell. The thin-lipped, slow-speaking youth brought the spectators to the edge of their seats with his testimony that he had seen Mrs. Gibson in De Russey's Lane "between nine and ten" on the night of the murders. He had been sitting with a girl in his Ford touring car, when the Pig Woman had ridden by on her mule. He was certain of Mrs. Gibson's identity because "I knew her personally, I have done business with her."

When Cleary gaveled Tuesday's session into being, the crowd in the courtroom was so great that extra state troopers had to be assigned to keep the aisles clear. But it was not until late in the day when William O'Rourke, a burly New Brunswick contractor, took the stand, that the hearing produced any news of note.

At 9 P.M. on September 14, 1922, the witness had been driving along Easton Avenue in the direction of Bound Brook. On the sidewalk near the Parker Memorial Home he had seen Hall and two women. The taller of the two women, who looked like Mrs. Hall, "was standing off from the other two, and I thought that she was kind of giving him a lacing out."

On cross-examination, however, the contractor was anything but positive as to the identity of the triumvirate. The man had "looked like" the minister, but he couldn't be certain.

Q. You would not say so?
A. In my mind, it resembled him, but I could not say.

He was equally indefinite as to the woman he had identified as the rector's wife. "Are you able to say whether the other woman was Mrs. Hall?" Pfeiffer demanded bluntly.

O'Rourke stared blankly into space for a minute. "No," he finally answered.

Because of the enormous crowd that vied for seats on the fourth day, the hearing opened thirty minutes late. Before Simpson called his first witness, McCarter introduced Clarence E. Case,[1] Somerset County's representative in the State Senate, to Judge Cleary. Case, a tall, dignified man in his late forties who bore a strong resemblance to Woodrow Wilson, had just been added to the legal staff of the defense in an apparent effort to furnish a Republican counterbalance to Democrat Simpson.

Witness followed witness with monotonous regularity. Dr. John F. Anderson, the director of the Squibb research laboratory, reiterated his opinion that Mrs. Mills' throat had been cut after her death. Alameda Harkins and Agnes E. Blust, the last two persons to have seen the murdered couple alive, had noticed first Mrs. Mills and then Hall walking rapidly along Easton Avenue toward the entrance to De Russey's Lane at approximately 8 P.M. on September 14. Both women were fairly certain that the choir singer had been carrying a package in one hand.

Peter Tumulty, a robust man with white hair and a ready smile who had been the Halls' man of all work in 1922, was now employed as Henry Carpender's chauffeur. He informed Simpson that at the time of the murders the Halls had owned two cars—a Dodge and a Case.

Q. And this Dodge was a sedan, wasn't it?

A. Yes, sir.

He didn't know whether the Dodge had been in the garage or not on the fatal evening because he had gone home before six o'clock. No, he had not washed the Dodge after the murders, only the Case.

After Miss Opie had testified that at seven thirty on the evening of the murders she had told Mrs. Mills that Hall had called that afternoon. Simpson called Lieutenant Edward Schwartz to the stand. In late October the fingerprint superintendent of Newark's Bureau of Records had found hoofmarks near the cedar tree where Mrs. Gibson claimed she had tied her mule.

Q. Was it a horse or a mule?

[1] Uncle of the present senior United States Senator from New Jersey, Clifford Case.

A. I should imagine a mule because the impressions were too small for a horse. It might have been a colt.

Q. Were they shod or unshod?

A. Unshod.

Detective James Mason, who had been Mott's chief investigator during the first investigation, had also seen "the footprints of either a horse or a mule there on the ground."

Q. Was it as large as a horse or was it more like a mule print?

A. It was smaller than a horse.

Lieutenant John L. Day, who had accompanied the two detectives to the Phillips farm, said that he had taken photographs of both the hoofmarks and the foliage. However, he had never developed the films because no one had asked him to do so.

Home News reporter Frank M. Deiner, who was destined to be the final witness of the hearing, had rushed to the Mills apartment fifteen minutes after he had learned that the bodies had been found. No one was home, but he had run into Jim Mills on Carman Street. "I asked him where I could locate Dr. Hall," Deiner recalled. "He said, 'Mrs. Hall told me he was doing institutional work in south Jersey.'"

The last news of the day came not from Somerville, but from Washington, D.C. The District's chief of detectives announced that he had just forwarded a handful of charred and torn fragments of a diary to the New Jersey State Police. The pages, which had been found at 7 A.M. on Monday, August 16, in an ash can in Tacoma Park, a suburb of the capital, by a sixteen-year-old girl, contained many references to the Hall-Mills case. Although it had rained two hours earlier, the papers were bone-dry.

The girl's mother said that the pages had been lying on top of a pile of rubbish in the can. "The handwriting," she said, "was that of an uneducated person, a woman, and misspelled words were plentiful. The woman showed a familiarity with the Hall-Mills case only an intimate of either family or a servant might develop. She wrote of things too intimate for an outsider to be familiar with. It was very evident an attempt had been made to destroy the entire diary by burning it."

Thursday's session lasted only twenty minutes. After Lieutenant Day had returned briefly to state sheepishly that he had been unable to locate the negatives of the photographs he had taken at the Phillips farm, Simpson announced that the state rested.

"That is all the evidence I care to present at this time to your Honor," he informed Cleary. "I think—I have no doubt at all in the matter—that I have established a prima-facie case to hold these men for murder."

Since, as McCarter conceded, the law did not permit the defense to call any witnesses, Cleary, who on Wednesday evening had promised a swift decision, was as good as his word. "I have come to the conclusion," he said solemnly, "that in this case a sufficient case has been made out by the state to justify its submission to a grand jury for its determination. I have reached the conclusion, therefore, that these defendants should be committed to await the action of the grand jury."

As the reporters rushed to telephone their city desks, Henry Carpender and Willie Stevens were returned to their cells. For the first time since the hearing began, the stockbroker's face was devoid of a smile.

Chapter 18

THE BAIL HEARING

(Thursday, August 26, 1926)

Reaction to Judge Cleary's ruling was as immediate as it was varied. Jim Mills, whom the reporters had come to regard as a minor bellwether, was all smiles. "I guess they've got the goods on 'em now," he said exuberantly. "I'll do all I possibly can to help Senator Simpson in his investigation."

In the county jail Warden James Major immediately canceled the special visiting privileges Carpender and Stevens had enjoyed since their arrest. "Now this case takes on a different complexion because a judge has held there is a prima-facie case of murder presented against them," he explained.

Within an hour after Cleary's decision chief defense attorney McCarter announced that he had scheduled a bail hearing before Justice Gummere in Newark on Monday, August 23. "We welcome another examination by a grand jury," he said confidently, "for it is our belief, from the evidence submitted before Judge Cleary and all other evidence that is available and was available if Senator Simpson had chosen to use it, no grand jury will indict either Mrs. Hall, Mr. Carpender, or Mr. Stevens."

Two Somerset County newspapers responded to Simpson's victory with hostile editorials. "To believe that one sensational New York newspaper could cause all the recent proceedings and expense," raged the Somerville *Democrat,*

144

"does not set well with Somerset County taxpayers." The
Unionist Gazette asked indignantly, "Must Somerset taxpayers pay bills for court proceedings over which they have
no control?" Taxation without representation, it supposed,
had gone out of style with the Boston Tea Party.

By nightfall the pages of the diary which had been found
in Washington had not yet arrived in Somerville. An enterprising reporter who learned that Louise Geist Riehl had
once kept a diary interviewed the former maid at her home.
"I have kept diaries since I was a child," Louise told him,
"but they have all been burned long ago. Besides, this one
in Washington couldn't be mine. That will be easy to prove
if they went to the trouble of comparing handwriting."

The diary pages were undoubtedly part of the "new leads"
which, Simpson had informed Cleary just before resting the
state's case, he was still checking out. Another came to light
when it was revealed by the Philadelphia police that a pistol
had been located in that city which might be the murder
weapon. Unfortunately, it all led to nothing when the gun
turned out to be .25-caliber instead of .32.

A third was inspired by a letter which the special prosecutor had recently received from a New Brunswick woman
whose name he refused to divulge. His correspondent wrote
that shortly after the discovery of the bodies Edward Tierce,
the proprietor of a local inn, had found a brooch near the
crab apple tree. He had promptly turned the piece over to
Middlesex County Detective Ferd David.

Simpson was sufficiently impressed by the contents of the
letter to drive to Tierce's home near Somerville. The inn-
keeper told him that he had gone to the Phillips farm on
September 17, 1922, with two friends. While they were walking over the area, his foot had struck the brooch, which had
been lying in the tall grass. The ornament had been circular
in form and slightly smaller than a half dollar. It had been
made of filagreed gold, with a Crucifix design in its center.

David recalled that someone had given him such a pin,

but that "it had ultimately been returned to its owner, who was not connected with the families of either of the murdered pair." According to the Middlesex detective, the owner's husband had identified the brooch as one that his wife had lost while sight-seeing at the Phillips farm, and it had been returned to him. As he remembered it, the pin, which was shaped in the form of a lovers' knot, with a small rose diamond in its center, was larger than a half dollar.

But David insisted that one portion of Tierce's story was patently untrue. "He could not have handed the brooch to me on Monday morning, September 18," he explained, "because I did not go to work on the case until Monday evening." In fact, he was certain that it had been "several days, or possibly weeks," after the murders that he had first seen the pin.

In New Brunswick, Mrs. Hall informed the press that she had never owned such a pin. Her statement was corroborated by Louise Geist Riehl. "Mrs. Hall never had a brooch like that," Louise said. "All of her jewelry consisted of fine old pieces such as are found in old families."

Jim Mills was positive that none of his wife's jewelry was missing at the time of her death. "As far as I can remember," he stated, "her jewelry was buried with her."

It wasn't long before the case of the missing brooch had turned into a minor donnybrook. First David claimed that he had told Simpson about the piece before Simpson had received the letter concerning it. This was angrily denied by the prosecutor. Then the detective insisted that he had turned the ornament over to Totten six weeks before the murders. "That's a lie!" Simpson thundered. "He told me that he had given the brooch to a man whose name he could not remember."

During the heated interchange a New Brunswick matron tried to clear up the mystery. "My son and his wife visited the scene of the crime on September 22 or 23," she said, "and my daughter-in-law lost the brooch then. My son saw a story in the New Brunswick *Home News* telling about the brooch. This story appeared on October 30, as I recall, and he went to Mr. David to claim the brooch."

The woman's story was substantiated by her son, who added that his wife no longer had the brooch. "In April of this year," he said, "there was an epidemic of robberies in the neighborhood where we live. My home was entered, and that brooch and a piece resembling it were among the articles taken."

Despite the explanation, Simpson accused David of obstructing the investigation and demanded that Governor Moore censure him. "No one can stand in the way of the investigation," the governor said angrily. "I made my stand clear to David—co-operate or get out!" David expressed surprise over Moore's outburst. He was being made the goat, he claimed, because Prosecutor Beekman was dead.

The diary pages, which had been mailed from Washington on August 18, finally reached Simpson. "I have turned the diary over to my chief investigator," the special prosecutor said. "We will make sure of the authenticity of the diary before we disclose its contents."

The New York *Times*, however, succeeded in obtaining some excerpts from the mutilated pages. On September 18 the unknown diarist had made her first reference to the Hall-Mills case. "I asked Frank today," she had written, "how terrible the killing of the Reverend Hall was. He said, 'Yes, I know something about it. I and Ben and Mike had a fire lit and we were shooting craps. We saw a man and woman walking toward us. We put out the fire.

"'An automobile came up and a woman and two men got out. The Pig Woman came along. She is the only witness. We heard shots. We saw the woman with the two men tear up papers and scatter them over the dead bodies. We saw the two men bury the gun. We dug up the gun.'"

On September 19, "Frank" had gone to New Brunswick

and sold the weapon to an unnamed buyer for fifteen hundred dollars. "We are going to Washington," the diary's owner wrote, "because the police know that Frank is a crapshooter and he is under suspicion." The last three entries published by the *Times* were appropriately intriguing:

"October 4. The baby hasn't come.

"October 10. The baby has come and it's a girl.

"October 10, 1922. Goodbye, diary, we are going to Washington. SARAH."

The diary, like so many other once-promising clues, soon proved to be the work of a crank. With it discredited, all the prosecution's new leads had come to naught. Now it was time to get down to the business of the bail hearing for Willie Stevens and Henry Carpender.

At ten on Monday morning, August 23, McCarter and Simpson entered Chief Justice Gummere's Newark courtroom. After sitting through an hour of civil motions Simpson could stand it no longer. "If the court please," he blurted out, "I am here in response to a telegram signed Robert H. McCarter. So I would like to know whether they are going to make a motion for bail or not."

Gummere turned to McCarter, who seemed stunned by the prosecutor's outburst. "What is your application?" he asked the chief defense attorney. "Our application is to admit to bail Mr. Henry Carpender and Mr. William C. Stevens," McCarter replied hurriedly. Since Justice Charles W. Parker would not return from his vacation until September, the defense had considered it necessary to apply to Gummere for the release of the two prisoners.

The chief justice deferred to his vacationing colleague. "Judge Parker," he said, "wrote, telling me that if at any time before his normal period of return any matter should come up which required his presence, he would be very glad to attend if notified to come to Somerville to hear it." If Mr. McCarter would wire Parker at Northeast Harbor, Maine, he was sure that a prompt bail hearing could be arranged.

As McCarter rushed off to find a Western Union office, Simpson returned to Jersey City. Before closing his door to the reporters who had followed him from Newark, he announced a new press policy. From now on he would answer only questions that were put to him in written form.

The surprised newsmen responded by submitting several to him.

What did he intend to do about Mrs. Hall's bail?

That depended upon Justice Parker.

Did he propose to ask for Parker's disqualification because the justice had praised the grand jury which had failed to indict Mrs. Hall in 1922?

Absolutely not.

The bail hearing opened in the Somerset County Court House at ten on Thursday morning. By the time that Justice Parker, who had returned from Maine the night before, had taken his seat at the bench, more than five hundred people occupied every available inch of sitting space in the stuffy courtroom. An extra chair had been placed behind the bench for Judge Cleary, who because of his familiarity with the case had been asked by his senior colleague to assist him.

McCarter's opening statement consumed almost two hours. After submitting an affidavit by J. Kearney Rice, Jr., a Highland Park resident who insisted that Henry Carpender had spent the entire evening of September 14, 1922, at his house, the chief defense attorney launched into a wholesale attack on the state's evidence. His short, stocky figure fairly quivered with nervous excitement as he warmed to his task.

As far as he was concerned, the whole case against Mrs. Hall and her co-defendants was based on "common gossip" and the "incomprehensible story" of Mrs. Gibson. For Parker's benefit he read aloud most of the Pig Woman's testimony at the preliminary hearing. In his opinion, there wasn't a shred of credible evidence to connect his client with the murders, and he was sure that no grand jury would think otherwise.

"If they indict," he concluded, "these people will answer the charge and prove their innocence. But I say, in the meantime, it is their right to have bail set because the proof is not evident, it is quite the contrary. We respectfully and confidently urge your Honor to grant this motion."

After an hour's recess it was Simpson's turn. The sharp-featured special prosecutor, who was dressed in a blue serge suit, broad striped shirt, and jaunty bow tie, began his argument in a moderate voice, which became more vibrant as the morning wore on. He was a study in motion, striding restlessly back and forth in front of the bench, one hand rattling the change in his pocket, the other running through his hair.

At the outset Simpson conceded that Mrs. Hall had not murdered her husband and Mrs. Mills. "Did she mean murder?" he asked. "No. I think Mrs. Hall meant to confront these people, but she was involved in this thing and the murder was done right before her eyes." He paused for a moment. "She was mixed up in it to the neck!" he hissed.

Suddenly the tension in the courtroom was broken by the sound of a fox trot emanating from a hurdy-gurdy on the sidewalk outside. With a half-smile on his lips Simpson looked pleadingly at Parker. The justice nodded and ordered a court attendant to stop the music. Several seconds after the attendant had left the room, the lilting melody came to an abrupt end with a saxophonic wail. Even McCarter joined in the laughter that greeted the song's precipitous climax.

"And when the poor man was murdered," Simpson continued, "she still loved him, and she did not want his body carried away like carrion thrown in a field, in a pit. She wanted him as soon as she could get him, and she put a card at his feet that anybody might know that this poor unfortunate man was not some tramp but that he was the rector of the church in New Brunswick."

There was an audible gasp in the spellbound courtroom as he pulled a small piece of pasteboard out of his coat pocket. "This," he explained, "is the calling card that was found leaning against the dead minister's left foot." With his free hand he pointed at Willie Stevens. "The man who put that card there," he said deliberately, "sits in this room."

Obviously Mrs. Hall's eccentric brother was "the colored man" Mrs. Gibson had seen walking along De Russey's Lane on the night of the crime. "He *does* look like a colored man," he observed, "with his kinky hair and his dark complexion."

Willie, whose growing nervousness had been emphasized by the rapidity with which he tapped his pudgy fingers with a yellow wooden pencil, became enraged at the prosecutor's reference. His eyes bulged and his face turned beet red as he struggled to rise from his chair. Only Tim Pfeiffer's firm hands on his shoulders prevented him from leaving his seat.

Simpson, seemingly unaware of the effect his words were having, continued without a pause. "It's all well enough for General McCarter to say that Mrs. Hall is a nice Christian woman," he said sarcastically. "I suppose only Mohammedans commit murder." But her guilt or innocence, or that of her brother and cousin, was not in issue. In order to deny the bail application, all that Justice Parker had to find was some proof on the part of the state. "I submit on the record," he concluded, "your Honor should not release these people on bail, but hold them without bail, to await the action of the grand jury."

Parker took only five minutes to reach his decision. "Our state constitution," he pointed out, "provides that 'all persons shall before conviction be bailable except for capital offenses when the proof is evident or the presumption great.' If a fairly substantial prima-facie case for the state appears, we deem the case to be within the constitutional exception. We are satisfied that such a case does appear. The application for bail is denied."

As Stevens and Carpender were led back to their cells, Pfeiffer rushed to a telephone to call Mrs. Hall. The widow exhibited no emotion as she received the news from Somerville.

Five blocks away, Jim Mills said, "It looks as though they must have something on them if they refuse to let them out on bail." His daughter, Charlotte, exclaimed gleefully, "Hurray! That's certainly good news. I think Simpson's great. Whatever he does is just right with me."

With the bail hearing out of the way, Simpson, who had decided to present his case against the three defendants to the September grand jury, asked Somerset County Prosecutor Bergen to begin his preparations. Bergen immediately ordered Sheriff Sanford W. Tunison to select the names of sixty prospective jurors for the drawing, which would take place in Judge Cleary's courtroom on September 10. The panel, which would be composed of the first twenty-three names drawn from the jury box, would be sworn in eleven days later.

The preliminaries were almost over.

The Reverend Edward Wheeler Hall. The minister in full clerical vestments standing before the Church of St. John the Evangelist.

Eleanor Reinhardt Mills. Mrs. James Mills sang in the choir at St. John's, where her husband was sexton.

Frances Stevens Hall. The principal defendant, Mrs. Hall, had this portrait taken for distribution to the newspapers shortly before she went on trial.

James Mills and Daughter Charlotte. "Dr. Hall was my best friend. He took care of me like a father," said he. "Mrs. Hall doesn't like flappers. I'm a flapper," said she. Note the newspaper headline.

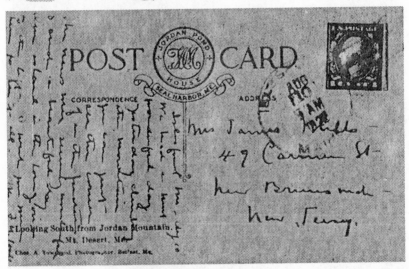

Private and Public Communications. *Above,* a fragment from Reverend Hall's diary, in which he refers to "sweet moments we had together." *Below,* a post card sent to Mrs. Mills by Mrs. Hall about a month before the murders. The post card, uncovered by the author, was never introduced as evidence.

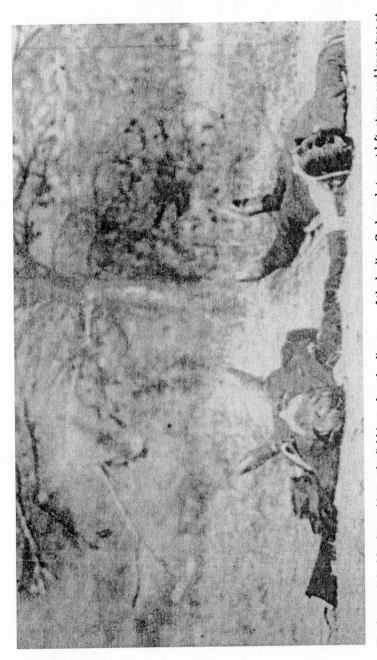

The Scene of the Murders. *Above*, the field just after the discovery of the bodies. Crab apple tree at left; stump and large tree at right referred to in the Pig Woman's testimony. *Below*, two detectives demonstrate the position of the bodies. Note that the crab apple tree has already been partially stripped by souvenir hunters.

State of New Jersey

STATE DEPARTMENT OF HEALTH	**BUREAU OF VITAL STATISTICS**

1 PLACE OF DEATH

County Somerset .... State....NEW JERSEY.......... Registered No............

Township Franklin .... or Borough ....

City Derusy Lane .... No........ .... St.,........... Ward

(If death occured in a hospital or institution, give its NAME instead of street and number.)

2 FULL NAME Edward W. Hall

3 Residence, No. Nichol Ave. .... St., ... Ward ....

(Usual place of abode.)

(If non-resident give city, town and State.)

Length of residence in city or town where death occurred ... yrs. ... mos. ... days. How long in U. S., if of foreign birth? ... yrs. ... mos. ... days.

PERSONAL AND STATISTICAL PARTICULARS	MEDICAL CERTIFICATE OF DEATH
4 SEX Male **5 COLOR OR RACE** White **6 Single, Married, Widowed or Divorced (write the word)** Married	**17 DATE OF DEATH** (Month, day and year) About Sept. 14, 1922.
7 If married, widowed or divorced HUSBAND of (or) WIFE of Francis Stevens (Give full maiden name)	**18 I HEREBY CERTIFY** That I attended deceased from ......19...., to ...., 19... that I last saw h.... alive on......., 19... and that death occurred on date stated above, at......m. Unknown
8 DATE OF BIRTH (month, day and year) 1881	The CAUSE OF DEATH was as follows: Pistol ball wound of brain (Possible Homicide)
9 AGE Years 41 Months .. Days .. If LESS than 1 day,....hrs. or ......min.	Contributory (Secondary)
10 OCCUPATION OF DECEASED (a) Trade, profession or particular kind of work Minister (b) General nature of industry, business, or establishment in which employed (or employer) (c) Name of employer	(Duration)... yrs. ... mos. ... ds. (Duration)... yrs. ... mos. ... ds. **19** Where was disease contracted, if not at place of death?
11 BIRTHPLACE (city or town) Brooklyn, N. Y. (State or country)	Did an operation precede death?... Date of .... Was there an autopsy?... Yes
12 NAME OF FATHER Edward W. Hall	What test confirmed diagnosis?....
13 BIRTHPLACE OF FATHER (city or town) (State or country) U. S. A.	(Signed) W. H. Long, County Physician (Address) Somerville
14 MAIDEN NAME OF MOTHER Fannie Hall	**20 PLACE OF BURIAL** Greenwood Cemetery Cremation or Removal Brooklyn, N. Y.
13 (a) BIRTHPLACE OF MOTHER (city or town) (State or country) N.Y.	Date or Burial Sept. 18 .'22 **21 Undertaker** J. V. Hubbard
15 SIGNATURE OF INFORMANT Mrs. E. D. Hall (Address) Nichol Ave.	Address New Brunswick, N.J. New Jersey License Number ---
16 Received..Sept. 21..... '22 John L. Totten LOCAL REGISTRAR.	

The Official Documents. *Above,* W.H. Long, County Physician, describes the cause of Reverend Hall's death as "Pistol ball wound of brain (Possible Homicide)." *Right,* in the autopsy reports, aside from the pistol ball wounds of both bodies, Dr. Long found in the case of Mrs. Hall the "entire anterior surface of neck decomposed due to some external violence."

TEL. CONNECTION

W. H. LONG, M. D.
40 SOUTH BRIDGE STREET
SOMERVILLE, N. J.

Copy of original notes made at   Sept 14. 2 2
Stephens Morgue

Body Rev. Edward Hall. Age 39. Weight
about 170. Height 5ft 6 in.   Body Badly Decomposed
Ext Marks Violence
Pistol Ball Wound 32 Cal. 3 in above Right Ear
1 1/2 in in front of Ear. probably wound of exit
Pistol Ball Wound 32 cal. directly behind, lower end
Lobe Left Ear 2 1/2 behind.
1. Small recent abrasion front surface Left Wrist.
2. Two (2) Small Scratches between 3 & 4 fingers Right
   Hand.
3. An apparently small abrasion on Neck posteriorly
   about 3 in to left from middle line

TEL. CONNECTION

W. H. LONG, M. D.
40 SOUTH BRIDGE STREET
SOMERVILLE, N. J.

Copy of original notes at   Sept 17. 2 2
Stephen Morgue
Body Mrs Eleanor Mills,
dead about 3 6 Hours.
Age 35 Weight 125 Height 5 ft 3 in
Ext Marks violence
Pistol Ball Wound 32. Cal 2 in above Bridge of nose
Median Line
Pistol Ball Wound 32 cal 1/2 in above and one
inch in front of Right Ear.
Entire anterior surface of neck decomposed, due
to some external violence
Entire Right Arm from Wrist to Shoulder abraded
and Lacerated
Left Elbow Abrasions
Abdomen & Operative Scars
Abdomen opened normal

The Hall Residence. The Halls shared this imposing mansion at the corner of Nichol Avenue and Redmond Street with Mrs. Hall's eccentric brother, Willie. *Photographed in 1980*

The Mills Residence. James and Eleanor Mills shared the second floor and attic of 49 Carman Street with their two children.

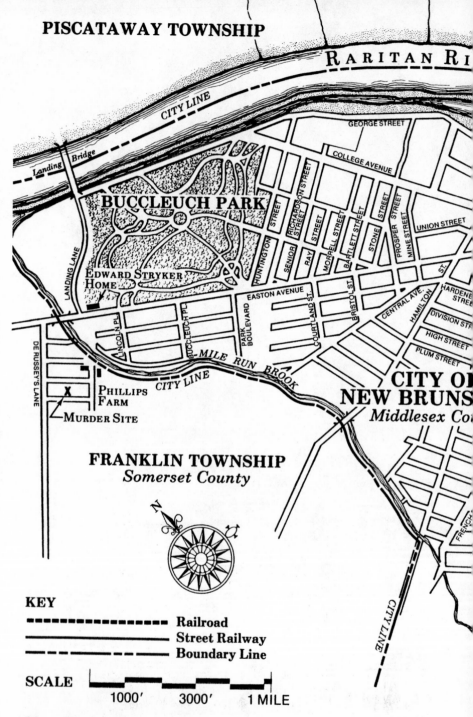

New Brunswick and Surrounding Areas in 1922
Showing Locations Associated with the Murders

BOROUGH OF
HIGHLAND PARK

MILLS RESIDENCE

CHURCH OF
ST. JOHN THE EVANGELIST

HALL RESIDENCE

RARITAN AVENUE

Bridge

WATER STREET

SPRING STREET

CURCH STREET

STREET

NEW ST.

PATERSON

BURNET STREET

CACHMANS STREET

WELTON STREET

GEORGE STREET

REDMOND STREET

TOWNSEND STREET

LIVINGSTON AVENUE

COWISE AVENUE

SUYDAM STREET

LEE AVENUE

REMSEN AVENUE

SEAMAN STREET

HANDY STREET

THROOP AVENUE

COMMERCIAL AVENUE

JONES AVENUE

NICHOL AVENUE

The Pig Woman's Residence. Jane Gibson shared this shack at the Hamilton Avenue end of De Russey's Lane with her weak-minded son, Willie.

Somerset County Courthouse. *Above,* this landmark was less than twenty years old when the most famous trial to take place within its walls began. (PHOTOGRAPH COURTESY JOHN T. CUNNINGHAM) *Below,* as the trial opened on November 3, 1926, Simpson (standing) addressed the jury.

A Family Portrait. As the trial opens, Mrs. Hall is flanked by her brothers and co-defendants, Willie (left) and Henry Stevens. In the left foreground is Clarence E. Case, Chief Assistant Defense Counsel

Opposing Counsel. *Left,* Robert H. McCarter for the defense; State Senator Alexander Simpson for the prosecution is studying an enlargement of a fingerprint (in a composite photograph).

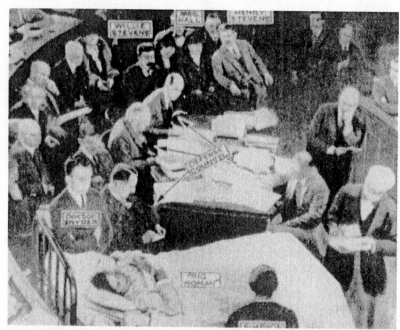

The Principal Witness *Above,* Jane Gibson, the Pig Woman, testifies from her sickbed in court. Defense counsel from top to bottom: Case, McCarter, Pfeiffer. *Below,* she is carried out of court and returned to the hospital.

The Physical Evidence. *Above,* Somerset County officials examine clothing, photographs, and models— including a carefully reconstructed skull. (PHOTOGRAPH COURTESY SOMERSET *Messenger Gazette) Left,* Dr. Otto Schultze explains the path of the bullets through Mrs. Mills' head.

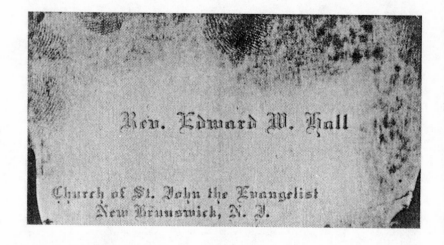

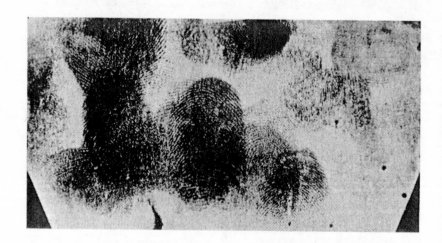

The Calling Card and the Fingerprint. *Above,* the mutilated visiting card found at the scene of the murders. *Below,* an enlargement of the fingerprints on the card.

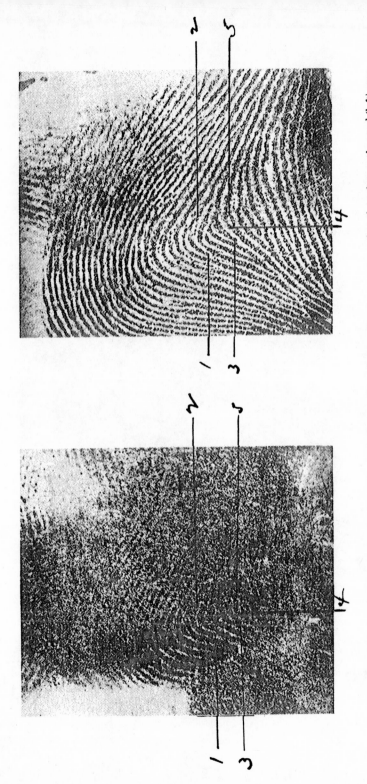

Willie's Fingerprint? On the basis of five points of similarity, three fingerprint experts swore that the print on the card (*left*) was that of Willie Stevens' left index finger (*Right*). The defense dismissed their testimony as unconvincing.

Willie on the Stand. The New York *Daily Mirror* of November 24, 1926 reflected general astonishment that the eccentric Willie Stevens remained imperturbable as a witness.

Henry Stevens' Diary. Stevens' alibi was based on his pocket diary, which showed that he had been fishing on the day of the murders.

The Pig Woman's Diary. Jane Gibson's diary, uncovered by the author and never used as evidence, contradicts parts of her testimony. On September 14, she wrote, "Mama got here 11 am had dinner followed thief lost him – open wagon lost moc[casin] Farmer fired 4 shots." On September 17, "Must have been what I heard and saw on 14th Willie 1.00." On the back of her entry for November 18 (partly covered by the fold): "Went to Sipels to see about cart, he said he was at Russels twice on Sep 14th at night and she was not there – he also mentioned being at the murder scene and saw a light in the lane from a car that pulled in then rubbing his hands together in a dry wash fashion said, you know Mrs Gibson I am a very busy man and my time is worth something and I cannot be running to court for nothing. Well I said, if you are an american citizen, and true to your color's you will come and tell all you know about this case. But we certainly do not want any lies or liars. and I left him suddenly, standing with his back against a rail back of his barn I got in my car and we rode away."

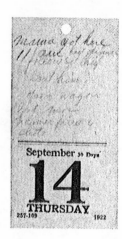

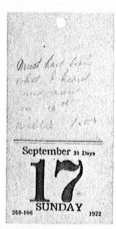

Chapter 19

THE ORDEALS OF HENRY STEVENS AND RALPH GORSLINE

(Tuesday, August 31, through Sunday, September 12, 1926)

The next two weeks, instead of providing a restful lull before the September grand jury convened, were as hectic as their predecessors. The excitement was generated by the entry into the case of two men who, up to this time, had played only minor roles.

Despite the fact that Henry Stevens, Mrs. Hall's oldest brother, and St. John's vestryman Ralph Gorsline had almost nothing in common, they did share one advantage. For more than four years both men had succeeded in remaining in the background. Now their relative anonymity was about to end abruptly.

Henry Stevens was the first to hit the headlines, when at the beginning of September teams of detectives suddenly began to commute daily from Somerville to Lavallette to question him. Although Stevens insisted that on the night of the murders he had been fishing on the beach in front of his house with some friends, it was obvious that no one in the prosecution camp believed him. "We're not impressed by his fish story," commented one detective.

Stevens was positive about the date because one of his companions had caught a large bluefish whose weight—six pounds—had been entered in a diary he kept for that purpose. Simpson, however, claimed that the man who was supposed to have hooked the giant blue couldn't remember when the catch had taken place. The fact that it might have occurred on the night of September 14 had been suggested to him by "detectives or reporters."

In addition to checking on Stevens' alibi, Simpson's investigators were interested in the station wagon he had driven in 1922. "There is a story about his car having run many miles on the night of the murder," one detective said. The new suspect promptly discredited the report. "The old Ford was literally falling to pieces," he claimed. "Its tires were almost off their rims, and nothing was in proper shape except the brakes."

It wasn't difficult for a stranger to find Henry Stevens' seaside house in Lavallette. Not only were there two Ocean County deputy sheriffs now regularly parked in front of it, but it was patrolled by a squad of reporters who had set up headquarters on the shore side. But if the cause of this attention was worried about its implications, he showed no sign of it. He spent almost every day fishing on Barnegat Bay.

As the days sped by without a new arrest, Simpson became increasingly irritable about the subject of Henry Stevens. On Saturday, September 4, the prosecutor was buttonholed by an inquisitive reporter.

"Does the state have testimony to place Stevens at the scene of the crime?" the newsman asked.

"Unless we could put the man at the scene of the crime," Simpson retorted, "there would not be much sense in trying to break his alibi. You will have to draw your own inference."

While the siege of Lavallette continued unabated, a major news story was developing in Somerville. For almost twenty-four hours Ralph Gorsline, who four years earlier had denied any knowledge of the crime, had been questioned relentlessly by relays of detectives. At the same time Catherine Rastall, a pretty member of St. John's choir, admitted that on the night of the murders she and Gorsline had been parked in the vestryman's car near the entrance to the Phillips farm.

Finally the police had something to report. On Friday, September 10, copies of statements made by Miss Rastall and Gorsline were distributed to the waiting newsmen. As they glanced quickly at the typewritten pages, the reporters realized that the first break in the case in almost four years had taken place. Gorsline had finally changed his story after being informed that Miss Rastall had altered hers. The gaunt vestryman had confessed that he, too, had been in De Russey's Lane on the night of the murders.

After picking up Miss Rastall in front of the YMCA he had driven west on Easton Avenue. "I turned into De Russey's Lane and started to back out and I heard one shot, then a pause and a woman's scream, then three shots," he had told his persistent questioners. "Then the scream died down to a moan, and finally stopped altogether."

The shots had seemed to come "from in back of the Phillips farm." Then he and his pretty companion had heard what sounded like "mumbling voices."

Q. What time did you hear the shots?

A. Ten twenty P.M.

Q. How long after the shots were fired did you hear voices?

A. About one or two minutes.

Later he and Miss Rastall had agreed to keep quiet about what they had heard.

Yes, he had taken her to De Russey's Lane before. He usually met her by appointment, but on September 14 they had run into each other by accident. "Do you know what I am doing now?" he had cried brokenly. "I am ruining my life. I have a wife, a thirteen-year-old daughter, and a nice home. I am going to lose all of this because I am going to talk.[1] I have kept silence for so long for one reason—I desired to protect Miss Rastall."

After Simpson had studied the statements of the vestry-man and the choir singer, he asked Justice of the Peace Sutphen to sign warrants for their arrests. The warrants, however, were rescinded shortly after they had been issued. "These two people are now unquestionably state's witnesses," Simpson explained, "and all we ask from them is assurance that they won't run away."

With the public's attention diverted elsewhere, Mrs. Hall suddenly broke her five-week silence and invited the press to her home. Sitting next to Tim Pfeiffer in her dim-lit Victorian parlor, the widow was a gracious and charming hostess. Although her hair had turned completely white, she appeared younger than she had in 1922. Dressed in white linen, she seemed completely at ease despite the fact that she had difficulty in being heard over a violent thunderstorm that was raging outside.

"My chief worry," she acknowledged with a smile, "has been reporters, but really the photographers have been the terrors. On some of the really hot days, however, I felt quite sorry for them. One day, in particular, I debated whether to send them out some cold lemonade, but I was informed that it would be misinterpreted either way." It had been this fear of publicity, she explained, that had kept her from visiting her cousin and her brother in the Somerville jail.

Before the interview ended, Mrs. Hall complained that she was not as aloof as the reporters had depicted her. "The trouble is," she said resignedly, "I am more or less an ordinary woman and that is not sufficiently picturesque. However, I am not going to cry about it. I'll make the best of it I can."

[1] He was right. After initially promising to stand by him his wife filed suit for divorce.

In New York, Henry Carpender's partners in McClave & Company called an emergency meeting. Since the broker was the company's only stock exchange floor member, his absence was costing his associates more than a thousand dollars a day in lost commissions.

The thrifty taxpayers of Somerset County weren't the only ones who were finding murder an expensive business.

Chapter 20

THE INDICTMENTS

(Tuesday, September 14, through
Sunday, September 19, 1926)

To everyone's surprise, the Hall-Mills case was presented to the hold-over April grand jury rather than to its September counterpart. Four years to the day after the murders, subpoenas were issued for some thirty witnesses to appear in Somerville the next morning. Although Simpson implied that it had all been Bergen's idea, it was obvious that the special prosecutor had been instrumental in summoning the April panel.

The hold-over jury, whose term was due to expire in a week, had as its foreman Carlton P. Hoagland, the outspoken publisher of the Somerset *Democrat,* a paper that had frequently criticized the investigation as being much too rich for the county's blood. In addition to Hoagland, the all-male panel consisted of three local officials, four merchants, a veterinarian, a title searcher, three retired businessmen, a bank official, three real estate brokers, a traveling salesman, an engineer, a mill foreman, and three farmers. It had not met since early June.

At nine thirty the next morning Foreman Hoagland led his twenty-two colleagues into the jury box of the Somerset County Court House. Thirty minutes earlier Simpson had burst into Sheriff Sanford W. Tunison's first-floor office. "May I use your telephone?" he had asked the sheriff.

The latter, who was angry because while he was making arrangements for calling the September grand jury the prosecution had been working behind his back to summon the April panel, had answered, "Nothing doing! Go to the prosecutor's office and use his phone! You can't use this one!" With an angry retort Simpson had turned on his heel and headed for Bergen's office.

His call completed, the prosecutor had hurried to the courtroom, where Judge Cleary and Justice Parker, in black silk robes, were just ascending the bench. As the senior judge, it was Parker's duty to welcome the grand jury, instruct its members on the law of murder, and order them to start their deliberations. "You have been recalled," he began, "for the special purpose of considering the evidence relating to the alleged murder of the Reverend Mr. Hall and of Mrs. Mills some four years ago, with a view of ascertaining whether indictments ought to be found."

After carefully explaining the legal aspects of the various degrees of murder, the justice concluded with the pointed admonition that no indictments should be voted unless the grand jurors were convinced by the evidence presented to them. "Adhere carefully to the letter and spirit of the oath that you took when sworn into service," he cautioned, "that you shall diligently inquire and that you shall present all things truly as they shall come to your knowledge to the best of your ability and understanding."

As soon as Parker had finished reading his instructions, the jurors were taken by a bailiff to their isolated room on the third floor of the courthouse. At nine forty Edward Garrigan, one of the two New Brunswick policemen who had arrived at the scene of the murders shortly after the discovery of the bodies, took the stand. He was followed, in rapid succession, by Mrs. Gibson and nine other witnesses whose all too familiar stories were old hat to anyone old enough to read a newspaper.

But Simpson's twelfth offering, a former chauffeur named John Stillwell, sent the reporters scurrying for the telephones. According to Stillwell, who had driven the hearse containing the murdered rector's body from New Brunswick to Brooklyn's Greenwood Cemetery on September 18, 1922, there had been scratches on Mrs. Hall's face that day. "They were on the widow's left cheek," he said emphatically. "I saw them at the cemetery and I saw them on the way back."

The testimony of Mrs. Marie Demarest was even more provocative. The tall, middle-aged woman said that she had seen Henry Stevens on a New Brunswick trolley car at 9:45 A.M. on Friday, September 15, 1922,[1] less than twelve hours after the killings. Mrs. Demarest, who had been a member of St. John's choir, also said that she had once heard Ralph Gorsline warn a tearful Mrs. Mills that he would expose her love affair with Hall unless she agreed to give up the rector.

At four twenty Simpson's presentation was complete. Ten minutes later Hoagland led his fellow jurors into the courtroom. The foreman handed Judge Cleary two indictments accusing Mrs. Hall, her two brothers, and Henry Carpender of the murders of the rector and the choir singer. Cleary read both documents hurriedly. "You have found these as true bills?" he asked the foreman. "We have, your Honor," Hoagland replied solemnly.

After the jurors had left the courtroom, Simpson, who was finding it difficult to control his jubilation, asked for a bench warrant for the arrest of Henry Stevens. Cleary promptly granted the prosecutor's request, and Captain Lamb was ordered to drive to Lavallette at once.

Bruce Rae of the New York *Times,* who had called Henry Stevens as soon as the indictments were announced, reported that the new defendant had received the news stoically.

---

[1] Stevens had consistently maintained that he had not left Lavallette until the evening of the next day.

"What do you know about that!" he had exclaimed. "Now I'll have to show them that they are wrong, won't I? I'm not worried. It may mean some discomfort to me, but it is no worse for me than for my brother and sister. I am not guilty. They have accused me. That is their side of the story. I got mine."

Lamb arrived at Stevens' home at 8 P.M. Mrs. Hall's brother, who, pipe in hand, met the big state trooper at the door, asked what he would be permitted to take with him. "You can take nothing with you," he was told, "with which you might inflict a wound, such as a silver pencil." He was given permission to pack his fountain pen and a safety razor, with the understanding that the razor would be brought to his cell whenever he wanted to shave.

It was after midnight when Lamb's police sedan, followed by several carloads of tired reporters, arrived in front of the Somerset County Jail. When Henry Stevens, a broad smile on his tanned face, alighted from the vehicle, he posed willingly for the photographers who filled the sidewalk in front of Warden Major's preserve. Shortly after he had been booked and taken to a cell, he was visited by Tim Pfeiffer.

In Jersey City the next morning a beaming Simpson graciously answered all questions about Henry Stevens. Although his newest defendant had seemed, at first, to have an iron-clad alibi, the six men on whom he had counted to support it had failed to do so.

Did he have a witness who had seen Stevens at the Phillips farm on the night of September 14? asked one reporter.

He most certainly did.

"I would not have allowed Henry Stevens to be indicted," the prosecutor explained, "if I did not have a witness who put him at the scene of the crime."

Toward evening Mrs. Stevens drove into Somerville. A pleasant middle-aged woman with white hair and a soft voice, she appeared tired after her sixty-mile drive from Lavallette. As she walked up the pathway to the county jail, she recognized many of the reporters who lounged near the entrance to the grim-looking building.

"I am glad to see you all," she said with a weary smile. "I have come to see the man I have lived with for the last twenty-five years. When you have lived together that long, it is hard to have a day go by without seeing each other. I plan to take a house here if I can get one and to visit my husband every day."

The arraignment of the four defendants was scheduled for 5 P.M. on Friday, September 17. By early afternoon Nichol Avenue was thronged with reporters, cameramen, and curious spectators, all waiting for the appearance of Mrs. Hall. At four o'clock Mrs. Edwin Carpender emerged from the shuttered house. "Mrs. Hall will come out on the porch for a moment and let you take her picture," she announced, "but please, if she does, be nice and don't all rush up like a mob."

Mrs. Carpender then stepped inside and led Mrs. Hall onto the porch. The reporters who had attended her press conference on September 3 were shocked at her haggard appearance. The woman who fourteen days earlier had exuded confidence and well-being was a shadow of her former self. Although her eyes mirrored her distaste, she consented to pose for the photographers. Finally she could stand it no longer. "I think you've had enough now," she said in a quavering voice.

In Somerville the courtroom had already begun to fill up. By three thirty the two boxlike galleries were completely occupied, and standees lined the side and rear walls. Even though it was only midafternoon, a thick blanket of gray clouds had made it necessary for the lights to be turned on.

At four o'clock members of the Stevens, Carpender, and Hall families filed into the room and took seats near the rail. Directly in front of them were four hard-backed chairs which had been reserved for the defendants.

The steady hum of conversation was suddenly interrupted by the arrival of Mrs. Gibson. As the short, stocky woman entered the courtroom, she paused for a moment to study its occupants. Although she did not appear to recognize anybody in the crowded room, the defendants' relatives were quite conscious of her presence. When Mrs. Theodora Bonner, one of the rector's two sisters, pointed out the new arrival to her companions, they turned and looked coldly at Mrs. Gibson, who seemed totally unaware of the stir her entrance had created.

Senator Simpson, accompanied by Somerset Prosecutor Bergen, entered the courtroom at four fifty-five and went directly to the prosecution table in the pit near the bench. Fifteen minutes later a court attendant informed him that Justice Parker, who had been delayed by traffic, would like to see him in chambers. After Simpson had left the room, the attendant, with a pointed glance in the direction of the crowded press table, warned that no pictures were to be taken in the courtroom.

Simpson's conference with Parker was extremely brief. As he returned to the courtroom, the door leading to the jail tunnel opened and Tim Pfeiffer led a black-clad Mrs. Hall and her three co-defendants through it. As they seated themselves in the empty chairs in front of the bench, the quartet nodded to their many friends and relatives in the room.

Willie Stevens, who was dressed in a black coat and blue serge trousers, seemed as phlegmatic as ever. Nattily attired in a blue suit with thin white stripes, Henry Carpender, whose prison pallor was quite noticeable, was nervous and ill at ease. In contrast to his brother and cousin, Henry Stevens, in gray, was deeply tanned from his recently curtailed daily fishing excursions on Barnegat Bay.

As soon as the defendants were seated, Parker and Cleary mounted the bench.

"Hear ye, hear ye," intoned the bailiff sonorously. "All persons having business with the Court of Oyer and Terminer for the County of Somerset, draw nigh and ye shall be heard."

Justice Parker, a tall, imposing figure of a man, brought his gavel down sharply. "Mr. Simpson," he began, "in the homicide case before me I understand that indictments were found." The special prosecutor nodded briskly. "They were, your Honor."

After the indictments had been docketed, Simpson adjusted his glasses and read them aloud. The one pertaining to Reverend Hall was first.

"The Grand Jury of the State of New Jersey and for the body of the County of Somerset, upon their oaths, present that:

> Mrs. Frances Stevens Hall
> Henry D. Carpender
> William Stevens
> Henry Stevens

On the 14th of September, 1922, with force and arms at the Township of Franklin, County of Somerset, and within the jurisdiction of this Court, did assault on one Edward Wheeler Hall; he then being in the presence of God and this State, and did willfully, feloniously and of their own malice aforethought kill and murder contrary to the form of the statute in such case made and provided against the peace of this State, the Government and the dignity of same."

The indictment as to the murder of Eleanor Mills was couched in identical language.

His reading finished, the prosecutor walked briskly to where the defendants were sitting. "William Stevens," he barked, "please stand up." Mrs. Hall's brother rose. "William Stevens," Simpson continued, "the Grand Jury of Somerset County has returned indictments against you for the murders of Eleanor R. Mills and Edward Wheeler Hall. How do you plead—guilty or not guilty?"

Willie's body stiffened. "I am innocent!" he shouted.

"But how do you plead—guilty or not guilty?" Simpson repeated.

"Not guilty!"

The same pleas were interposed by the other defendants. Henry Stevens answered in a low voice that could not be heard as far as the first row of spectators. Several reporters noticed that as he replied to Simpson's question his hands were clenched tightly behind his back. Carpender's low-pitched but distinct tones were clearly audible in every part of the courtroom. Lastly Mrs. Hall replied, "Not guilty," in a firm, precise voice.

"Is there anything else, Senator?" Parker asked. "Nothing else," Simpson replied with a quick glance at Senator Clarence Case, who in McCarter's absence was acting as chief defense counsel, "unless there is an application for bail for Mrs. Hall."

Case looked momentarily flustered. "I hadn't understood that it was necessary," he told Parker. "We were prepared for some increase in her present bail of fifteen thousand dollars, and that was all." Simpson smiled benignly. "Senator Case is too good a lawyer," he said, "not to know that Mrs. Hall on her arraignment here had her bail automatically canceled."

The state, he continued, had no objection to allowing Mrs. Hall to remain at liberty, because "her position is different from the others." However, he felt that in view of the indictments, her bail should be raised to twenty-five thousand dollars on each of the two counts. When Case indicated that a total bail of thirty thousand dollars would be more than enough, Parker promptly compromised the sum at forty thousand.

While a representative of the United States Fidelity & Guaranty Company of Baltimore was drawing the new bonds, the widow was escorted to the anteroom of the jail. Five minutes later she signed the two twenty-thousand-dollar bonds, and after having dinner in jail with Henry

Carpender and her brothers, was driven back to New Brunswick.

Mrs. Henry Stevens, who hadn't attended the arraignment because of a shopping trip to New York, returned to Lavallette late that evening. "Henry is behaving like a lamb!" she exclaimed to the few reporters still stationed near her house. "His principal worry seems to be that there is no peg in his cell on which he can hang his washcloth, so I'm going to take him up some twine tomorrow with which to rig up a line to hang it on."

As the tumultuous week drew to a close, cars containing thousands of curious spectators choked the road between Somerville and New Brunswick. The site of the Phillips farm, which was now dotted with small frame houses, was crowded with eager sight-seers. Some drove down De Russey's Lane to Mrs. Gibson's farm, but were prevented by state troopers from getting as far as her gate. Those who expressed a desire to see Jenny, the celebrated mule, were told that the animal had been retired to an upstate pasture.

Chapter 21

SIMPSON'S UPS AND DOWNS

(Monday, September 20, through Saturday, October 2, 1926)

On Monday, September 20, while most of the country's attention was centered on Miami, which had been all but destroyed by one of the most devastating hurricanes ever to strike the Florida peninsula, Simpson was busy tying up some loose ends.

The special prosecutor, whose single-mindedness had already become legend, was determined to avoid a Somerset County jury. Accordingly, he had scheduled an application for a "foreign jury," for the following Thursday. Under New Jersey law, such a request had to be presented to the Supreme Court of the state.

There were, Simpson told the press, at least three good reasons why an out-of-county jury should be called in. First, the original investigation had been conducted by the officials of Middlesex County, "where three of the four defendants live and their family connections and business connections are of great importance." Second, Somerset Sheriff Sanford W. Tunison, who had been a member of the 1922 grand jury, was "manifestly antagonistic to the investigation." Third, the three leading Somerset County newspapers had opposed the investigation from the beginning. "They wanted the matter to remain as it was, with no one indicted," he added bitterly.

The foreign jury hearing took place in Trenton. While three Supreme Court justices listened attentively, Bergen began the proceedings by reading several affidavits aloud. The first, by the Somerset County prosecutor himself, claimed that Sheriff Tunison wouldn't talk to him after the case had been reopened and had been hostile to Simpson's investigation from its start. In another a detective swore that the sheriff "had ordered one of the investigators out of the room, and even refused permission for the special prosecutor to use a telephone when he so desired."

Finally, a clerk in Simpson's law office related how he had clipped certain editorials from Somerset County newspapers since the revival of the case. As Bergen finished his twenty-minute reading of the stiffly worded legal documents, he handed copies of the many editorials referred to in the last notarized statement to the three justices.

When Bergen sat down, McCarter rose and read two affidavits by Tunison into the record. In one the sheriff denied that he was prejudiced against the investigation or that he had been reluctant to talk to Bergen. In the other he maintained that after he had refused to let Simpson use his telephone on the day the April grand jury met in Somerville, the special prosecutor had cursed him out soundly.

With the formalities out of the way, Simpson urged the court of three justices to grant his motion. "This murder occurred four years ago," he began. "It was a brutal and horrible murder. Four years ago, when a grand jury made an investigation, sixty-two witnesses were called before the only eyewitness was summoned. Four years have gone by, and this woman whose throat was cut after death has lain in her grave and not a hand has been raised. The case has slumbered on and on, and justice has not been administered."

Since the beginning of his investigation the Somerset

County newspapers had been influencing public opinion against the prosecution, he said.

"I would not take the responsibility for trying this case in Somerset County while the eyes of the nation are on New Jersey without first obtaining an opinion from the court. I say Somerset County is not the kind of county to administer justice in this case. The trial of the case should be like Caesar's wife—above suspicion."

McCarter was far more subdued than his flamboyant adversary. "This is not a case of hysterics, nor of quotations from Caesar," he said quietly. "It is a case of the law. No effort has been made here to show that the 250 members of the Somerset County Petit Jury are prejudiced. I defy the state to show that the names are prejudiced."

After a brief conference at the bench the three justices promised to rule on Simpson's motion shortly. Two days later they announced that there would be no "foreign jury." The court's members had not been convinced by the prosecution's affidavits. They had been equally unimpressed by Simpson's argument that the newspapers of Somerset County had made it impossible for a local jury to reach an impartial verdict.

In denying the motion the three justices pointed to the fact that the editor of one of the very newspapers cited by Simpson had been the foreman of the April grand jury, which had indicted the four defendants. "This circumstance alone," they ruled, "is sufficient to convince this court that the fear which counsel for the state apprehends that a petit jury will be influenced by the published clippings is more chimerical than real."

Simpson took his first significant legal defeat philosophically. "It took four years to get indictments in this case in Somerset County," he observed, "and it seems to me that I am not going to be sure of the fair and impartial trial I might have obtained with a jury from outside of Somerset

County. I am not surprised, but I have no criticism to offer. My hands are clean. I have done all I could."

On Saturday, September 25, Simpson called a press conference at his Jersey City office to discuss his future plans. "I have until the third Tuesday in December to move this case for trial," he said. "The date will depend entirely on whether Justice Parker is available and when we can obtain a sufficiently large courtroom in Somerville. I do not plan to make any application until I have some idea of these things."

He thought it would take only a day or so to clear up these details, and he planned to ask Justice Parker on Saturday, October 2, to set a trial date.

The following Tuesday, Frances Hall gave the most unusual interview of the four-year-old case. In the morning she had driven to Somerville for a strategy conference with her co-defendants and their six-man legal staff. After lunch with Tim Pfeiffer at the Somerset Hotel she and the lawyer invited two reporters to join them on the drive back to New Brunswick. As she steered her car through a steady rainfall, Mrs. Hall willingly answered all questions asked by her inquisitive passengers and even volunteered a few observations of her own.

Did she intend to go to Europe after the trial? The widow laughed. "It is impossible for me to make any plans at the present time," she answered. "I used to be a good American and I still am a good American, but I am getting skeptical. I have just reached the conclusion that New Jersey is not a fit place for decent people to live in. I don't know whether I shall continue to live here or not."

Reaching the outskirts of Somerville, Mrs. Hall increased her speed markedly. There was silence in the car as the stocky, white-haired woman maneuvered her sedan over the wet pavement.

"The newspapermen and the photographers seem to be

the most amusing persons in the case," she blurted suddenly. "You see, I am quite frank and always truthful—even if some people don't believe it. When I read of the mythological Mrs. Hall, the Mrs. Hall in the newspapers, I always feel that I am reading about some other person. That Mrs. Hall is such an unpleasant, hard, cool person! I don't at all like the mythological Mrs. Hall!"

"Do you think the crime will ever be solved?" one of the reporters asked. "How can one tell?" the widow answered. "I am glad, however, that it is going to trial. That will end it. I am innocent and I have nothing to fear."

What was her opinion of Simpson's investigation? She didn't think much of it. "It is simply intended to link myself and my family to the murders. I am surprised that the state did not issue blanket warrants for my whole family."

As the car entered Bound Brook, the rain was falling so heavily that it was difficult to see the road. Near the railroad station Mrs. Hall scraped the side of a truck parked alongside the road. She brought her vehicle to an immediate halt. "Is everything all right?" she asked the driver. "Yes, ma'am," he replied. "Go ahead." With a relieved smile she started her car and drove slowly out of town.

What did she think about the calling card that had been found leaning against her husband's foot? "I heard four years ago," she replied, "that reporters placed that card there. There must be many fingerprints on it. I heard that everyone handled it."

Had she lost any friends because of her indictment? "I have many friends. I consider them the best in the world. If anyone who calls himself a friend left me at this time, I would no longer consider him a friend."

Mrs. Hall slowed down as the tall trees on both sides of the road indicated that she was approaching New Brunswick. Did she have any comment about her midnight arrest? It was "perfectly outrageous."

As the car turned into the Hall driveway, one of the reporters hurriedly asked the last question of the ride. "How do you regard Mrs. Gibson, the Pig Woman?" he queried. "I don't regard her at all," the widow snapped. "I never did."

That evening Henry L. Dickman finally arrived in New York from the Alcatraz Disciplinary Barracks on the army transport *St. Michiel*. One of nineteen prisoners who had made the trip from California in the ship's brig, the former state trooper was taken at once to the stockade on Governors Island. As soon as he learned of Dickman's arrival, Simpson announced that one of his detectives would interview him immediately.

Three days later the prosecutor jubilantly revealed that Dickman had signed an affidavit in which he claimed that he had been bribed to abandon his investigation of the Hall-Mills case. "Dickman swore that he was the last man working on the case and that he was paid a large sum of money to leave New Jersey," Simpson said. "We have corroborative detail which is being checked now, so that his statement on the matter does not stand alone."

Simpson was not prepared to identify the person who had offered the bribe. He would go no further than to state guardedly that Dickman had done so in his statement. "He named the person or persons concerned in the payment of a large sum of money. It was in cash. He gave new names, but he did not name any new defendants. He was told to 'get out' of the state."

Shortly before dark on Friday, Tim Pfeiffer, who had decided that he had to work more closely with McCarter, completed the transfer of his office from Manhattan to McCarter's Newark suite. He had nothing but scorn for Dickman's claim that he had been bribed to leave New Jersey.

"I was the only attorney for the defense four years ago," the tall shirt-sleeved lawyer told the handful of reporters who were watching him unpack his books and papers, "and I can say that neither I nor anyone else associated with the defendants bribed or attempted to bribe this man Dickman."

During the night former Middlesex Prosecutor Joseph E. Stricker, who had been recuperating from an appendectomy in Long Branch's Monmouth Memorial Hospital took a sudden turn for the worse. The fifty-six-year-old former prosecutor, who had one of the most lucrative law practices in the state, died at 7 A.M. of what was eventually diagnosed as peritonitis. Members of his family reported that his last words had been "Ambition, ambition, what does it amount to?"

In Somerville the next morning Simpson rose to make the first of three motions. "My first application," he informed Parker and Cleary, "is for a severance. The state asks that Henry Carpender be tried separately, as the evidence against him is different from the evidence against the others."

McCarter argued desperately that his clients were entitled to a joint trial. "When you consider the expense that another trial would involve, not only for the county but for the defendants, every course urges that they be tried together. We most respectfully pray—nay, beg—that the order of severance be not granted."

The two judges huddled briefly at the bench. "It may be that the state has important evidence not yet disclosed," Parker declared. "I accede to the request that an order of severance be issued."

There was a broad smile on Simpson's face as he approached the bench once more. "I now notify the defense," he boomed, "that I shall move the trial of Mrs. Hall, Willie Stevens, and Henry Stevens first." Parker's nod indicated that this motion, too, had been granted.

The prosecutor's third request was for a struck jury, a panel to be selected from a special list of prominent residents of the county. However, he demanded more than the usual forty-eight names from which to choose his jury. In view of the fact that each defendant was entitled to twenty peremptory challenges, he wanted a large enough panel so that it would not be exhausted before a jury was finally seated. "Motion granted," Parker said.

McCarter had a request of his own to make. "We have given notice of a motion in the case for a speedy trial for the defendants," he said. "We ask this as their constitutional right. We are ready to go to trial on a moment's notice."

When Simpson, who explained that one of his material witnesses lived in California and would not be available for a month, suggested November 3, the defense attorney's chin dropped a full three inches. "I am shocked," he spluttered, "that the prosecution should ask for a date a full month away." Parker looked up. "What would you do, Mr. McCarter," he asked, "if you had a material witness for the defense who would not be available before then?"

With the trial of Mrs. Hall and her brothers scheduled for November 3, McCarter moved for an inspection of the minutes of the 1922 grand jury. The prosecution should have no objection to this request, he said hopefully, since it had already turned the minutes over to the *Daily Mirror*. Simpson was livid.

"That is untrue!" he screamed. "That is a lie, and he is not going to get away with that while I am in the court!"

Parker brought his gavel down sharply. When the prosecutor had subsided, the justice turned back to McCarter. "How do you know, Mr. McCarter," he inquired, "that the state gave them to this newspaper?" When the defense attorney started to explain that the stenographic notes had been in Simpson's possession, the prosecutor sprang to his feet again. "That is a lie!" he reiterated. Parker intervened quickly and denied McCarter's request.

The defense had one more motion to make. It wanted an opportunity to examine the calling card which had been found near the dead minister's left foot. Simpson protested strenuously. Three weeks ago, at the preliminary hearing for Willie Stevens and Henry Carpender, he had tried to introduce the card in evidence but the defendants' attorneys had blocked his efforts. Now the prosecution objected to letting the card out of its possession.

Parker nodded. "Senator McCarter's motion is denied," he intoned.

With six straight victories behind him, Simpson tried one more gambit. He wanted the court to charge the newly sworn September grand jury as to the law of accessory after the fact of a murder. "We have evidence which we want to present to this grand jury which has come to our attention within the last few days," he said, "and we want to be sure the grand jury is properly instructed as to just how to indict."

There was no objection from the defense table, and Parker's gavel ended the proceedings exactly one hour after they had begun.

Chapter 22

LAST-MINUTE PREPARATIONS

(Saturday, October 2, through Tuesday, November 2, 1926)

Minutes later the reason for Simpson's last request became clear. Parker having left the bench, he asked Cleary for a warrant for the arrest of Felix De Martini as an accessory after the fact. De Martini, the New York private detective who had been hired by Mrs. Hall in 1922, had been actively assisting Pfeiffer since the revival of the case.

Simpson buttressed his request with an affidavit accusing De Martini of intimidating and influencing witnesses for the state. No sooner had the county judge signed the warrant than it was handed to two of the prosecution's investigators with instructions to arrest the private detective. A little more than an hour later they were stationed outside De Martini's Brooklyn home.

Just before midnight their quarry, accompanied by Pfeiffer, surrendered at Brooklyn Police Headquarters. Shortly after he had been booked and lodged in a detention cell, a team of New York lawyers retained by Pfeiffer began preparing a writ of habeas corpus. Early the next morning an obliging Supreme Court justice signed the writ and scheduled a hearing for eleven thirty that morning. Even the most ardent courtroom buffs could not recall when a similar hearing had been scheduled for a Sunday.

For the next two weeks De Martini's frantic efforts to remain out of Simpson's clutches were front page news. After he was released in ten thousand dollars bail, Simpson appealed to Governor Smith. Although Smith promptly signed an extradition order, De Martini was permitted to remain in New York until the determination of his habeas corpus application.

When the writ was eventually dismissed, De Martini's attorneys asked the Appellate Division to reinstate it. After a brief hearing the five-judge court refused to interfere with the lower court's ruling. A week later, however, the Court of Appeals, New York's highest tribunal, voted to free the detective, whose bail had been revoked after Smith's extradition order. "We think the affidavits fail to charge the appellant with the commission of a crime," read its unanimous opinion.

The defense was quietly jubilant over De Martini's victory. "We repeat now, as we have stated all along," Pfeiffer said, "that De Martini will be a witness for the defense at the trial. We will bring De Martini into New Jersey. We have not done so because we wished the courts to establish that his arrest was unjustified and that the charge made against him at the instigation of Senator Simpson was without foundation."

Governor Moore was deeply disappointed by the court's action. "The defense now has an opportunity to make good its boast that De Martini would voluntarily come to New Jersey if he was let out of jail," he said when news of the detective's release reached him.

Simpson's sarcastic comment revealed the reason for his Herculean efforts to extradite the elusive De Martini. "Now that he is free," he said, "he may want to face Mrs. Gibson, who said that he is the man who advised her to leave the state."

With November 3, the first day of the trial, fast approaching, the rival camps were busy preparing their cases. The defendants' six-man legal team, which had rented a large house in South Somerville as its headquarters, began holding daily strategy conferences.

A ballistics expert, hired by McCarter, was examining the bullets which had been responsible for the deaths of the minister and the choir singer, while defense handwriting specialists studied the love letters found between the couple's bodies.

As for Simpson, he had decided to exhume the two corpses once more. In order to obtain the necessary authorizations, he had applied to the appropriate courts in Somerville and Brooklyn. As soon as he received word that Justice Parker had signed an order with reference to Eleanor Mills, he disclosed that Dr. Otto Schultze, New York County's medical examiner, had been asked to perform both autopsies.

Before dawn one day, four gravediggers, working with the aid of flashlights, raised Mrs. Mills' coffin and carried it to a little shed at one end of North Brunswick's Van Liew Cemetery. When the simple pine box was opened, Jim Mills was asked to identify the body. "Yes, that's my wife," he whispered hoarsely. His grisly task done, he was driven home by a policeman.

The autopsy took almost three hours. When Schultze emerged from the shed, the waiting reporters asked him whether the persistent rumors that Mrs. Mills' tongue had been removed were true. "I can't say just now whether the tongue was cut out or not," the physician replied, "but it seems likely that it may have been done." But it would take a complete laboratory analysis of the dead woman's organs before he could give a definite answer on this score.

At eight the next morning the choir singer's body was returned to its resting place. As early traffic began to clog the Philadelphia–New York highway that ran past the cemetery, three workmen quickly shoveled the loose earth over the coffin. When they had finished their task, Jim Mills, the only spectator, placed a fresh wreath on the unmarked grave.

Several hours later a Brooklyn judge authorized the removal of Hall's body from Greenwood Cemetery. After a four-hour autopsy by Dr. Schultze and a pair of assistants at a nearby funeral parlor, the coffin was returned to its vault. All that Simpson would reveal to the press was that Schultze had been convinced by his examination that the minister had been shot "while either bending over or kneeling."

Simpson had also been busy on other fronts. One afternoon, armed with a search warrant, he had swooped down on Henry Stevens' Lavallette house and searched the building from cellar to roof. Mrs. Stevens, who arrived home just as the special prosecutor was leaving, announced that two butcher knives, an old straight-edged razor, a child's saw, and a broken fish knife were the only missing items. "They've evidently not taken the Frigidaire and the furnace!" she cried.

Four days later the special prosecutor sent several policemen to Minnie Clark's house with a warrant for her arrest as an accessory to Eleanor Mills' murder. Although Mrs. Clark insisted that she was too sick to accompany the officers to Somerville, she was escorted to a waiting car when a physician, thoughtfully supplied by Simpson, signified that she was in excellent health. Within the hour she was lodged in the Somerset County Jail.

She was not destined to remain there long. After a brief hearing in which the only significant evidence against her was testimony that she and Ralph Gorsline had been seen "spying" on several trysts of Hall and Mrs. Mills in Buccleuch Park, bail was set at five thousand dollars. Mrs. Clark was released when her husband put up his house as security.

As a last-minute precaution Mrs. Gibson had been spirited out of town. The Pig Woman had been suffering from a

minor stomach ailment for several weeks, Simpson explained, and he thought that a change of scenery might help
to restore her health. Accordingly, she had been taken to
an unidentified house near Somerville, where she would remain until her services were required at the trial.

Mrs. Hall's preparations for her pending ordeal were confined to sitting for some new portraits at the studio of a
Princeton photographer. "The reason I'm having these pictures taken," she declared, "is to correct the injustice done
to me through snapshots showing me as a terrible ugly
scheming woman. They will have pictures at any cost, and
I decided that I might as well submit and have a picture to
show me as I know I am."

"I don't want to go on the stand," she confessed, "but I
shall do so. I would do anything in the world to avoid the
possibility. Every time I see my name spread across a newspaper or see my picture in print, it fills me with horror."

As far as she was concerned, the *Daily Mirror* was responsible for her predicament. "It was a matter of malicious prosecution of myself and my family," she said bitterly, "insti-
tuted by a tabloid to increase its circulation, abetted by
politicians to advance their own ends."

She was supremely confident that she would not be convicted. "I expect an acquittal, just as I have ever since the
investigation was started," she said with a smile. "I am not
guilty, and therefore I cannot see how there could be any
other result."

The widow's belief in her eventual vindication was shared
by two hundred New Brunswick matrons who published a
letter of confidence in the *Home News*. The body of the letter was the same as the one that had been signed by seventy-
six women on the eve of the first grand jury hearing, four
years earlier. "We desire to place on record," the ladies
wrote, "the same firm belief in Mrs. Hall's absolute innocence."

On the official side, there remained only the challenging of the struck jury panel. Early in October, Parker had selected the names of sixty prospective jurors from a list of almost three times that many, prepared by the county's jury commissioner. Five days before the trial was scheduled to begin, lawyers for the prosecution and the defense went over the list with the justice. By the time they called it a day, twenty-four names had been stricken from the list by peremptory challenges.

Somerville could hardly wait for November 3. Like Dayton, Tennessee, which a year earlier had completely refurbished itself to accommodate the crowds attracted by the Scopes anti-evolution case, the Somerset County seat was ready for what its Chamber of Commerce hoped would be an avalanche of free-spending visitors. There were so many jerry-built refreshment stands along Main Street that according to one observer, the thoroughfare looked like "a country fair."

White parking lines had been painted on both sides of Main Street near the white stone courthouse with its stately Ionic columns and colonnaded cupola. The town's police chief predicted that his seven-man force would have no difficulty in handling the anticipated crowds. "If all of New Jersey comes to Somerville, my men will be ready," he said confidently. "As soon as we see any sign of traffic congestion around the courthouse, we'll just cut it off."

The second-floor courtroom boasted 275 fixed seats that fanned out in ever widening circular rows from a pit which contained the bench, the jury box, and several oak counsel tables. In order to increase the room's capacity, a hundred camp chairs had been placed against the rear and side walls. Although at least three hundred reporters from every major newspaper in the United States and Europe were expected, only the first hundred seats had been reserved for the press.

The newsmen were having space problems in other directions. The few furnished rooms which were still available in Somerville were renting at such fantastic prices that many correspondents planned to check into Manhattan hotels and commute to their labors at the Somerset County seat. One enterprising group of reporters had rented a house near De Russey's Lane which they promptly christened "Crab Apple Acres."

With the trial only hours away, telegraph and telephone installation crews were swarming over the courthouse. The mass of wires that clung to the outside walls of the building made it look more like a power plant than a hall of justice. The 129-position switchboard that had been used to report the recent Dempsey-Tunney heavyweight championship fight had been shipped directly from Philadelphia's Sesquicentennial Stadium and installed in the cellar. Fifteen special operators had been hired to man the mammoth board.

Both Western Union and Postal Telegraph had hired additional telegraphers who would be stationed at the courthouse on a twenty-four-hour basis. A New York radio station was preparing to broadcast the trial from a microphone located in a building across the street. A fleet announcer was expected to run back and forth between the press table and the makeshift studio to air significant portions of the testimony.

The outside world would not have to wait long for news from Somerville.

PART III

Chapter 23

THE TRIAL—FIRST WEEK

*(Wednesday, November 3, through
Saturday, November 6, 1926)*

At 10:10 A.M. on Wednesday, November 3, 1926, four years and fifty days after the deaths of Edward Wheeler Hall and Eleanor Reinhardt Mills, the trial of three of the four persons accused by the State of New Jersey of their murders began in Somerville's Court of Oyer and Terminer. At precisely that moment Bailiff John Bunn, who had been court crier for some twenty-eight years, announced the arrival in the courtroom of Parker and Cleary, who had decided to continue their bench partnership through the trial.

"Hear ye, hear ye," Bunn boomed in his sonorous voice. "The Court of Oyer and Terminer for the County of Somerset is now in session. All those having business before this court draw near and ye shall be heard. God bless this honorable court and the State of New Jersey."

As Bunn began to call the roll of the struck jurors, the three defendants entered the courtroom. Mrs. Hall, who was dressed in a black corded silk coat with a squirrel collar and a black ribbon hat, led her two brothers to the row of seats directly in front of the rail, where they were immediately joined by several relatives. During the afternoon, however, the relatives were banished to the spectators' section when Simpson protested that the jury would have difficulty in

identifying the defendants if their "kinfolk" were permitted
to sit among them.

To everyone's amazement, a jury was selected in little
more than an hour. Although its elderly foreman, great-
grandfather Frank A. Dunster, was George Totten's father-
in-law, he passed muster with both sides. The eleven jurors
who followed him into the cramped box on the left side of
the courtroom were all married men, ranging in age from
thirty-five to sixty and hailing from eight of Somerset
County's towns and villages.

Simpson's opening was mercifully short. After pointing
out that the three defendants were on trial only for the murder of Eleanor Mills, he proceeded to blame the tragedy on
Mrs. Hall's desire to catch her husband and the choir singer
in *flagrante delicto*. On September 14, 1922, when she overheard her husband making a date to meet her rival in De
Russey's Lane that evening, she had asked her two brothers
to accompany her there. Unfortunately for the defendants,
their crime had been witnessed by Mrs. Gibson.

Moreover, there were a host of other suspicious circumstances which pointed conclusively to their guilt. The calling
card which had been found leaning against Hall's left foot
bore Willie Stevens' fingerprint; Mrs. Hall, who was seen
entering her house in the middle of the night, had called
the police to inquire about "casualties"; the brown coat she
was wearing that evening had been sent to Philadelphia to
be dyed black; and one of her private detectives had tried
to bribe key witnesses against her.

"Now then, we have other evidence which will develop in
time," the prosecutor declared. "I am not going to detail it,
but if we prove that evidence, if we prove to you these facts
which I say in my opening—and you must remember that
when a man tells you in his opening what he is going to
prove you must rely on the witnesses—the witnesses may say
exactly what he says, or substantially what he says, or the witnesses may not.

"We will attempt to prove these facts to you by evidence, then the defendants take the stand and explain the evidence, and then the case is closed. Then it is time enough for us to argue with you as to what conclusions you may draw. You may draw guilt or you may draw innocence, but surely you have to draw the conclusion that with this evidence it is perfectly right—nay, it would be wrong not—to put these three defendants on trial."

Even to those who had followed the case closely, the name of the first witness for the prosecution meant nothing. John S. Dickson, a forty-year-old accountant for a Wall Street brokerage firm who lived in North Plainfield, a small community ten miles due north of New Brunswick, testified that at eight thirty on the night of the murders Willie Stevens had stopped at his house "and asked to be directed to a place called the Parker House."

Q. You did not know any Parker House?

A. The name was unknown to me then. I asked him what it was. He said it was a house for the aged,[1] an institution, and he had relatives there.

Because Willie seemed so confused, Mr. Dickson and his wife had walked with him to the trolley stop at the corner. "There I inquired what time it was with a view to finding out what time he could make a Bound Brook trolley," the accountant recalled. "He pulled out an open-faced watch, and it was exactly a quarter to nine then."

Q. Did you see him or didn't you take the trolley car?

A. Before returning we stood for a moment or so and looked back up the sidewalk to see if he crossed the bridge that he would have to cross to take the car, but to the best of my knowledge, I never saw him cross that bridge.

After only twenty-seven questions Simpson turned the witness over to Senator Case. The defense attorney established

---

[1] The only such institution in the area with that name was the Parker Memorial Home for the Aged on Easton Avenue, near De Russey's Lane.

that Dickson had been sitting in his dining room when he heard "a scuffling sound" at the front door. Upon investigation, he had found Willie standing on the porch.

Q. What did he say about the Parker House?

A. He insisted it was down the lane.

At first Dickson had thought that the defendant was drunk. "He was agitated," he said. "He was anxious to get out of the neighborhood." On the way to the corner Willie had informed him that he was an epileptic.

The accountant had noticed that Willie was wearing a black derby and a "loose-fitting" dark suit.

Q. Did he have any ornaments on?

A. He had a watch and chain.

Q. What kind of a watch and chain?

A. The watch I noticed when I asked the time was an open-faced gold watch.

When he walked with the defendant to the corner, Dickson had taken his hand. "It was a very soft hand," he remembered. "I would say one that is not in the habit of doing hard work."

Like her husband, Mrs. Dickson also had felt Willie's hand, which she described as "soft, but very cold and clammy." On cross-examination, Senator Case wanted to know whether the defendant's hands "seemed to you to be unusually soft." The courtroom exploded with laughter when Mrs. Dickson stated that she had never felt a man's hand before.

It took several minutes before the staccato authority of Parker's gavel could restore order. "I want to say to this audience," the justice warned, "that this is a murder trial that is being tried, and if there is going to be any hilarity the courtroom will be cleared, and cleared without compunction."

Charlotte Mills was next. Now twenty years old, she was an attractive, self-possessed young lady who was covering the trial as a special Hearst reporter. Under Simpson's tender guidance, she identified sixteen of her mother's letters to Hall. She revealed that it had been the murdered woman's habit to leave notes for the minister in a large book in his study.

Q. Where was the large book?

A. The second shelf from the bottom of the bookcase.

After dinner on September 14, 1922, Mrs. Mills had clipped an article by Dr. Percy Stickney Grant, a well-known Episcopal clergyman who had long advocated liberalization of the church's divorce canons, from that day's New York *World* and taken it to Hall's study. She had returned home at seven fifteen and told Charlotte that she had met Miss Opie at the trolley stop.

The dressmaker had informed her "that a phone message had come for her in the afternoon but that she was unable to make her hear, and the phone call, she said, was from Mr. Hall, so my mother left her and came down to me and told me that she was going to the phone up the street to find out if there was anything Mr. Hall wanted."

Q. Did you see her again alive?

A. I saw she came from the church, went up to the house, got a nickel to phone, and went around the corner to phone and told me to wait for her; and that was the last I saw of her.

After the discovery of the bodies Charlotte had gone to Mrs. Hall's house. "I rang the bell," she said in her soft voice, "and the maid came to the door and directed me that Mrs. Hall was around the back, and as I started for the back I saw somebody running to the house, but I could not tell who it was. I came around and I thought I would leave, but just at that time I heard heavy footsteps on the front porch and it was Mr. Pfeiffer, and he asked me what I wanted."

When she explained that she wanted to see Mrs. Hall, the lawyer said that in view of what had happened, he thought such a meeting "would not look right." He suggested that Charlotte might be better off in "an institution or religious home of some kind" until the excitement had died down. Simpson then handed a second package of letters to the girl. Was she familiar with Hall's handwriting? She was. And were the letters he had just shown her written by the clergyman? They were.

Q. Where have you seen these before today?

A. In a crocheted bag of my mother's, hanging on the back of our living room door.

The bag had also contained a diary kept by Hall.

McCarter conducted Charlotte's cross-examination. Had he understood her to say that her mother had left a letter in Hall's study on the night of her death? "I do not recall a note, but I do recall a clipping," the girl replied.

The silver-haired lawyer's tone hardened. "Do you remember, Miss Charlotte," he snapped, "going down to Mount Holly in the month of January, 1923, and making a statement there to Mr. Ellis Parker?"[2] She did.

Q. Do you remember that you stated as follows: "She [referring to your mother] expected a call to come to Opie's next door. She went to the church and put those newspaper clippings on the desk. I saw some clippings and a letter she had for Mr. Hall"? Do you remember saying that?

A. I do not.

Q. And were you at the same time asked, "What was the letter, Charlotte; did you see it?" Answer: "No, I saw her writing it earlier, but didn't know what was in it." Did you make that statement?

A. I did not.

Suddenly McCarter turned his sights on Jim Mills. Had Charlotte seen her father between 7:30 P.M. on September

[2] This was the first public indication that the celebrated Burlington County detective had been working for the defense. The prosecution had learned of Parker's secret affiliation a month earlier, when it had unearthed a letter dated August 2, 1926, from the detective to Henry Stevens. "Dear Friend Henry," it began. "If there is anything I can do privately in the way of advising her [Mrs. Hall] or assisting Mr. Pfeiffer, will be only too glad to respond without any cost to them, with a proviso that I be kept incognito."

14 and the next morning? She had not. Wasn't it true that he had been given five hundred dollars for Hall's letters and diary? It was.

Q. By whom?

A. By a newspaper company.

No, she didn't know whether Mills had ever read the letters which had been kept in the crocheted bag.

On redirect, Simpson, who had seemed surprised by the testimony about Ellis Parker, asked Charlotte who had taken her to the office of the Burlington County detective. It had been a newspaperwoman.

Q. Was anything said about why you were taken there?

A. They told me he wanted to solve the murder; he wanted me to help him, and I voluntarily went with them, and he took me in a room alone and asked me all kinds of questions, and I told him to the best of my ability the things he asked me, and he accused my father of doing it and I objected—

McCarter broke in with an objection of his own. "I move," he roared, "that her evidence touching on what occurred between Ellis Parker and herself in this separate room be stricken out!"

Simpson's face turned livid. "I want to be heard on this," he insisted. "Am I not entitled to prove that the purpose of her being there at the time she is alleged to have made the statement was to fasten the crime on her father? Then I can connect Ellis Parker with Henry Stevens and show that Ellis Parker was working for Henry Stevens in an endeavor to falsely fasten the crime on her father.

"We have certainly the right—they cannot open the door and then shut it in my face. This jury is entitled to know who Ellis Parker is, what was he trying to do before us, was he trying to do something for one of the defendants, was he trying to falsely accuse a man of murder. All that we are entitled to know!"

Despite the vehemence of his argument, the special prose-

cutor subsided meekly when McCarter pointed out to
Their Honors that what might have occurred between Charlotte and Ellis Parker out of the stenographer's presence was
not part of the conversation to which he had alluded on
cross-examination. "I withdraw that question!" Simpson said
abruptly.

Thirty seconds later McCarter erupted again when his
doughty adversary continued to press Charlotte as to what
had taken place in Ellis Parker's office. Justice Parker finally
put his foot down. "I think it is not proper redirect," he
ruled. "You may find some other way of proving it."

The next morning Anna L. Hoag mounted the stand. A
tiny woman of uncertain vintage whose pallor was accentu-
ated by brown curls which peeped out from the brim of a
modish turban, Mrs. Hoag, said that on September 14, 1922,
she had lived across De Russey's Lane from the Phillips
farm. A few minutes after ten that night she had heard
four sharp reports coming from the direction of the Phillips
farm.

Q. What did they sound like?
A. Pistol shots.

There had been a single shot and a cluster of three, but
Mrs. Hoag couldn't remember the order in which they had
occurred.

After the murders the witness had moved to the Phillips
farm. One hot afternoon in August 1923 a man whom she
identified as Henry Stevens had visited her home. Immacu-
lately dressed in a dark suit and a Panama hat, he had asked
for directions to Raritan.

"I asked him to sit down, and he sat down on the porch,"
Mrs. Hoag related in her precise manner. "I thought the
man was sick because he trembled so. And then he got
talking that he had been in Florida that winter and he talked
on Florida for a while. Then all at once he said, 'Wasn't

there a tragedy on this place?' and I said, 'I know nothing about any tragedy.' And with that I ran into the house because I was frightened."

After Mrs. Hoag left the porch, her unexpected visitor had walked to the pump for a drink of water. "Then I came out to watch him. I had my dog with me, and I watched him up the lane and the man nearly collapsed—when he passed the place where the bodies were found, he nearly collapsed."

Although Stevens had told her that he was out for a hike, Mrs. Hoag was convinced that there was a car waiting for him in De Russey's Lane. "He must have had a car, because he was immaculate," she explained.

At the preliminary hearing in August, Mrs. Hoag had testified that the order of the shots had been three and then one, and Case wasn't going to let her forget it. Did she remember saying that? he asked. The witness nodded her head briskly. She did.

Q. And do you remember Mr. Pfeiffer asking you, "That is entirely clear in your mind?" To which you answered, "It is very, very clear"?

A. Well, there was four shots.

Case's voice was suddenly harsh. "Did you say it or did you not say it?" he demanded. "I did say it," Mrs. Hoag replied sheepishly.

By all odds, Ralph Gorsline was the day's most eagerly awaited witness. The gaunt, soft-spoken vestryman was the object of every eye as he shuffled up the center aisle of the courtroom to the witness stand. There was a brief flurry of laughter among the spectators when in his nervousness Mr. Gorsline raised his left rather than his right hand to take the oath, but a stern glance from Justice Parker cut it off abruptly.

On direct, Gorsline admitted that at 10:15 P.M. on September 14 he and Catherine Rastall had parked in De Russey's Lane.

Q. And what was the first intimation you had that there was anything wrong?

A. We heard—I heard a mumbling of voices which sounded like men's voices.

This had been followed, in quick succession, by one shot, a woman's scream, and three more shots.

Q. Then what did you hear?

A. And a moaning.

"Now will you describe, as you described it for the grand jury," Simpson asked, "what you saw and heard, with the same gestures you described it for me to the grand jury?"

McCarter was on his feet in a flash. "One moment," he interjected. "I don't think that is proper."

Before Parker could rule on the objection, Simpson interrupted. "I want you to cut your throat for these men the same as you did for the grand jury!"[3] he shouted at the perplexed witness.

As McCarter spluttered in helpless rage, Parker ruled in favor of the defense. "I have already said that what took place before the grand jury is not material or relevant at this time," he admonished Simpson, "and the witness should not be asked what took place there."

Properly abashed, the prosecutor changed course abruptly. "On the first of October, 1922," he began, "at the Burns Detective Agency in New York City, didn't you go there and see a man named William Garvin, and tell him that your conscience troubled you, that you were in De Russey's Lane on the night of September 14, 1922, and that on that night you saw Henry Stevens there with a revolver, and that you ran up the bank and Henry Stevens said, 'What the hell are you doing here? This is none of your affair. Get the hell out of here!', and fired two shots in the ground, and you got away as fast as you could, and that afterwards you were

[3] When he testified before the April grand jury, Gorsline had evidently indicated, with graphic gestures, how he thought Eleanor Mills' throat had been cut.

taken to some lodge room and made to swear that you would never tell it? Did you make such a statement as that at that time and place and to that person?"

Gorsline's answer couldn't have been more explicit. "Absolutely no!" he retorted sharply.

The defense wasted no time on the vestryman, whose testimony had not lived up to its advance billing, and released him after establishing that he and Miss Rastall had left De Russey's Lane as soon as they had heard the gunshots. His companion on that night, a slight, soft-spoken brunette, said that she, too, had heard "mumbling voices" shortly after Gorsline had parked his car and turned out its lights.

Q. Did you hear anything else besides the mumbling voices?

A. Right after that I heard one shot and a scream, and then three shots.

The shots were "quite a distance away" from the vestryman's car.

Tall, heavy-set George D. Totten testified with the aplomb of a man who had performed the same function in more courtrooms than he cared to remember. In a concise, matter-of-fact manner he described the two bodies he had first seen more than four years ago under a crab apple tree on the Phillips farm.

There was little interest in the crowded courtroom until Simpson started to question the former Somerset County detective about the calling card which the prosecution claimed contained Willie Stevens' fingerprints.

When Totten first saw it, it had been standing on its edge in the grass, some eight inches away from the minister's left foot.

Q. What held it up?

A. It stood up on the edge, undoubtedly supported by tufts of grass or a weed.

Simpson handed him a small pasteboard card. "Have you ever seen that card before?" he asked. The detective studied it for a moment. "That is the card that lay between the feet of the two bodies," he replied.

The card, along with other exhibits in the case, had been picked up by Sheriff Conkling and brought to Prosecutor Beekman's office in Somerville. The following Tuesday they had been taken to New Brunswick and turned over to someone in Stricker's office.

Q. And they never came back?

A. No, sir.

In fact, he had never seen the card again until the preliminary hearing before Judge Cleary, three months ago.

When Simpson offered the card in evidence, Case was granted permission to question Totten before Parker ruled on its admissibility. In an exhaustive cross-examination, the Somerset County senator established that Sheriff Conkling had wrapped all of the exhibits that had been found near the bodies in a brown paper bag before taking them to Somerville. That evening Totten had looked at the card and noticed nothing significant about it except that it was "fly-specked."

When he and Beekman took the exhibits to Stricker's office, they had been put into the Middlesex prosecutor's safe. During the next few days the witness had been present while William Fitzpatrick, Middlesex County's fingerprint expert, had examined the card under a low-power microscope.

Q. There were others present then?

A. Yes, sir. Mr. David was there. I saw them both examining the various exhibits.

No, he had not seen any fingerprints on the card until the preliminary hearing. Case pointed to some black smudges above Hall's name. "Were they on at the time you last saw it prior to the August hearing?" he asked. Totten snapped out his answer. "They were not there," he said.

As soon as Case had finished with Totten, Parker admitted the card as State's Exhibit 17. When the defense attorney insisted that he and his colleagues should at least be allowed to examine the card before Simpson called fingerprint experts to testify about it, the prosecutor flew into a rage.

"I have never heard," he shouted angrily, "of the trial of a criminal case of any importance being halted so that the defendants may have the opportunity to pore over the exhibits of the state. When this card is in evidence, these men can take the card. They can take it at four o'clock. They can photograph it. They can eat it, if they want to, for all I care. But that I should be embarrassed, that I should be halted, that my train of reasoning should be subject to the whims and frivolities of these men, is unfair to the prosecution."

When McCarter joined the fray with the suggestion that the defense be permitted to examine the card in the presence of the state's experts, Simpson gave substance to a rumor that had been bruited about New Brunswick since early morning. Mrs. Gibson, who had collapsed outside the courtroom yesterday, was now seriously ill in the Somerville General Hospital.

"They can take the card," he said earnestly, "and take it to a spiritualistic medium if they want to for a week and examine it and then examine the witness's evidence in connection with it and cross-examine. I have no objection to that, but if your Honor says that I have to go to another branch of the case, I have not the witnesses here."

"We have not said that," Parker replied quietly. "What we are proposing to do is to let you go on with your fingerprint testimony to your heart's content, subject to a reasonable intermission before the other side has to cross-examine." Simpson snorted. "My heart will very little enter into it," he countered.

With the fireworks over for the time being, Lieutenant Fred Drewen of the Jersey City Police Department mounted the stand. Drewen, who boasted of ten years' experience in reading fingerprints, had taken Willie Stevens' prints in August. Several days later he had compared the print on the back of Hall's calling card with that of Willie's left index finger.

Q. Is it or is it not a print of William Stevens?

A. It is.

Drewen was followed by Edward H. Schwartz, a thin, bald-headed man who for more than two decades had headed the Bureau of Records of the Newark Police Department. He had first seen State's Exhibit 17 in New Brunswick during the week of September 18, 1922. Two months later, after the refusal of the first grand jury to indict, the card had been sent to him and had remained in his possession "up to the time of this investigation."[4]

Q. Will you tell me whether or not this card contains any fingerprints of William Stevens?

A. The card contains the left index finger of William Stevens.

Joseph A. Faurot was easily the most impressive of Simpson's three fingerprint experts. During his more than twenty-five years of experience the former New York City deputy police commissioner had studied the science of criminal identification in most of the capitals of the world. Like his predecessors on the stand, he readily identified the finger-print on the calling card as that of Willie's left index finger.

To illustrate his point, he produced some transparencies of Willie's fingerprints, which he projected on a small screen while he meticulously explained the reasons for his conclusion.

Mr. Faurot was still testifying when Simpson suddenly interrupted him. He had just received word, he told Parker and Cleary, that Mrs. Gibson was at death's door. "Therefore I want to request the court to go where she is," he asked, "to take this jury and counsel for the defense and take her testimony because her testimony is of vital importance to the state." He was prepared to put her physicians on the stand, who would substantiate his claim that his star witness was expected to sink into a coma shortly.

---

[4] Schwartz later admitted that in June 1926 he had given the card to *Mirror* editor Phil Payne, "with the distinct understanding it would be turned over to the state."

Faurot, who was still sitting in the witness chair, was hurriedly excused to make room for the prosecution's medical men. Dr. Aaron L. Stillwell, an attending surgeon at the Somerville Hospital, stated that because of Mrs. Gibson's high temperature and fast pulse rate it was his opinion that she was "in a serious condition." Dr. Thomas Flynn felt that the Pig Woman's condition was "serious" and that she would be unable to take the stand for some time. Dr. A. Anderson Lawton thought that forcing Mrs. Gibson to testify "would be dangerous to her life."

After a brief conference in chambers Parker and Cleary announced that they would adjourn the trial briefly while they visited the sick woman at the hospital.

At five thirty-five the two judges returned to the courtroom. "We have seen Mrs. Easton or Gibson," Parker said. "The witness is a very sick woman and in no condition to testify here or there. However, the doctors do not think the feared coma will set in, and are hopeful of recovery. We have therefore concluded that no examination of this witness will be had today. Tomorrow morning we will see how the matter has developed."

Mrs. Gibson's condition was unchanged the next morning, and Simpson improvised by calling Jim Mills as his first major witness of the day. The former sexton, who was dressed in a wrinkled gray suit, had changed only slightly in the four years since his wife's murder had precipitated him into sudden prominence. With his sunken cheeks, his long, pointed nose, his veined, gnarled hands, and his pallid complexion, he still looked like a man on the verge of inevitable and total defeat.

The prosecutor deftly led him through his marriage to his wife, the birth of their two children, and Mrs. Mills' growing preoccupation with church affairs. His wife had begun singing in the choir, he said, a year before her wedding, and at the time of her death had been one of its most active members. In fact, she had been given one of the five keys to the front door of the church, the others being distributed to Hall, Minnie Clark, the organist, and himself.

Q. Would those keys admit you to any part of the interior of the church?

A. Any part of the church inside.

On the night of his wife's murder he had arrived home from work at six fifteen. After supper he had started working on some window boxes on the back stoop. Eleanor had left the house at seven thirty, and he had never seen her alive again.

At nine forty-five he had almost finished riveting the box slats together, and since it had gotten dark, he had decided to finish his work "under the light, on the table on the back porch." A few minutes later his daughter and son, who had been visiting an aunt, had returned home.

He had then gone downstairs, where he sat on the front porch until "pretty near eleven o'clock." Five minutes later, after a stop at a nearby grocery store for a glass of soda water, he had arrived at St. John's.

Q. Why did you go to the church?

A. To close the windows.

He had returned home at eleven twenty, and after leaving the kitchen light on for his absent wife, had gone to bed.

Mills had awakened at 2 A.M. and gone upstairs to the attic bedroom which Eleanor and Charlotte had shared for several years. When he saw that his wife had not returned home, he had donned his overalls and walked to St. John's.

Q. What did you do?

A. I took and threw the light on, went all around the seats, looking, because I thought my wife might have went in the first part of the evening and fell with a fainting spell.

Failing to find her, he had retired for the night.

The next morning he had prepared breakfast for his children and reported for work at the Lord Stirling School across the street. During the day he had seen Mrs. Hall four times. Their first meeting had occurred in the minister's study "be-

tween half past eight and nine o'clock that Friday morning."
When Mrs. Hall said that her husband had not been home
the previous night, Mills said that his wife was also missing.

"Do you think they eloped?" he had asked. "God knows,"
she had replied. "I think they are dead and can't come
home."

At noon and at 5 P.M. that Friday the minister's wife had
visited him at his home to inquire whether he had heard any
news about his wife. He had last seen her on her front porch
that evening when she confessed that she had run into "a
blank wall" as far as her husband's whereabouts were concerned.

Q. Was anything else said?
A. Before I went away, I said, "I don't know what to
make of it, Mrs. Hall," and she said to me, "They must be
dead or they would come home."

That was the last time he had ever spoken to Mrs. Hall.
McCarter's cross-examination of Mills began after the
noon recess. From the moment the lawyer asked his first
question, it was obvious that pre-trial predictions that a
major part of defense strategy would be to imply that the
theory that the witness might be the real killer had a great
deal of validity.

In its issue of November 2 the *Daily Mirror* had revealed
that some two months earlier Tim Pfeiffer had written to
Bernadine Szold, a former New York newspaperwoman then
living in Paris, in order to determine whether Mills had confessed to murdering his wife and Hall during a press-inspired
seance at Miss Szold's Manhattan apartment in 1922. She
had never answered the lawyer's letter.

"You were by trade, I think, a shoemaker?" McCarter began softly. "For over twenty some years," was Mills' listless
answer. "Did you have a kit of tools?" the lawyer demanded.
"No," the witness replied, "I just carried a knife, that is all—
knife and stones, like that, for cutting purposes."

Q. Do you mean a shoe-cutter's knife?
A. Yes.

Wasn't it true that he had used this knife to take care of his family's shoes? No, it was not. He had worked with "a different kind of a knife."

With a quick look at his rapt jury, McCarter immediately changed the subject. After establishing that Mills had had the run of the church during his tenure as sexton, the defense attorney turned to the night of Eleanor Mills' death. Hadn't he and his wife quarreled that evening?

For the first time since he had begun testifying, Mills showed a little fire. "We didn't have no words at all," he retorted. "Only she said to me, 'You are late for your supper,' and I said, 'I couldn't help it.' That was all was said, and I sat down and had my supper."

He had first discovered that the article about divorce by Dr. Grant had been cut out of the New York *World* when he had looked through the paper after completing his work paper," he recalled. "I turned the paper over on the table, on the window boxes. "It was a part missing from the but I did not read it. I seen part of the paper was missing. I did not have time. It did not bother me."

The next morning he had seen the missing article on Hall's desk.

Q. And you read that clipping when you found it in the church?

A. I didn't read it, I just seen the heading of it.

The last he had seen of his wife was her disappearing back as she had left the house at seven thirty on the night of her death. When he had asked her where she was going, she had replied tauntingly, "Follow me and find out."

Q. Did you follow her?

A. No, sir, I did not.

A few days earlier he had seen some letters which were wrapped in his wife's scarf. "You read those letters enough to realize that they contained the words 'dear' and 'honey'?" McCarter asked ominously. "I had seen a good part of them," Mills admitted.

In view of the fact that Mills had testified on direct that

he had gone to the church at two in the morning because he was afraid that his wife might have fainted, McCarter decided to explore the extent of his husbandly concern. Did he make any inquiries about her on Friday? No, sir, he did not.

Q. How many relatives had your wife in New Brunswick?
A. Two or three.
Q. You had not made a single inquiry of them, had you?
A. No, sir.

"Why was it," McCarter demanded, "that all Thursday night, all Friday, and down to Saturday morning, you did not make an inquiry at a hospital, a police station, or a single place concerning the unexplained absence of your wife?" The witness shrugged his thin shoulders. "Well, my wife used to go away sometimes a day or two away from home," he explained, "and that is why I did not pay any attention to it."

Mills had been on the stand for almost six hours when McCarter drew to a close. Was it true, the lawyer wanted to know, that he had received a check for five hundred dollars for Hall's diary and letters? It was. And who had signed this check? The New York *American*.

Q. That is one of the Hearst papers?
A. I think it is.
Q. And the New York *Mirror* is also a Hearst paper, is it not?

Before Mills could answer what proved to be McCarter's final question to him, Simpson leaped to his feet. "I object to this," he piped. "We are not trying the *Mirror*, nor are we trying Mr. Hearst. We are trying three people for murder and cutting a woman's throat. If Mr. Hearst can stop murder, he is doing good work."

The defense attorney started to say something, thought better of it, and sank wearily into his seat. "No further questions," he sighed.

Forty-eight-year-old Marie Demarest was the last witness of the long day. The tall, stout housewife testified that

Henry Stevens, whom she had known since childhood, had been in New Brunswick, and not Lavallette, as he claimed, on September 15. At nine forty-five that morning she had seen him in a car at the corner of George and Hazard streets. "I glanced at the car," she said in her precise voice, "and I thought at first I knew the face, and I took a second look and I seen it was that gentleman right there, Henry Stevens."

The sharp-eyed witness had also spied Mr. Hall and Mrs. Mills sitting on a bench in Buccleuch Park twice in May 1922. On both occasions Minnie Clark and Ralph Gorsline had been standing alongside a car parked on Easton Avenue and "looking in the direction of Dr. Hall and Mrs. Mills."

Q. Did that state continue when you passed?

A. They were.

Since McCarter and Case were alternating in their cross-examination of the prosecution's witnesses, that of Mrs. Demarest fell to Case. In the brief time remaining before adjournment the Somerset County senator established that Mrs. Demarest had never spoken to Henry Stevens and that she had not seen him for many years before September 15, 1922.

Q. Then, Mrs. Demarest, the fact is that you never had a speaking acquaintance with him?

A. No.

But she was positive that Henry Stevens had been in New Brunswick the morning after the murders. She remembered the day well because "it was the day my cousin was at my mother's, and the day before my mother was hurt."

It was five forty-five when Parker interrupted Case. "Is this examination to be protracted?" he asked. When the lawyer assured him that it was, the justice called it a day.

As the crowded courtroom began to empty, the Associated Press representative in Trenton sent out a flash that Arthur S. Riehl, whose annulment suit had led to the reopening of the investigation, had just discontinued the action. His wife took the report philosophically. "It proves that he merely filed suit to aid a newspaper in reopening the Hall-Mills case," she said.

Mrs. Demarest was back on view the next morning.[5] Case asked if she could tell what kind of a car Henry Stevens had been driving when she saw him in New Brunswick. "That I could not do," she answered sharply, "because I looked at the man but not at the car."

Q. Might not it have been a wagon?

A. No. There would have been horses if it had been a wagon.

When Case asked her if anybody had been with her that morning, Mrs. Demarest fairly screamed "No!" at him. "Why do you say it just like that, Mrs. Demarest?" the defense attorney asked. The witness was far from abashed. "I am rather a loud talker, that is all, and quick," she barked.

Charlotte Mills was recalled briefly to identify two letters which Simpson handed to her as being in Mrs. Hall's handwriting. Over McCarter's objection the letters were quickly admitted in evidence. Both letters had been written to Henry Stevens shortly after the arrests of Willie and Henry Carpender on August 12. In one Mrs. Hall complained that she had been "greatly embarrassed" by her brother's failure to come to New Brunswick.

On August 30 she had asked Henry's permission, as one of Willie's co-trustees, to use Willie's money for his legal expenses. "I will have to dig down deep into my capital, and now the expense of all this legal business," she had written. "All I want is your sanction and signature to using Willie's own money for his own expenses."

As soon as Simpson had finished reading the two letters into the record, he called Anna K. Bearman, an extremely tall woman who bore a striking facial resemblance to Mrs. Hall. Mrs. Bearman, who seemed completely at ease in the witness chair, said that on September 25, 1922, Mrs. Hall

5 By agreement between Simpson and McCarter, full Saturday sessions had been scheduled.

had asked her to send a brown coat and a dark blue scarf to A. F. Bornot & Company in Philadelphia to be dyed black.

The reason for this request, Mrs. Bearman informed McCarter on cross, was that "she was wearing mourning and would be wearing mourning for some time." Yes, she had looked at the coat before sending it to Bornot's, and there was "not a spot" on it.

When Bailiff Bunn called out the name of Henry L. Dickman, there was an excited hum of voices in the courtroom. Escorted by two military policemen, the lean former state trooper walked briskly up the center aisle and took his place in the witness chair.

Under the supervision of prosecutors Beekman and Stricker, he had interviewed Henry Stevens in Lavallette, in early 1923. Although the defendant maintained that he had been fishing on the beach on the night of the murders, "he seemed nervous at the time, and evasive."

Q. Will you tell what you mean by "he seemed nervous and evasive"?

A. I asked him a question, and he tried to evade the answer.

Case didn't even try to keep the contempt out of his voice. "You got all the information you wanted from Henry Stevens, got everything you wanted to know?" he demanded. "Yes," Dickman answered.

Q. What he said to you was satisfactory?

A. Yes.

Q. And you went away thoroughly satisfied?

A. Yes.

Q. Notwithstanding he was evasive?

A. Yes.

Before the noon recess Case succeeded in extracting from the witness the fact that in addition to his recent desertion from the Army, he had also taken French leave from both the Navy and the New Jersey State Police.

It wasn't until the end of Dickman's one-hour stint that the long-anticipated subject of the bribe by Beekman was finally brought up. Why, Simpson asked on redirect, had the witness deserted from the New Jersey State Police? He had been given "an inducement" by Beekman.

Q. What was the inducement you were given?

A. Twenty-five hundred dollars.

Q. Did he say why he gave it to you?

A. He told me to get out of the case and stay out.

On re-cross, Case's voice was bitter. "You say that Azariah Beekman paid you twenty-five hundred dollars as a bribe to leave the state?" he asked. "He did," Dickman replied tersely.

Q. He is now dead?

A. I believe he is dead.

"That is all," the defense attorney said.

The last witness of the first week of the trial was John E. Toolan, who as Stricker's assistant prosecutor had interviewed Mrs. Hall in her home nine days after the murders. It took Toolan thirty minutes to read the questions he had asked the widow and the answers she had given him more than four years ago. The story of Mrs. Hall's nocturnal excursion to St. John's with her brother Willie early on the morning of the fifteenth[6] was too well known to excite any interest, and the courtroom had begun to empty long before Toolan had finished his dreary recitation.

Shortly before midnight Dr. Lawton issued a bulletin on Mrs. Gibson's condition. "It is approximately the same as it has been for the past two days," the bulletin read. "There was a slight improvement in her general condition and a slight decrease in temperature during the day. She is taking some nourishment and is resting comfortably. There is no immediate prospect that she will be able to leave the hospital or undergo examination for her testimony."

The physician's bulletin proved to be the last he was ever to issue as far as Mrs. Gibson was concerned. At eleven the

6 According to Totten, Mrs. Hall did not mention this trip until he informed her that she had been seen coming home by watchman Phillips.

next morning a sedan containing Simpson and several police officers pulled up in front of the hospital. A minute later a Jersey City ambulance with a doctor and a nurse sitting on its front seat parked behind the prosecutor's vehicle.

With almost military precision the little group marched into Mrs. Gibson's private room. When Simpson announced that he expected to move his star witness to Jersey City, Dr. Lawton objected strenuously to the thirty-two-mile trip. "I didn't come down here to discuss the matter with you!" Simpson snapped as the Pig Woman was transferred to a stretcher and carried to the waiting ambulance.

One hour later Mrs. Gibson arrived at the Jersey City Hospital. She was immediately examined by a resident physician, whose diagnosis differed markedly from those advanced by his Somerville confreres. "Mrs. Gibson is suffering from a gynecological condition," he said. "She is not dying, and her life was not prejudiced by the trip from Somerville to Jersey City in the ambulance. She will not be able to leave this hospital for at least three weeks, I think."

Simpson was far more optimistic than the physician as to when Mrs. Gibson could testify. "I hope to put her on the stand Thursday or Friday," he said. "I removed her so that she could be under the care of our own doctor. As a result of a report I received on her condition, which had her very ill and might have to remain for quite a little while, and having been told by Jersey City physicians that she was not very sick, I decided to have her put in a place where I could be informed of her condition."

Dr. Lawton was apoplectic over the transfer. "I want to make it clear that the removal was over my definite protest," he shouted. "Senator Simpson didn't even have his own physician with him to examine her before the long trip. In twenty years of medical practice I have never heard of anything as outrageous. At 8 A.M., Mrs. Gibson's temperature was 102⅖, her pulse was 84, her respiration 22, all figures above normal."

Chapter 24

THE TRIAL—SECOND WEEK

*(Monday, November 8, through
Saturday, November 13, 1926)*

Monday started out slowly with the testimony of Charles
Russell Gildersleeve, a tall, lanky young man who in 1922
had been a lay reader at St. John's. In his five minutes on the
stand he said that he had seen Hall and Mrs. Mills in New
York City in "the late summer of 1921."

Q. Where did you see them, what part of New York?

A. Near the corner of Forty-ninth Street and Broadway.

Gildersleeve looked quite relieved when Case growled,
"No questions."

But the next witness—a slender youth in his early twenties
—was destined to spend an uncomfortable two hours as Mc-
Carter attempted to break down his simple story that he had
seen Mrs. Gibson riding her mule in De Russey's Lane several hours after dark on the night of the murders.

At the beginning of his long cross-examination Robert
Erling, a New Brunswick millwright, struggled valiantly to
withhold the name of the girl who had been with him in his
Ford touring car that fateful night. He didn't want to reveal
her identity "because she is married and she has two children now, and she has a husband, too, and I feel that by me
giving her name it will bring something on the children
and on her."

209

Parker, however, ordered him to answer, and the name of
Jenny Lemford became an ineradicable part of the burgeoning record, which already exceeded one thousand pages.

Under McCarter's deft probing, Erling said that after supper at Miss Lemford's house he and the girl had driven into
De Russey's Lane just before dark. When the lawyer reminded him that at the preliminary hearing he had estimated the time to be approximately eight thirty, Erling
owned that it was "just at that time."

The couple had parked opposite a little spring to the
right of the roadway, and after talking for an hour, had gone
for a walk in the direction of Hamilton Street.

Q. And you got back into the car after your walk at about
what time?

A. It might have been an hour or an hour and a half, I
could not tell you exactly.

It was then that he had seen Mrs. Gibson, astride of Jenny,
riding toward him from the Easton Avenue end of De Russey's Lane. He had recognized her at once because he had
often taken his laundry to her house "to have it washed by
people on the place."

He and Miss Lemford had remained in the lane until
"somewhere about eleven o'clock." No, he hadn't heard any
shots or screams, and he hadn't seen "a noisy rickety wagon
go by."

Q. So as far as you know, except for your pleasant evening
with Miss Lemford and your seeing Mrs. Gibson, nothing
unusual occurred there at all?

A. The only thing I saw while I was there, just before I
left there were two other cars in the lane, one was a sedan
and one was a large touring car.

Although he had testified at the preliminary hearing that
he had first mentioned the incident to Nellie Lo Russell in
1924, he now remembered that he had discussed it with his
parents on the following Sunday.

Q. Why did you swear before Judge Cleary that you had

spoken to no one about it except Mrs. Russell about two
years before the time you were testifying?

A. I did not think at the time. It passed my mind—it
passed my memory at the time.

McCarter couldn't keep the disbelief out of his voice.
"Oh, it passed your memory," he echoed scornfully.

The defense attorney had one more conversation to investigate before he released the perspiring witness. In August
1926 hadn't Erling met a friend of his named Willard Staub
and said, "Staub, if you will say that you were out in De
Russey's Lane the night of September 14, 1922, you'll get
some money out of it"? No, sir, he had not.

Q. You did not say that to Staub?

A. He talked to me.

Q. One moment. You did not say that, or substantially
that, to Mr. Staub?

A. I don't remember saying it.

"Will you say you did not say it?" McCarter demanded
harshly. "I don't remember saying it," Erling repeated doggedly.

After the luncheon recess William Garvin, a rotund, bald-
headed man in his middle fifties, waddled to the stand. Looking anything but the private investigator he professed to be,
Garvin said that in 1922 he had been the manager of the
New York office of the Burns Detective Agency.

Q. After the murder did you ever see a man named Ralph
Gorsline?

A. I recognized that man recently as having come to me
with a story.

On October 1, 1922, the vestryman had visited his office
in the Woolworth Building and said that "his conscience
troubled him, that he was in De Russey's Lane on September
14, 1922, and that on that night he said he saw Henry Stevens
there with a revolver and that he ran up the bank and Henry
Stevens said, 'What the hell are you doing here? This is none

of your affair. Get the hell out of here!', and fired two shots
in the ground, and that he got away as fast as he could, and
that afterwards he was made to swear that he would never
tell it."[1]

McCarter, whose face had turned beet red as Garvin an-
swered Simpson's few questions, started out with a rush.
"Are you the man that is commonly known as 'Greasy
Vest'?" he demanded.

"I object to that!" roared Simpson.

"I don't care about that," Garvin drawled.

"I know, but I do!" snapped the prosecutor. "Unfortunately, you are not trying this case. I object to that on the
ground that it is not proper cross-examination. He may be
known as Ali Baba, but that would not make him Ali Baba."

Parker cut him short. "The question is overruled," he
ordered.

McCarter turned back to the bemused witness. "Were you
alone when Gorsline told you all this?" he asked. Garvin
nodded vigorously. "I was," he replied.

Q. So that your story is that a perfect stranger came in to
see you, wanted to be alone, and told you that story.

A. That is customary.

Q. Never mind about what is customary, is that a fact?

A. That is a fact.

He had not seen Gorsline again until "a couple of months
ago," when at the prosecution's request, he had gone to New
Brunswick to identify the vestryman as the man who had
visited him in his office.

Q. You were not sure, were you?

A. He resembled the man very much.

It was only when he had seen Gorsline in Somerville during the grand jury session last September that he had felt
"pretty sure" he was the same man.

Simpson, who had already demonstrated a remarkable flair

[1] Four days earlier Gorsline had testified that such a meeting had never
taken place.

for the dramatic, was at his histrionic best when McCarter relinquished the witness. His right hand jangling the keys in his pocket, the prosecutor turned and walked briskly toward the rear of the courtroom. "Is Gorsline here yet?" he asked. "He is in the back of the courtroom," Cleary said.

Seconds later the harried vestryman ran down the center aisle with what one reporter described as "the expression of a man, out of training, who had run fast and long."

Simpson turned back to Garvin. "Is this the man who came to your office and told you the story?" After taking a good look at Gorsline the witness was certain. "That is the man," he said simply.

Before adjourning for the day Parker asked Simpson for a report on Mrs. Gibson's condition. "I am not a physician," the special prosecutor replied tartly. "All I know is the physicians say she is improving."

A press bulletin issued by the Jersey City Hospital that morning had indicated that the Pig Woman was on the mend. "Her temperature is lower and her general condition somewhat improved. Her greatest need at the present time is rest in bed, to be followed by such other treatment as is deemed appropriate. In the opinion of the attending physicians, she will be confined to the hospital for at least two weeks."

Mrs. Gibson, who now referred to herself as the "Babe Ruth" of the prosecution, told a *Times* reporter who had managed to invade her room that her testimony would convict Mrs. Hall and her brothers. "I have nothing but the truth to tell," she said fervently, "but God knows how I want to tell it."

The Pig Woman refused to discuss the attitude of her mother, seventy-six-year-old Mrs. Salome Cerenner, who had missed no opportunity since arriving in Somerville as a prospective defense witness to brand her daughter as a liar. "I can't say anything about her. I don't understand why my own mother should be so hateful, but then, she alone can speak out about that."

Tuesday, November 9, the sixth day of the trial, dawned cold and rainy. A cold wave from the west was about to end one of the mildest falls in recent years. Through the court-room windows, which were latticed by the bare and bowing limbs of the elms and maples that dotted the lawn, early arrivals could see clouds of dead leaves being driven by vio-lent gusts of wind. When Justice Parker mounted the bench, he immediately ordered Bailiff Bunn to turn on the inade-quate bank of lights that hung in a semicircle from the high ceiling.

For the first five hours the testimony was as uninspiring as the weather. First Schwartz and then Faurot valiantly de-fended, in highly technical terms, their conclusion that Ex-hibit 17 bore the print of Willie Stevens' left index finger.

Under a merciless cross-examination by McCarter, who had obviously done his homework well, both experts ad-mitted that the impressions on the minister's calling card might have been impaired by its peregrinations since it was found in the grass near the crab apple tree on the morning of Saturday, September 16, 1922.

Faurot agreed with McCarter that the presence of a for-eign substance on Exhibit 17 might prevent the formation of a perfect print. "If something interfered," he said, "it is going to interfere with your print." He also conceded that there were discrepancies between Willie's print and those found on Exhibit 17 "caused by this card lying there in at-mospheric conditions for one and one half days."

On re-direct, however, he assured Simpson that there was no doubt in his mind that the prints were the same.

It was three in the afternoon when Dr. Otto H. Schultze, a tall, well-built man in a double-breasted blue serge suit, succeeded the former deputy commissioner. After stating that he had performed an autopsy on Eleanor Mills' body in a New Brunswick garage on October 28, 1926, the New York

County medical examiner carefully opened a bulky brown paper carton he had carried to the stand with him and removed an object wrapped in excelsior.

"What is this, Doctor?" Simpson asked innocently.

"This is a manikin," Schultze replied in his coldly professional tone. "It is a model of a head, neck, and the beginning of the shoulder of a human subject."

As Schultze began to point out with a red crayon the three bullet holes he had found in the slain woman's head, Mrs. Hall hurriedly averted her eyes to her lap, opened her black pocketbook, and began to examine its contents methodically. A few minutes later she raised her head, turned in her chair, and stared intently at the rear of the courtroom.

Willie, on the other hand, seemed hypnotized by Schultze's gruesome demonstration, and kept his bulging eyes fixed on the manikin. There was no sign of emotion on Henry Stevens' impassive face.

With awesome precision the clear-speaking physician illustrated the path of each one of the .32-caliber bullets that had penetrated the dead woman's skull. One bullet had entered the forehead "two inches above the level of the brow"; another had pierced the right cheek "four tenths of an inch below the level of the external angle of the right eyelid," and a third "the right side of the head 2.2 inches above the opening of the ear."

Q. Would any of these wounds be sufficient to cause death?

A. Either one of the three could have caused death.

There were visible shudders in the courtroom as Schultze, with a sweeping gesture, described the gaping cut he had found in the dead woman's neck. "The wound was found from the left side of the rest of the neck, forward and around the neck, just above the collarbone, or a distance of five inches to the middle line, and a distance farther of one inch across the middle line on the right side of the skin of the neck. At this point the wound continued four tenths of an inch from its ending, producing a further wound around the neck. That passed for a distance of 3.6 or a little more inches, toward the right and rear to the muscle that joins the shoulder and the back of the head."

Because of the lack of blood in the lungs Schultze was positive that Mrs. Mills had not taken a breath after her throat was cut.

The witness caused a ripple of excitement when he reported that "the upper part of the windpipe and the larynx and the tongue were missing."

Q. Those were all, of course, organs used in singing.
A. Yes.

Could the doctor tell how the missing organs had been removed? "There was no indication as to how they had been taken out," he answered. "They were gone, they were missing, but I think I can state they could not have been pulled out. They had to be cut out."

Hall had been killed by a bullet that entered the right side of his head "four inches above the level of the opening of the ear."

Q. The bullet was not in the wound, was it?
A. No. There was a wound of exit in the skin of the neck at the back on the left side.

It was highly possible, Schultze declared, that Hall and his killer had been struggling for the gun at the moment the fatal bullet had been fired.

When Senator Case took over for the defense, Schultze admitted that Hall might have been killed "in a half dozen different ways."

Q. And what you have enumerated now is just a guess that anybody might make?
A. That is what I said before; not a guess, but anybody could see how it might occur.

But he was certain that with the exception of one bullet, all of the shots had been fired from the right side of the victims' heads. The exception was the bullet wound in the middle of Mrs. Mills' forehead. Because of the absence of powder marks he concluded that the murder weapons had been held "at least a foot from the bodies."

He had noticed several other wounds on both cadavers. The knuckle of Hall's right forefinger had been bruised and there was "a scrape or burn" on his right middle finger. He had also found a "very superficial" puncture wound in Mrs. Mills' lip. Neither body had been mutilated, but there had been a cut in Mrs. Mills' abdomen which extended "from the navel to the privates."

Parker, who had been following Dr. Schultze's testimony as avidly as everyone else in the courtroom, suddenly realized that time for adjournment had arrived. His gavel brought an immediate end to the day's session.

According to her doctors, Mrs. Gibson would not be able to testify for some time. "The physicians in attendance upon Mrs. Gibson," their daily bulletin read, "examined her this morning, and as a result of the examination, the diagnosis of yesterday was confirmed. Her general condition is simply improving. At the present time her stay in the hospital is indeterminable."

Simpson pooh-poohed the report. "If Mrs. Gibson tells me she is feeling well enough to go on the stand to testify," he proclaimed, "I will have her brought to Somerville, where she can tell her story. I will do this regardless of what the doctors say."

Before calling his first witness on Wednesday, Simpson had a request to make. "I want to ask your Honor," he began, "if you would order this jury, sometime during the state's case, taken by competent showers to the scene of the alleged crime, and have the place exhibited to them." Parker wondered whether this could be done without causing a large crowd to congregate at the Phillips farm. "They could be taken," the prosecutor replied, "some day after adjournment of court, and nobody knowing except the court and the showers."

When Case pointed out that the terrain had changed greatly during the four years since the murders, Parker said that he and Cleary would mull over the state's request.

Dr. Runkle Hegeman, the Somerville physician who had conducted the 1922 autopsies, echoed most of Schultze's findings. But he couldn't tell whether Mrs. Mills' windpipe, larynx, or tongue were missing. "I did not open the mouth," he insisted when pressed by Simpson, "and I do not know what was in the mouth."

Case confined his cross-examination to the condition of Mrs. Mills' neck. "This wound in the neck, it almost severed, did it not, the head from the body?" he asked. "Yes, sir," the physician replied. In fact, it had severed everything except one muscle, the backbone, and "a few inches of flesh extending on each side of the backbone."

Q. What have you to say as to whether it would need to be a sharp instrument to inflict the wounds you saw in the neck?

A. Either very sharp, or else a great deal of pressure was used. The line of the skin cut was smooth, and not jagged, as it would be if it were dull or a nicked instrument.

Dr. Edward I. Cronk, the New Brunswick health officer, was Simpson's next offering. A small, cadaverous-looking man whose hair was parted in the middle and carefully combed over his temples, he was thoroughly badgered by the prosecutor, who was determined to find out why the physician had opened the sutured wound in Mrs. Mills' abdomen. Cronk insisted that he had done so "in order to determine whether any organs were missing, and also to determine whether she was in a condition of pregnancy."

Q. Who requested you to do that?

A. I was requested by Mr. Hubbard, the undertaker, to make the examination and identification of the body.

"That is not my question," Simpson retorted. "Who requested you to open the wound?" Cronk stared long and hard at the stained-glass ceiling. "No one," he finally replied.

He had not intended to examine the corpse when he first entered Hubbard's mortuary. While he was there, the undertaker had received a telephone call from William E. Florence, who was then acting as Mrs. Hall's attorney.

Q. As a result of something Mr. Hubbard said after he phoned, you did what you did?

A. Yes, sir.

After being informed by Hubbard that there had already been an autopsy in Somerville, he had decided to look for "concealed evidence" in the dead woman's abdomen.

"Concealed evidence of what?" Simpson persisted. "Whether any organs were missing or whether she had been pregnant," Cronk replied testily.

The prosecutor's ears perked up.

"Was she pregnant?" he inquired.

"She was not."

Before the afternoon session began, Parker announced that he and Cleary had decided that the court would not sit on Armistice Day. "The day is a legal holiday, and there appears to be a very considerable sentiment," he explained. "We understand that the jury makes no protest, and we wish to express our appreciation of the patriotic stand taken by the jury in that regard."

Under those circumstances, Simpson promptly suggested, perhaps Foreman Dunster and his eleven colleagues could be taken to the Phillips farm during the holiday. "That is a matter which is still under consideration, Senator Simpson," Parker replied. "The court has not determined just what to do about that. You may now go on."

Dr. Arthur L. Smith had removed Mrs. Mills' right kidney on January 16, 1922. He had set a fee of two hundred dollars for the operation, which Hall had agreed to pay in twenty monthly installments of ten dollars each.

Q. And were you paid?

A. Partly.

Q. How much?

A. Thirty dollars.

During the four weeks Mrs. Mills had spent in the Middlesex General Hospital, Hall has visited her "every day or so."

Like Dr. Hegeman, Smith, who had attended both of the 1922 autopsies, hadn't looked to see if Mrs. Mills' larynx, tongue, and windpipe were intact.

Q. And as far as the autopsy was concerned, no organs were removed from Mrs. Mills' body?

A. No.

He recalled that three bullets had been found in the dead woman's head and that he had given them to Totten. No, he couldn't swear that the bullets which Simpson showed him were the ones which had killed Eleanor Mills. "But they probably are," he added quickly.

Case's approach was hardly subtle when he took over. Was it Dr. Smith's opinion that it would require a "firm grip" to inflict the gaping wound in Mrs. Mills' throat? It was.

Q. Now, a razor—we are speaking of the old-type razor— has a very flexible joint, hasn't it, between the handle and the blade?

A. Yes.

But the physician was positive that by holding the razor a certain way it was possible to cause the wound he had seen at the autopsy. With the help of two pencils he demonstrated for the defense attorney how the cut might have been made.

On re-direct Simpson gave Smith an old-fashioned straight-edged razor and asked him to show the fascinated jurors how Mrs. Mills' throat could have been cut. With two quick slashes in the air the witness all but decapitated an imaginary victim.

Then the prosecutor returned to the question of the missing larynx. Had the doctor seen any portion of this organ? Yes, he had.

Q. What did you say a moment ago on cross-examination —you were not sure whether you saw it?

A. The lower portion. The upper portion was retracted.

That was what he had meant to say in his autopsy notes when he had written "Windpipe severed and retracted."

Charles J. Alpaugh, who was as nervous as he was earnest, followed the self-possessed medical man on the witness stand. On the night of the murders he had been driving a busload of Somerville firemen home from a dance in Red Bank. As he drove out Easton Avenue, he had seen a Dodge sedan and a Cadillac coupé parked near De Russey's Lane. Suddenly "two or three" persons had slid down a bank on the side of the road in the direction of the Dodge.

Barbara Tough, who said that her last name was pronounced "Too," was the state's final witness of the day. The thin, angular domestic, whose horn-rimmed glasses and floppy hat gave her the appearance of a female Harold Lloyd, kept everyone in the courtroom in smiles with her full-throated Scottish burr.

In her more than six years as a maid in the Hall household Miss Tough had seen and heard a great deal about the minister's affection for Mrs. Mills. "I could easily see," she told Simpson, "that Eleanor was one of his favorites." On one occasion she had discovered the choir singer sitting on Hall's knee in the guild room of the church.

On September 14, Barbara had left the house at 2:30 P.M., and after spending the day with relatives and friends, had returned home "at ten sharp." She had been somewhat surprised to see that "there was a bright light in the library and one in the lower hall and one in the second hall and one in the kitchen." She had gone directly to her third-floor room without seeing any member of the family.

Four hours later she had been awakened by the sound of Mrs. Hall's footsteps. "I heard her walk from her own room to the bathroom and from the bathroom back again, and it was only a few minutes when I heard the big clock downstairs strike two."

The next morning she hadn't seen Mrs. Hall until shortly after nine o'clock. "She came upstairs and she said, 'Oh, Barbara, Dr. Hall has not been home all night,' and I said, 'So

the girls tell me.' And then I said to her, had she notified
the police, and she said no, she had called up the Middlesex
Hospital and asked whether there had been any accidents or
casualties, but she had not given her name."

At seven thirty that evening she had heard Mrs. Hall call
Agnes Storer, the church organist, and say, "Oh, Agnes, Mr.
Hall won't be down to choir practice this night as he is out
of town."

Early the next morning Mrs. Hall had handed a pair of
white silk socks to the maid and asked her to "wash these for
him."

Q. What happened then?

A. About four o'clock Mrs. Hall came into the sewing room
and asked me to give her a box. I asked her how large a box,
and she said a box to hold some clothing for him. Then she
asked me if those white socks were dry and I said, "Yes,
they are right here." I gave her the box and the white silk
socks and she walked out of the sewing room.

"What was her manner then?" Simpson wanted to know.
"Well, she was quiet," Barbara replied.

Henry Stevens had last visited the Halls in June 1922.
"How often did he come to the house?" the prosecutor demanded. The witness thought for a moment. "Well, just in
flying visits, occasionally, not often to stay," she answered.

Q. Did you notice what the relations were between Henry
Stevens and Dr. Hall?

A. They were friendly in a cold sort of friendly way.

Q. What do you mean by "in a cold sort of way"?

A. They were just on friendly terms, not considering
they were brothers-in-law.[2]

Barbara knew that Willie owned a small rifle and a revolver because she had often seen them in his room. No, he

---

[2] Paul F. B. Hamforszky, the former Hungarian Reformed minister who,
four years earlier, had claimed that Hall had told him that Henry Stevens had
threatened to kill him because of his affair with Mrs. Mills, had mysteriously
disappeared on the eve of trial.

hadn't owned a razor; he had always gone downtown for his shaves. In fact, the only razor in the house belonged to the minister, who kept it in the bathroom cabinet.

Q. What kind of a razor was it?

A. One of the old-fashioned kind, not a safety razor.

Simpson held up the razor he had shown Dr. Hegeman. "When you say old-fashioned kind, you mean this kind?" he asked. He winced when the girl replied, "Yes, but I think it was a tiny bit smaller than that."

With the exception of the proprietors of the refreshment stands on Main Street, everyone in Somerville welcomed the Armistice Day respite. Judge Cleary took advantage of the crisp fall weather to go hunting in the neighboring countryside. The jurors, who had been locked up in the Colonial House, an austere hostelry several blocks from the courthouse, spent the day reading in their rooms under the watchful eyes of three deputy sheriffs.

After an early morning drive with Tim Pfeiffer to her lawyers' headquarters in South Somerville, Mrs. Hall spent the rest of the day catching up on her household chores. It was open house at the Somerset County Jail, where the Stevens brothers and Henry Carpender were deluged by visitors.

The daily bulletin on Mrs. Gibson's condition indicated that she was mending slowly. "She is showing some improvement. Her temperature was lower this morning, and the physicians are of the opinion that if the improvement continues it will be possible to produce her as a witness before the state rests its case."

That evening, however, the Pig Woman suffered a sudden relapse, and a transfusion was ordered for early the next morning. "This transfusion," said one of her doctors, "is performed to correct a moderately severe secondary anemia which was found and reported on Mrs. Gibson's admission last Sunday." It would be several days, the physician estimated, before the success of the operation could be determined.

On Friday there was more than a little interest in the testimony of Philip A. Payne, the man who many people believed was responsible for the trial.

A slender man in his early thirties who was somewhat hard of hearing, the *Daily Mirror* editor had first seen the dead clergyman's calling card in a Newark hotel "around the first week in July." The card had been given to him by fingerprint expert Edward H. Schwartz, and after being photographed by *Mirror* cameramen, had appeared in the tabloid's issue of August 27.

Q. Did you give Schwartz any financial consideration or anything of value for the card?

A. Nothing of financial value.

McCarter couldn't wait to get at Payne. "When did you become acquainted with Mr. Schwartz?" he blurted out before Simpson had returned to his seat. "Several years ago," Payne replied suavely. It had been Schwartz who had made the appointment to meet the editor at the St. Francis Hotel in downtown Newark to discuss turning over the calling card.

Q. Why wasn't it a good place to meet at his office, right down at police headquarters?

A. Better ask him that, I don't know.

After three or four meetings in the vicinity of the St. Francis, Schwartz had given him the card "in a taxicab, going from the hotel."

"You say you gave him nothing whatever for the card?" McCarter asked incredulously.

"Nothing financial, no," Payne repeated blandly.

"Well, if it wasn't financial," the lawyer roared, "what did you give him?"

Payne stared blankly at the ceiling.

Finally McCarter's patience gave out. "Why don't you answer me?" he barked.

Payne smiled. "I can think while I answer just as well as you can think while you ask me a question."

Q. Does it require a great deal of thought to remember what it was?

A. No.

Q. Why don't you answer?

A. I told Schwartz that if he would help clear up this crime, he was doing a service to the State of New Jersey. That was the only consideration he got.

From the stricken look on McCarter's face, it was obvious that Payne had carried the round.

Until August 17 the calling card, which had been kept wrapped in wax paper, had reposed in a locked filing cabinet in the editor's office. On that day he had asked one of his reporters to take the card to Middletown, New York, so that Commissioner Faurot could inspect it.

Q. Then you suggested it, didn't you?

A. I told him.

Q. Certainly, you don't suggest, you command, is that it?

A. I did not command. I am not the Queen of Rumania. I just told him to go.

Q. Oh! You are the Queen of the *Mirror?*

A. Unfortunately, I am not. My sex is masculine.

As the courtroom erupted in laughter, Parker, struggling vainly to hide a broad smile, ordered both men to "conduct this examination in good order."

Payne had indeed been present at the midnight arrest of Mrs. Hall on July 28. McCarter pounced. How had he known that Mrs. Hall would be arrested at that late hour? The police had told him.

Q. Who told you?

A. Captain Walsh, and I think Sergeant Burke is his name.

In fact, he had been tipped off by those same two officers that Justice of the Peace Sutphen had signed the warrant for her arrest.

Before relinquishing the witness McCarter attempted to

force him to disclose just how much money the *Mirror* had spent in its investigation of the murders. When Simpson objected, the defense attorney argued long and loud that the question was a proper one. Despite the fervency of his plea, however, he was unable to convince Parker, who sustained the prosecutor's objection. Only William Randolph Hearst's auditors were ever to know the extent of the publisher's interest in the four-year-old murders.

After lunch John V. Hubbard took Payne's place in the witness chair. An elderly man with silver hair, the undertaker said that he had sent one of his employees to Somerville on Sunday, September 17, to pick up Eleanor Mills' body. Although he was the Middlesex County coroner, he hadn't bothered to order an autopsy.

Q. You knew this had been a murder, didn't you?

A. Well, it was supposed to be so.

Q. What did you think when you saw a woman with her throat cut and three bullet wounds in her head?

A. I supposed it was.

On the day that the bodies were found, Hubbard had gone to the Somerset County seat and picked up the minister's corpse. The body had been buried in Brooklyn's Greenwood Cemetery at one o'clock the following Monday afternoon.

Q. So that the body was buried within forty hours after the time you got it in New Brunswick?

A. Well, we got it out Saturday and it was buried Monday. Approximately forty hours.

Although he knew that Hall had been murdered, he hadn't asked anyone whether it was permissible to inter the body out of the state.

Case's cross was brief. Wasn't it true that the undertaker had recommended that both bodies be buried quickly? Yes, sir, he had.

Q. On account of the decomposition?

A. Yes, sir.

But the minister's body had not been interred, had it?

No, sir, it had not. "It was placed in a receptacle for the body in the vault," he explained. At Mrs. Hall's instruction, he had placed the coffin on the lowest of three racks in the vault.

Vivacious and pretty Louise Geist Riehl was a welcome change from Mr. Hubbard and his talk of death and decomposition. The slender ex-maid, who was a picture of high style in her scarlet hat, becoming dress, and high-heeled pumps, perched in the chair the undertaker had just vacated and glared at Senator Simpson as she waited for his first question. She snapped out her answers in an emphatic manner that left no doubt that she had very little love for her doughty inquisitor.

Simpson was primarily interested in the telephone call that had come for Hall after supper on the night of his death. Louise had answered it on the second-story extension, which was located some twelve feet away from the stairwell. The early evening caller, whom she recognized as Mrs. Mills, had asked for the minister. Thinking her employer was downstairs, the maid had walked to the head of the stairs and looked over the banister.

Q. What did you see when you looked down?

A. I saw Mrs. Hall. She was coming in, and had just lifted the receiver off the hook, had it halfway up her body.

"Just then," she continued, "Mr. Hall called from the bathroom. I said, 'Oh, it is all right, he is up here.' She placed back the receiver and turned around and walked out."

Simpson, who seemed crushed by the impairment of his pet theory that Mrs. Hall had overheard her husband and the choir singer making a date to meet at the Phillips farm, quickly shifted course.

He now wanted to know what Willie Stevens had said to Louise early the next morning when the maid met him in the dining room. "I says to him, 'What are you doing up so early?' He said, 'I would rather not tell you, I would rather have Mrs. Hall tell you.' I said, 'What are you doing up so early, what is the matter?' He said, 'There was something terrible happened last night, and Mrs. Hall and I have been up most of the night.' "

Q. Did you ask him what the terrible thing was?

A. No, sir.

Willie, who seemed "a little nervous," had begged Louise not to tell Mrs. Hall what he had said.

The maid had served breakfast to Mrs. Hall, Willie, and Frances Voorhees, the minister's ten-year-old niece who was spending a few days in New Brunswick. "Mr. Hall was not there," she told Simpson. "I waited quite a while for him to come down, and then I came in and asked her if I should keep the things warm or was he going to have his breakfast in bed; and she said, 'Louise, Mr. Hall has not been home all night. I don't know where he is.' And I asked her if she had called up the police, and she said yes, she had called up the police and asked if there were any casualties or any accidents and she also said she had called up a hospital, I think, but I am not sure."

That evening the witness had overheard an interesting conversation between her mistress and Willie Stevens. "As I got to the second landing," she recalled, "Mrs. Hall and Mr. Stevens had just gone up before me, and Mrs. Hall said, 'Good night, Willie,' and he said, 'Are you going to bed, Frances?' She said, 'Yes. I thought he would come last night, but I know he won't come tonight. I know he must be dead, or else he would communicate with me, and I am going to bed.' Words to that effect."

Senator Case had only a few questions. "Was Mrs. Hall crying that Friday morning?" he asked gently. "Well, her eyes were red," Louise replied. "I could see she had been crying. She did cry. Tears came to her eyes. Of course, she did not cry real loud. The tears came to her eyes, and I could see that she was worried. She played with some keys or something. She was rather nervous."

When had she last seen Mrs. Hall on Thursday evening?

She was "almost positive" that the widow had rung the bell
that was the signal to close up the house "between nine
thirty and ten." After fastening the window shutters in the
dining room the maid had entered the library. "Mrs. Hall
was in the library," she said, "sitting at the table, playing
cards. I presume she was playing solitaire, because she was
playing all by herself."

Finally, had Mrs. Riehl overheard any part of Hall's conversation with Mrs. Mills earlier that evening? She had.

Q. And what was his conversation? What did he say?

A. "Yes, yes, yes; that is too bad. I was going down to the
church a little later. Can't we make arrangements for later,
say about a quarter to eight?"

Q. And that was all that was said?

A. Yes, sir.

She thought that the conversation had taken place at
about 7:15 P.M. Twenty minutes later the minister had left
the house. "I heard him tell Mrs. Hall he was going out, he
had to go out for a little while. He was going out to see
about the Mills bill."

Inquisitive Miss Opie closed out the long afternoon. The
stout seamstress had been delivering telephone messages
from Hall to Mrs. Mills for "a couple of years." On the day
of the murders the minister had called "in the middle of the
afternoon," but Miss Opie had been unable to locate Mrs.
Mills.

She hadn't delivered the message until seven fifteen that
evening, when she had met her pretty neighbor at the
George Street trolley stop. "I told her I was going to take
a trolley car to a friend's house, and I told her if she wanted
to go down to use my telephone she could."

Q. What did she say?

A. She did not say a word and did not say whether she
would or not, but we talked until the car came.

That was the last time she had seen Eleanor alive.

At two on Saturday afternoon Miss Opie had watched as

Edwin Carpender parked his dark coupé in front of 49 Carman Street. Minnie Clark got out of Carpender's vehicle and
walked up the front stairs to the Millses' apartment.

Q. In Mr. Carpender's car did you see anything when
Minnie Clark went into the house?

A. Why, I saw a lot of papers in the back like in boxes or
letter drawers.

"Drawers of what kind?" Simpson demanded. "Well, the
only thought I had was file drawers, something like that,"
Miss Opie stammered.

Saturday's session was inaugurated by a long and bitter
exchange between Simpson and McCarter over the admissibility of Hall's diary and twelve of his love letters to Mrs.
Mills. The prosecutor, in offering the exhibits, maintained
that they were both relevant and material to the state's case.
"The conversations between them, and correspondence, and
the possession of Dr. Hall's diary written by him, detailing
his great affection for this lady, certainly are competent evidence," he argued.

Although McCarter protested that the diary and the letters had been located long after the murders, Parker admitted them all. "They are, in our judgment," he ruled,
"competent on the question of motive."

With the diary and letters marked in evidence, Simpson
laid aside the tantalizing exhibits while he called several
minor witnesses.

Harry A. Kolb, who in 1922 had driven a milk truck for
the Paulus Dairy, said that at 2 A.M. on Friday, September
15, he had found an open door at the rear of the Hall mansion.

"How much was it open?" Simpson asked.

"It was open that far that I had to run ahead of it and
close it or my left front wheel would have struck it."

In the five months that he had been delivering milk to
the Halls, that particular door had always been closed.

Bill Grealis, a pink-cheeked, blond youth who couldn't have been more than eighteen, had worked as a delivery boy for a New Brunswick clothing store in the summer of 1922. Two days after the murders he had delivered a new suit to Willie Stevens. The defendant, who appeared to be "very nervous," had met him in the front driveway and asked him to come to the back door.

"He explained that he was bringing me around the back way because they had trouble in the family—he didn't want to bring me to the front door," Grealis said. After giving the boy a bundle of clothes to be cleaned, Willie had insisted that he leave by the side entrance.

When Grealis arrived back at the cleaning store, he and his brother had untied the bundle. Both boys had immediately noticed some dark spots on the garments.

Q. Where were the spots?

A. Down on the front of the vest and around the waistline of the trousers.

On cross, he admitted he knew that Willie habitually dropped food "on the front of his clothing and that it had to be frequently cleaned."

After lunch Simpson finally got around to reading Hall's letters to the jury. As the prosecutor's strident, high-pitched voice carried to every corner of the courtroom, Mrs. Hall sat quietly with her gloved hands in her lap and her head held to one side. At one point, when Simpson came to one of the minister's more passionate declarations of love for the soprano, he took a quick look at the widow. She stared directly at him, her only sign of emotion being a slight flush that colored her neck and cheeks.

The evening bulletin released by the Jersey City Hospital indicated that Mrs. Gibson's emergency blood transfusion had been eminently successful. Signed by the hospital superintendent, the terse report was made public at 8 p.m. "Mrs. Gibson is under the constant care of two nurses and a physician, and seems to be resting comfortably," it read. "She appears to be in no immediate danger, and the transfusion has added greatly to her strength."

The second Sunday of the trial was marked by the deaths of two prospective witnesses. Nicholas Bahmer, with his daughter, Pearl, at his bedside, died of tuberculosis at the Bonnie Burn Sanitarium in Scotch Plains. The saloonkeeper, who had once been a major suspect, had not been in the news since 1923, when an incest charge filed by Pearl was dismissed.

An hour after Bahmer's death sixty-year-old Charles E. Waite, one of the prosecution's ballistics experts, was stricken with a fatal heart attack in his hotel room. Waite, who had developed a system of bullet identification, had been expected to testify as to the make and type of the gun which had killed the unlucky lovers. According to Simpson, the dead man's partner was prepared to take his place in the witness chair.

For the first time since the revival of the case the lane that led to the Phillips farm was closed to traffic. A development of small homes had been constructed on part of the property, and its owners had complained to the police that the thousands of curious spectators who flocked to the area each week end were despoiling unsold houses in their frenzy to obtain souvenirs of their visit. Two state troopers, who had been stationed in the lane since dawn, turned back everyone who could not prove that he had a legitimate reason to enter the property.

As Somerville's inhabitants settled down to a long, lazy Sunday, there was no doubt that the town was reaping a financial bonanza from the trial. All of the lunchrooms near the courthouse had been forced to hire extra help, and one that had been on the brink of bankruptcy three months ago was now solidly in the black. The manager of the local telegraph office said that since morning he had distributed thirteen hundred dollars in money orders to the newsmen who haunted the town.

The proprietor of one men's furnishings store announced gleefully that he had sold eighteen overcoats to reporters alone during the last three weeks. "As for the number of shirts, ties, and socks, well, all I can say is, business is good."

Chapter 25

THE TRIAL—THIRD WEEK

*(Monday, November 15, through
Saturday, November 20, 1926)*

New Brunswick cab driver Alfred Butler was Monday's first
significant witness. At 10:40 A.M. on Saturday, September 16,
1922, he had driven a woman from the Pennsylvania Railroad station to the Hall residence. He had not been able to
discharge his passenger at the front door because a green
car was blocking the driveway. As he pulled to a stop, the
cabbie had noticed Henry Carpender "coming off the
porch."

Q. What was he doing?
A. He had a bundle under one arm and three or four
boxes under the other arm.

After placing his burdens in the green car Carpender had
driven away at once.

Butler was followed by John Stillwell, the chauffeur who
had driven the hearse containing Hall's body from New
Brunswick to Brooklyn after the minister's funeral. He testified that while the funeral procession was crossing New
York Harbor on the Staten Island Ferry he and several other
drivers had left their vehicles in order to stroll around the
boat. As they passed the car in which Mrs. Hall was seated,
the widow had raised her veil.

Q. What did you observe about Mrs. Hall?

A. We could see a little scratch on the left side of her face.

The scratch, which looked fresh, had been "about an inch and a half or two inches long."

According to stoutish Elsie P. Barnhardt, one of the murdered woman's sisters, Eleanor had made no secret of her feelings toward the rector. She had often told Mrs. Barnhardt that she intended to elope with him to Japan as soon as Charlotte had graduated from high school.

Q. What did Mrs. Mills say about Dr. Hall?

A. She told me that she thought more of Mr. Hall's little finger than she did of her husband's whole body.

Eighteen months before the murders Mrs. Barnhardt had accompanied Eleanor on a church outing to Bound Brook. "When we arrived at the church, Mr. Hall placed me and Eleanor in his car, and Mrs. Hall objected to it. She acted as though she objected, because she finally did not come in our car; she went with Mrs. Anna Bearman."

Q. You say she would not go in your car—what do you mean by that?

A. She acted very angry at the way Mr. Hall arranged the persons in his car.

For the rest of the day Mrs. Hall had avoided both her husband and Mrs. Mills.

This was not the first time that Mrs. Hall had been angry with the couple. At a Halloween party in the Sunday school room she had "stayed by herself" when she saw her husband dancing with Mrs. Mills.

Q. Did she stay away from everybody or just from Dr. Hall and Mrs. Mills?

A. No, she stayed away from them.

Mrs. Hall, who had been the only unmasked woman at the party, had spent the whole evening "watching what was going on."

Q. How many times did Dr. Hall dance with your sister?

A. I think mostly all evening.

In fact, with the exception of two sets with Mrs. Barnhardt, the minister had danced only with Eleanor.

There had been bad blood also, Mrs. Barnhardt said, between her sister and Minnie Clark. "She told me that Minnie Clark liked Mr. Hall, too, and that Minnie was very jealous at times, that Mr. Hall paid her—that is, Eleanor—attention and that whatever Eleanor did for Mr. Hall, Minnie would try to go her one better, and Minnie had stopped being friendly with Eleanor because Mr. Hall had shown favoritism to Eleanor."

On cross, McCarter succeeded in eliciting the information that Eleanor had not been above criticizing her husband's inadequacies in his presence. "You spoke of a conversation that occurred between Mrs. Mills and you, in which she said that she cared more for Mr. Hall's little finger than she did for her husband's body?" the lawyer purred. "She made that remark," Mrs. Barnhardt replied nervously.

Q. She made that remark to her husband, didn't she?

A. Yes, and Charlotte and Daniel were there.

It was almost time for the luncheon recess when Bailiff Bunn called out the name of Elisha K. Soper. The witness, a gray-haired, swarthy man in his early fifties, had passed the Easton Avenue end of De Russey's Lane at midnight on September 14. En route to New Brunswick, Mr. Soper had seen a "dark-colored open touring car" with dimmed lights parked on the right-hand side of Easton Avenue.[1]

Q. Could you say whether there were any persons in it or getting into it or getting out of it?

A. There was two men in the car, and a lady in a light coat on the back seat.

No, he had not recognized anybody in the car.

Simpson, whose face had turned the color of red brick at Soper's last statement, spun on his heels and barked out the name of Ira Nixon.

---

[1] The driver of the automobile in which Soper had been riding later swore that he had not seen any such car that night.

As soon as Nixon had been sworn, the prosecutor asked him if he and Soper hadn't worked as salesmen for a Newark oil company on September 23, 1922. Yes, sir, they had. And wasn't it true that they had discussed the Hall-Mills case on that day? It was.

Q. And did [Soper] in that conversation say that he was in the vicinity of De Russey's Lane the night of the murder, that he saw an automobile whose lights were so bright that the man driving the car had to slow down, and that he recognized the people in the car, a woman and two men, as Mrs. Hall and her brothers?

A. I say that he did.

"That is all." Senator Simpson gloated.

"Why are you here today?" Case began softly. "For the simple reason that for the last four years I have had the information that I am giving the State of New Jersey today," Nixon replied earnestly.

Q. Why didn't you give that information up earlier?

A. For the simple reason that I did not want to get mixed up in something, that I would not have to be harassed and stay up around this courthouse for two or three weeks like Mr. Soper.

"Hmph!" snorted the defense attorney.

Those who had begun to suspect that there was little logic to the sequence in which Simpson was calling his witnesses had their suspicions confirmed when Samuel T. Sutphen, the Somerville undertaker who had first examined the bodies, mounted the stand. The corpses had arrived in his morgue at 2:45 P.M. on September 16. Hall's had been removed by Hubbard three hours later and that of Mrs. Mills the next morning.

When he had searched the minister's body, he had found two handkerchiefs and sixty-one cents in change, all of which he had turned over to Sheriff Conkling. "When I was disrobing the body of Dr. Hall," he added, "a bullet dropped down when I was removing his coat."

At nine fifteen the next morning Dr. William Long, the Somerset County physician, had made an incision in Mrs. Mills' abdomen.

Q. What part of the body was cut?

A. About two inches below the navel.

After a brief examination Long had sutured the incision. During the operation Sutphen had noticed that there was a little wound on the dead woman's lip and that her arm was bruised, but neither he nor Long had opened her mouth to see if the tongue was intact.

Before court adjourned, Simpson asked Parker whether he had reached a decision as to whether the jurors would be permitted to visit the scene of the murder. The justice had.

"First, we are fairly well satisfied that it would be of no substantial advantage to this jury to go and look at the place as it is now. Second, we are equally well satisfied that if any attempt were made to take this jury down there to give them a chance to look at the place, it would be next to impossible to prevent interference with the jury, and on these two grounds we conclude that it would be highly inadvisable to send them there."

That evening both Case and Simpson attended an executive meeting of the New Jersey Senate in Trenton. When the session ended, the prosecutor was asked to comment about a report from the Jersey City Hospital that it might be some time before Mrs. Gibson would be able to make the trip to Somerville. "I think that Mrs. Gibson will be able to give her testimony on Wednesday," he replied. "I shall hear tomorrow at noon as to the probability of her being able to make the trip."

Until her marriage in June 1920, Marie M. Lee, another of Eleanor's sisters, had lived with the Millses. On Tuesday morning she testified that the murdered woman had often confided in her that she expected to marry Hall and go to Japan with him. "She said that she was going away with him, that he was going to try to get a divorce and they were going away when it was possible for him to do so."

Q. What did she say to Mills in your presence about her love for Dr. Hall?

A. She told him she cared for him, and would not do anything to disgrace his name, and when she was ready to go she would tell him.

After Mrs. Mills' kidney operation her relationship with Minnie Clark had deteriorated rapidly. "Mrs. Hall and Eleanor were not friendly," Mrs. Lee declared, "and she suspected Mrs. Clark of telling Mrs. Hall things that would make her feel that way toward her."

Q. What was that date?

A. That was the last visit I made in 1922, April.

Dr. Schultze was recalled briefly to give his opinion as to the necessity for Hall's hasty burial. "There would have been no need for haste in burying the body," he declared. "I have known bodies to be kept for a month or more."

On cross-examination, however, the physician readily conceded that in reaching his conclusion he had not taken into consideration either the weather or the condition of the minister's body when it was found.

Sharp-tongued Marie Demarest followed Dr. Schultze. Mrs. Demarest had been brought back to describe Felix De Martini's visit to her home in October 1922. Simpson was content to give his locquacious witness her head, and after asking her to recount her conversation with the private detective, sat down while she complied willingly.

"He said, 'Now, you told about seeing Henry Stevens on Friday morning.' I said, 'Yes.' He asked me to explain just where I saw him. I told him, and he said, 'Now, about your cousin Minnie Clark,' he says, 'what about her?' And I explained to him just about my cousin going to the Mills house. He says to me, 'Now, I am working on this case, but do you know that you are hurting your cousin?' I said, 'I don't know as I am.'

"'Listen,' he says, 'you have not seen Henry Stevens in

New Brunswick.' I says, 'Oh, but yes, I have.' He said, 'Oh, no, you did not. You know you are hurting him, too. Now, you have just taken over this place. You have got a mortgage on this place of twenty-five hundred dollars.' I says, 'How did you know? I never told anyone.' He says, 'I found it out. How would you like to have twenty-five hundred dollars and a little bit more to it to keep your mouth shut?' I said, 'No, thank you. If I wanted to clear the mortgage off on this house, I would rather go to work in a factory, in preference to taking Dr. Hall's blood money to keep my mouth shut.' "

Case's cross-examination was brief but thorough. Had Mrs. Demarest ever reported the bribe attempt to the police? She had not. Had anyone been present during her conversation with the detective? No one. When had she first learned his name? After he offered her the money.

Q. A man whom you had never seen before and who, so far as you know, had never seen you before comes and offers you twenty-five hundred dollars and a little more to buy your soul?

A. Sure.

Had she ever seen De Martini again? Yes, sir. Six weeks ago a state policeman had driven her to Brooklyn to take a look at the detective during his extradition proceedings. "I would not want to identify him as the man who had come to see me," she explained, "until I saw him personally."

Mazie Clemens, an attractive young lady who spoke in a rich contralto, succeeded the stern, raspy-voiced Mrs. Demarest. Miss Clemens, a New York *World* reporter, had arrived in New Brunswick several hours after the bodies had been found. At nine the next morning she had driven into the Hall driveway, where she saw Mrs. Bearman sitting in the front seat of a parked automobile.

Q. What happened after that?

A. After waiting a few minutes I saw a man come out of the house with a bundle of papers. He put them in the back of the car.

Q. Do you know who he is?

A. Henry Carpender.

Miss Clemens had watched as the broker made three trips. "The first trip he carried a bundle of papers tied up with a string, or what seemed to be a string; and then he went back and brought out some newspapers. The third trip he brought out a box, no top on it, and some papers on the top."[2]

Simpson, who was anxious to catch the 4:03 to Jersey City, had no more witnesses. While the special prosecutor was jamming papers into his already bulging brief case, Bergen was pressed into service to read Hall's diary to the jury. Dated consecutively from July 31 to August 12, 1922, the thirteen entries, which had been written for Mrs. Mills' benefit, covered the period of the minister's summer vacation on Islesford, a small island off the coast of Maine.

In order to be able to communicate with each other, the lovers had agreed that Mrs. Mills would address her letters to General Delivery at nearby Seal Harbor, where the minister was to post his to her. In the main the diary referred to the frantic efforts of its keeper to get to the Seal Harbor post office despite the dense fog that characterized the area.

"Another disappointment today, dear," he wrote on August 4. "I had hoped surely to get to Seal Harbor, but the fog set in thick very early. Just waiting for tomorrow, when I will go to Seal—fog or no fog. I know there is a letter waiting for me."

When Bergen finished his reading, Simpson informed Parker that Mrs. Gibson would be able to testify on Thursday morning. "She could appear in court tomorrow at ten," he said, "but the doctors think it would be better for her that she appear at ten o'clock on Thursday. So I would ask your Honor to adjourn over to Thursday instead of tomorrow morning."

With effusive apologies to the jurors for keeping them in-

2 Miss Clemens was undoubtedly the passenger whom cabbie Alfred Butler had driven to the Hall residence on Saturday afternoon, September 16, or Sunday morning, September 17, 1922. Although Butler fixed the time as Saturday morning, he was obviously mistaken.

carcerated for the extra day, Parker acceded to the prosecutor's request.

Late the next afternoon Simpson sent a detective to the
Jersey City Hospital to prepare Mrs. Gibson for her impending trip to Somerville. Despite her sunken eyes and waxen
complexion, the Pig Woman's voice was strong as she assured the prosecutor's emissary that she was able and willing
to testify. Earlier she had given the hospital a signed release,
in which she acknowledged that she was about to leave
against the advice of her physicians.

Senator Simpson scoffed at reports that the hospital authorities would refuse to release his star witness. If she were
not allowed to leave the next morning, he threatened, he
would ask Justice Parker for a writ of habeas corpus. However, he didn't think that this drastic step would be necessary, as the hospital superintendent had assured him Mrs.
Gibson could make the trip to Somerville.

Thursday, November 18, was the day on which George
Bernard Shaw refused to accept the forty thousand dollars
that went with the 1925 Nobel Prize for Literature because,
as he put it, "I already have more money than is good for
me." It was also the day that Jane Gibson rode into Somerville in a white ambulance.

At 7:35 A.M. four Jersey City policemen carried her out
of the hospital on a specially built air cushion to the waiting
vehicle, where she was joined by a physician and two nurses.
Sandwiched between two Jersey City police sedans and followed by six cars filled with reporters and photographers,
the ambulance headed slowly out of town. Because its driver
had been advised to drive slowly, it took almost four hours
to cover the thirty-two miles to Somerville.

Despite the early hour and a steady drizzle, the route was
lined with curious onlookers.

"Do your stuff, Jane!" one man shouted as the convoy
crawled through Newark.

"Now's yer chance, Jane, to do yer squealin'!" yelled a shrill-voiced Elizabeth matron.

In Scotch Plains a woman held her small son above her head so that he could get a better look at the ambulance. "Hurray!" the boy cried. "There goes the Pig Woman!"

There was only one stop—at Plainfield, where two bottles of ginger ale were purchased for Mrs. Gibson.

When the procession pulled into Bound Brook, it was met by a messenger from Senator Simpson, who urged the ambulance driver to waste no time in getting to Somerville as court was already in session. The impatient prosecutor had sent the county seat's only motorcycle policeman to keep the last section of road open. At ten fifty the white vehicle rolled cautiously through the crowd of reporters, photographers, motion picture cameramen, and bystanders who had been waiting in front of the courthouse since early morning.

As soon as the driver had cut his engine, a detective rushed into the courtroom and informed Bailiff Bunn that the Pig Woman had arrived.

"Bring her right in!" Bunn ordered.

A deputy sheriff opened the rear doors, and as everyone in the packed room turned to watch, four policemen carried in a stretcher which seemed to contain nothing but a bundle of sheets and blankets. It was only when the contents of the stretcher had been transferred to the iron hospital bed which faced the jury box that Mrs. Gibson's wasted face could be seen.

Her eyes remained closed as the jurors filed into the courtroom. Seconds later Cleary and Parker took their places on the bench. Just as Parker gaveled for silence, one of the investigators for the defense steered Mrs. Salome Cerenner, the Pig Woman's mother, to a front-row seat. "Sit there and don't let nobody move you," he ordered. "Watch her as she testifies, that's all."

Mrs. Cerenner, who wore a black dress that must have been at least thirty years old, was not aware that she had stolen the spotlight from her celebrated daughter. The aged woman, her gnarled hands clasped in her lap and her pointed chin moving slowly up and down, blinked uncertainly as she watched the Jersey City physician checking the witness's pulse.

"She is a liar!" she blurted out suddenly. "A liar, liar, liar! A liar, that's what she is! Ugh!"

If Mrs. Gibson had heard her mother's caustic comment, she gave no sign. She lay with her eyes closed as the court clerk, Bible in hand, walked over to the bed. "Do you solemnly swear to tell the truth, the whole truth, and nothing but the truth, so help you God?" he intoned. Mrs. Gibson's "I do" could hardly be heard.

"Before you proceed with the examination," Parker said to Simpson, "I was wondering whether Mrs. Easton's[3] voice is sufficiently strong for the jury to hear." His suggestion that the stenographer repeat the Pig Woman's answers aloud was enthusiastically seconded by the prosecutor.

In general, Mrs. Gibson's story was much the same as the one she had told to Mott, Simpson, two grand juries, and scores of newspaper reporters. Shortly before eight forty-five on the night of the murder her dog, which had been tied to a tree between the house and the road, began to bark. "I went outside and I walked down where the dog was and listened, and when the dog stopped barking I walked back and I sat on the swing and listened."

Several minutes later "a rickety old wagon that rattled and rattled and rattled went down the road right through the middle of my cornfield." Because thieves had plundered some twenty rows of her corn the preceding Sunday, Mrs. Gibson saddled her mule and followed the wagon up De Russey's Lane toward Easton Avenue.

Just as the wagon turned right into Easton Avenue, an automobile had entered De Russey's Lane. In the glare of its headlights the mounted woman had seen a bareheaded

[3] The witness was sworn as "Mrs. Jane Easton," which was probably her right name, but she was referred to throughout the trial by counsel for both sides as "Mrs. Gibson."

white woman and "a colored man" standing at the side of the road.

Q. Do you know who the woman was?

A. Yes, Mrs. Hall.

Q. Have you learned who the man was who was with her?

A. Yes. Willie Stevens.

When she reached Easton Avenue, Mrs. Gibson could no longer see the wagon. "I turned around to try to locate it, but I could not find it," she said weakly. Thinking that the wagon had doubled back across the fields, she re-entered De Russey's Lane and rode until she reached the entrance to the little path that led to the Phillips farm. She had then turned to the left and walked slowly down the darkened lane until she reached "two little cedar trees and a stump," where she tethered her mule.

Q. After you tied her, where did you go?

A. I walked slowly toward De Russey's Lane. I was going to look for the wagon and follow him on foot.

Suddenly she had heard a "rumbling of voices" to her left.

Q. Men's voices?

A. Men's voices and women's voices.

As the owners of the voices came closer to her, she had heard a woman shout, "Explain these letters." Then all hell had broken loose. "Somebody was beating, beating, beating. I could hear somebody's wind going out, and somebody said 'Ugh!' Then somebody said, 'God damn it, let go!' Then somebody threw a flash toward where they were hollering. I see something glitter and I see a man and I see another man, like they were wrestling together. One was Henry Stevens."

Seconds later a shot had shattered the night air.

Now thoroughly frightened, Mrs. Gibson had run toward where she had left her mule. "There were two women," she recalled. "One said, 'Oh, Henry,' very, very easy, and the other began to scream, scream, so loud, 'Oh, my; oh, my!' So terrible loud. I ran for the mule after the first shot, but that woman was screaming, screaming, trying to run away or something, and I just about got my foot in the stirrup when Bang! Bang! Bang! Three quick shots."

She had ridden home as fast as Jenny could carry her.

After she had stabled the animal, she discovered that one of her moccasins was missing. Several hours later she had decided to go back to look for the lost slipper. In the light of the newly risen moon she had returned to the cedar grove. As she searched for her moccasin, she was startled to hear what she first thought was the hoot of an owl.

"I heard it again, and I said, 'Something is the matter out here,' and then I listened, and then I heard the voice of a man. It seemed kind of like a woman hollered along there or someone, and I heard the voice of a man, and the moon was shining down very bright, and so I heard it again, and I looked right at the cedar, and I crossed over the lane right at the cedar, and I seen a big white-haired woman doing something with her hand, crying, something."

The woman, who had been kneeling, was Mrs. Hall.

Simpson, who appeared quite satisfied with Mrs. Gibson's testimony, concluded his direct examination with a series of questions about Felix De Martini. Had the witness ever seen the private detective before? She had—he had come to her house shortly after her story became public in 1922. "He said, 'You had better keep your mouth shut; it will pay you better to keep out of this.' I jumped up and I said, 'Who are you?' So I took my gun and banged it on the floor. I said, 'Move, and move quick!' He began to move. I was afraid of him."

As Senator Case walked over to the hospital bed, the witness's physician hurriedly checked her pulse and temperature. The defense attorney waited patiently until the doctor signified that Mrs. Gibson was ready to be questioned once more.

"Now, Mrs. Gibson," he began suavely, "you remember testifying at the preliminary hearing held in August 1926, in this courtroom?" She did. At that time had she identified Henry Carpender as one of the men she had seen near the cedar grove? Yes, sir, she certainly had.

Suddenly Case turned on his heel. "Will Henry Carpender stand?" he demanded. The stockbroker, who had been brought into the courtroom during Mrs. Gibson's direct examination, rose to his feet.

Q. And is this the gentleman that you then identified?
A. That is one of the men.

The veins on Case's neck bulged. Why hadn't she mentioned at the preliminary hearing that there had been other men present? "Nobody asked me," the supine woman replied quietly.

The lawyer turned to something else. Since she had been sworn as Jane Easton, he wanted to know what her correct legal name was. It was Easton, but people had begun to call her Mrs. Gibson shortly after she had purchased her farm. "They always got Gibson's Farm products," she explained, "and they got to calling me Mrs. Gibson and I never said nothing."

Q. But you took title to your farm under the name of Jane Gibson, did you not?
A. I sure did.

Q. Therefore if you took title to the farm as Jane Gibson, how do you explain what you have already said?

Simpson's prompt objection saved Mrs. Gibson further embarrassment.

For the next thirty minutes Case hurled his questions at the Pig Woman with such rapidity that she often had difficulty in keeping up with him.

How many husbands had she had?

Only one—William H. Easton.[4]

Hadn't she married a Frederick Kesselring in 1890?

[4] Four years earlier Mrs. Gibson had just as emphatically denied that she was married to Easton.

That was not true.

And didn't Kesselring divorce her for adultery in 1898?
"No," she replied tartly. "That is mixed up with somebody else. That man was a married man and had a wife and
baby."

Had she ever lived with a man named Harry Ray?
No, she had not.

Did she know a man named Stumpy Gillan?
No, sir.

Why, Case demanded, had Mrs. Gibson-Easton waited
more than two weeks to divulge what she had seen at the
Phillips farm?

"I had trouble enough without getting mixed up in anybody else's," she explained patiently. "Nobody wants to get
mixed up with anybody and accuse anybody of murder,
even though they do see it. Besides, I thought the authorities
were slick enough to find out who did do it."

Case's next question was interrupted by Mrs. Gibson's doctor, who decided to take her pulse again. "It's nothing but
chatter, chatter, chatter, and talk, talk, talk," the Pig Woman
muttered to the physician as he completed his examination.

Five minutes later the defense attorney concluded his
cross and court adjourned until Friday morning.

As four policemen transferred her from the hospital bed
to a stretcher, Mrs. Gibson rose on one elbow and pointed a
trembling finger at the three defendants. "I have told the
truth, so help me God, and you know I've told the truth!"
she gasped.

For a brief moment a faint smile appeared on Mrs. Hall's
normally impassive face. Willie, who appeared fascinated by
Mrs. Gibson's outburst, rubbed his nose vigorously as she
was carried out of the courtroom. His brother, who was
somewhat deaf, did not appear to have heard the Pig Woman's remark.

Mrs. Gibson fell asleep as soon as she had been placed in
the ambulance. She awoke at Maplewood and said that she
felt greatly refreshed. The ambulance stopped at Irvington

for five minutes so that the now wide-awake woman could enjoy a pint of ice cream.

It took three hours to make the return trip to Jersey City, and Mrs. Gibson was back in her private room shortly after five thirty. "I feel better tonight than I have at any time during the last four years, now that I've got that out of my system," she told the doctors and nurses who came in during the evening.

Major Calvin H. Goddard, a firearms expert,[5] testified on Friday that the bullets which had been found in the bodies of the dead couple had been fired from the same weapon.

Q. How do you determine that?

A. I placed them under what we term a comparison microscope, by which the image of two objects may be fused into one. By using this microscope I have determined the fact that they had all issued from the same gun barrel.

He was fairly certain that the gun involved had been a .32-caliber Colt. "A summary of my measurements of all the bullet markings link them up with bullets fired through the Colt pistol rather than those fired through any other type of pistol, but I do not wish to make that statement without some qualification on account of the poor condition of the bullets."

Simpson's next witness, a young man named David D. Nagel, caused immediate consternation at the defense table. Nagel, who had been working as a photographer's helper for the New York *American* in 1922, swore that he had been on the same ferry as Hall's funeral cortege. At that time he had noticed a scratch on Mrs. Hall's face.

"Where was Mrs. Hall when you saw this scratch?" asked Simpson.

"She was sitting in the car. The door was open, and there was a lady standing out in front right by the door, and they were laughing and joking," was the answer.

5 Major Goddard had replaced his partner, Charles E. Waite, who had died of a heart attack five days earlier.

Alfred D. Scholz, Jr., the *American* photographer for whom Nagel had been working, confirmed the youth's story. He, too, had seen a scratch on Mrs. Hall's face. It had been on the left side, "just about the bone of the cheek down."
Q. Did it look fresh or old?
A. Well, quite fresh.

"I was assigned to watch Mrs. Hall, to get a picture of her," he explained, "and I had a big baseball camera with me, and they opened the curtain in the window of the car, and some of the relatives, or some people, got out of the car ahead of my car and came over toward Mrs. Hall's car, and they stood around. Mrs. Hall smiled and said, 'How do you do?' and they started to laugh and smile and joke."

In 1922, Frank Caprio had worked as a confidential investigator for Azariah Beekman. In November of that year, shortly after the first grand jury had refused to indict, Caprio had visited the Somerset prosecutor's office, where he had seen State's Exhibit 97—a straight-edged razor—wrapped in a fingerprint identification card. At the same time he had noticed what appeared to be "a German automatic" on Beekman's desk.

With the latter's permission, the witness had taken the razor with him when he left that day. Four years later he had turned it over to Senator Simpson in Jersey City.
Q. And you delivered it to me in the same condition you got it from Mr. Beekman?
A. Yes, sir.

The bald-headed witness, who wore a striped suit and large solitaire, grew truculent under McCarter's biting cross. Hadn't he been convicted in Monmouth County of the crime of obtaining money under false pretenses and sentenced to three years at hard labor in the New Jersey State Prison? "I didn't do no three years in State Prison!" Caprio retorted.

"I want an answer to my question," the lawyer demanded. "Were you convicted as I asked you and as I now repeat?" His quarry looked helplessly in Simpson's direction. "Yes," he finally admitted. "But Monmouth County is a place where they sentence prisoners for nothing."

By the time McCarter finished with Caprio, even Simpson had lost all faith in the veracity of his witness. "I refuse to rely on Caprio's testimony," he announced. "I have withdrawn the razor."

The shifty-eyed witness sat for a moment in the chair, looking bewildered at the special prosecutor. Finally he uncrossed his well-tailored legs, stood up, and walked rapidly out of the courtroom.

Simpson waited patiently until the double doors had closed behind the thoroughly discredited investigator.

"The state rests," he said simply.

The courtroom clock read one fifty-five.

Senator Case's opening for the defense consumed the rest of the day. Considerably better organized than Simpson's effort seventeen days earlier, it promised that ample and compelling evidence would be presented to prove that none of the defendants had been anywhere near the Phillips farm on the night of the murders.

"We are trying to prove to you that we did not do it," Case explained. "The defendants, gentlemen of the jury, and none of the defendants, were there. None of the defendants knew anything about it, either before or after the sad tragedy—knew nothing about and had nothing to do with it. When you hear their stories, your conscience and your minds will be free to acquit them."

At ten o'clock the next morning Henry Stevens walked briskly to the stand. Despite the fact that he had spent almost two months in jail, he still exhibited traces of the deep summer tan he had acquired on Barnegat Bay. His black, gray-streaked hair was carefully combed, and his stubby mustache and amber-rimmed spectacles made him look more like a Rutgers scholar than the inveterate outdoorsman he was. His voice, as he began to answer Case's questions, was clear and forceful, and his aplomb never deserted him as the day wore on.

Stevens' alibi was hardly a state secret. Ever since the murders he had insisted that he had spent the entire day of September 14, 1922, in Lavallette. "In the morning I was downtown, tending to the usual things that I did around town. In the afternoon I made a short trip to see an old friend of mine who lived at Seaside Park, three miles below. I was only there a short while, and I came back and fished some more. I did not fish very long, and came in and had supper in the neighborhood of six o'clock.

"After supper I went out on the beach, fishing. Along about dusk Arthur Applegate came along with a good-sized bluefish, and I weighed it for him. It weighed six pounds." He had left the beach at 10 P.M. and returned one hour later. Then he had walked to the home of the Wilsons, his next-door neighbors, and offered them "a couple of bluefish."

Before returning home he had agreed to drive Mrs. Wilson and her two daughters to Point Pleasant early on Friday afternoon so that they could catch the train to Jersey City.

The next morning he had risen early, and after casting for mullet along the beach, had returned home for breakfast. "I went downtown about traintime because I usually went down to meet the train and get the morning mail and the morning paper," he continued. "I went to the station and was there when the train came in."

After lunch he drove the Wilsons to Point Pleasant, did some household errands, and then returned to Lavallette.

He had spent the remainder of the day fishing on the beach near his home. "I had supper and retired about the same time as the night before, or possibly a little earlier," he recalled.

After lunch the next day he had received a telegram from Edwin R. Carpender, informing him that Hall had been killed. He had taken the afternoon train to New Brunswick, arriving there "about six thirty, or maybe a little later."

Case ended with a flourish. "Were you on the night of the fourteenth of September, 1922, or the morning of the fifteenth day of September, 1922, at or near the City of New Brunswick?" he demanded. "No," Stevens replied firmly.

Q. Did you in any way, directly or indirectly, participate in the killing of either Edward Hall or Eleanor Mills?

A. No.

Q. Did you procure that to be done by anyone else?

A. No.

Q. Have you any knowledge relating thereto?

A. No.

There was a faint smile on the lawyer's face as he turned to Simpson. "You may cross-examine," he said quietly.

The prosecutor got nowhere with the imperturbable witness. Stevens maintained that his experience with firearms had been limited to rifles and shotguns. "I have never fired an automatic in my life," he insisted. No, he had not attended his sister's wedding, but he had not objected to the marriage.

Mrs. Hall had never told him that she suspected her husband of having an affair with Mrs. Mills, and he had never met or even heard of the choir singer. He had not remained away from both Somerville and New Brunswick after the arrest of his brother and sister because he was afraid that someone would recognize him. "I never had any idea of that kind," he protested.

Just before lunch Stevens admitted that he often used "a sheath knife" to clean fish. Simpson, remembering the implications raised by Case's references to Jim Mills' leather-cutting knife, decided to take a leaf out of the defense attorney's book. Pulling over the papier-mâché manikin on which Dr. Schultze had demonstrated the results of his autopsies, the prosecutor asked the defendant to indicate how he would clean a bluefish.

"Can you make the slash on the throat of this woman that you make on a bluefish?" he asked sharply.

Stevens looked horrified.

"I could not," he answered.

Simpson picked up Stevens' diary, in which the witness had indicated that Arthur Applegate had caught a six-pound bluefish on September 14, 1922. When had he made that particular entry? "It might have been two or three days later; it might have been only one day," Stevens answered. "I have no recollection whether it was before or after the murders had been discovered."

If he entered such trivia as the weight of his friends' fish, why hadn't he been interested in recording his brother-in-law's funeral? "It was unimportant to put in a diary," Stevens said doggedly. "That diary was kept as much for a record of fish and game as anything else."

Four eyewitnesses attempted to corroborate Stevens story. Thaddeus S. Mellinger, a Philadelphian who spent his summers in Lavallette, had seen him fishing on the beach "from around nine o'clock to about ten thirty" on the night of the murders.[6]

Q. Now, did you know anything about his movements on Friday, the following day?

A. Only this. About after my breakfast I saw him drive by my house, which is the third house down on the right from his.

Robert E. Stoneback, a commercial paper dealer who had been Mellinger's guest on the fatal night, recalled that Stevens had been on the beach "between eight thirty and nine thirty, about twenty feet away from us, fishing." William H. Eger, whose summer cottage was a block away from the defendant's house, had fished with him "from seven thirty to nine thirty." Lavallette's Mayor Enoch T. Van Camp had watched Stevens weighing Applegate's bluefish "between eight forty-five and nine o'clock."

Although Simpson could not shake Stoneback or Eger, he

---

[6] Two months earlier, however, Mr. Mellinger had executed an affidavit for Simpson in which he had sworn that it had been Friday and not Thursday night when he had seen his neighbor on the beach. His explanation: "I made a mistake in it."

made mincemeat out of Van Camp's testimony. It seemed that the portly mayor had signed an affidavit on September 3, 1926, in which he stated that it was impossible for him to remember when Applegate had caught his big fish.

Q. Will you say under oath whether you on the third of September took your oath that you could not say what day of the week and what day of the month that you saw this fish weighed, did you say that, yes or no?

A. I recollect, which I am trying to get into my head, Mr. Simpson—

Q. All right, sir?

A. That I don't remember swearing to that, that I did not know the date.

Q. That is your signature, isn't it?

A. That is my signature.

Q. But I want to get you clearly on the record that you say now either that you don't remember or that you did say under oath on the third of September, 1926, that you could not say what day of the week or what day of the month it was you saw Henry Stevens weigh the bluefish.

A. Well, if it is in there, I certainly said it. I don't think I swear to anything false, to the best of my knowledge.

Because of the incessant laughter generated among the spectators by the mayor's awkward attempts to explain away his damaging affidavit, Parker angrily ordered everyone except newspapermen out of the room five minutes before the last session of the week drew to a close.

The Jersey City Hospital announced that despite all reports to the contrary, Mrs. Gibson was doing "remarkably well." The Pig Woman, whose room was filled with congratulatory letters, baskets of fruit, and floral bouquets, was in excellent spirits. "It was a wonderful thing," she chortled, "to be able to go down there when I was needed."

She drew the attention of her many visitors to a vase of tuberoses which stood on her night table. "They're from Charlotte Mills," she said proudly.

Chapter 26

THE TRIAL—FOURTH WEEK

*(Monday, November 22, through
Saturday, November 27, 1926)*

The fifteenth day of the trial opened with the testimony of Anna Evanson, a gentle old woman with mild blue eyes whose voice still bore a trace of her Swedish origin. Mrs. Evanson, who had been working as a cook for the Stevenses for six years, said that she had served Henry his supper at six o'clock on the night of the murders. When she left the house, an hour later, she had seen her employer fishing on the beach.

The following morning she had reported for work "between half past nine or nine." Her first chore had been to wash and dry the wet clothes he had been wearing earlier that morning when, he informed her, he had attempted to catch some mullet for bait.

Howard Price, a spare man with thinning gray hair, stated that he lived two blocks away from the Stevens house. At 9:55 P.M. on Thursday, September 14, 1922, he had been walking along the beach.

"As I came to the Stevens cottage," he said, "I stopped to see what time it was, and as I was looking at my watch I raised my head and there was a man passed about eight or ten feet in front of me, crossing my path at a right angle and going toward the beach."

Q. Who was it?

A. Henry Stevens.

Price was succeeded by Arthur Applegate's wife, Mazie, a stylishly dressed woman whose flashing eyes and red cheeks spoke well for Lavallette's vaunted climate.

At 7 P.M. on September 14, Mrs. Applegate had taken her eight-year-old son to the beach, where her husband was fishing. "Henry Stevens was on the beach all the time," she asserted, "and he was there when we came back, and it was ten o'clock or after, and we said good night to him."

Q. Had any incidents taken place while you were down at the beach that you remember?

A. Yes, sir. My husband caught a bluefish, and Mr. Stevens weighed it for him.

She distinctly remembered that "it was dark, so we had to have a light."

Carpenter Arthur Applegate took his wife's place in the witness chair. A husky man with enormous work-lined hands, he wore a heavy brown sweater under his dark gray coat. On the night that he had caught his giant bluefish, Henry Stevens had been casting "directly in front of his house, sitting on his fishing box." Because Applegate had been having a run of bad luck, Stevens had given him a new hook. A few minutes later the carpenter had hooked his blue.

Q. Quite a sizable fish, was it?

A. Fairly good size, yes.

Q. Who weighed it?

A. Mr. Stevens.

With Mrs. Evanson, Mr. Price, and Mrs. Applegate, Simpson had contented himself with questions designed to indicate that it was passing strange that each witness was able to remember so clearly what had happened that Thursday evening four long years ago. But Applegate was not to get off that easy. Armed with the minutes of the April grand jury and an affidavit which the witness had executed on September 3, 1926, the special prosecutor swarmed all over the gap-toothed carpenter.

Wasn't it true, he demanded, that on both occasions Applegate had sworn he couldn't remember when he had caught his six-pound blue and that detectives or reporters had suggested to him it might have taken place on the night of the murder? He couldn't recall whether he had said that or not.

Q. Don't you think you have rather a peculiar memory?
A. I think I am about as peculiar as you are.

Despite all of Simpson's badgering, Applegate insisted that he couldn't remember what he had said earlier about his bluefish. Of one thing he *was* certain. "It was caught on the night of the murder," he repeated doggedly.

On September 13, 1922, real estate salesman John Piard had been taken ill in Philadelphia with a strangulated hernia. Thinking that the cool air of Lavallette might relieve his pain, he had taken the train to the seaside resort the next evening.

Q. And you arrived at Lavallette at about what time?
A. Quarter to six.

He, too, had seen Henry Stevens fishing from the beach that night. "I saw him on the beach at about a quarter to seven until dark on Thursday night," he said.

Early Friday morning Piard had returned to Philadelphia. "I was sick, and I went to University Hospital," he recalled. "I got there about a quarter of ten, and they operated on me about half past eleven." While he was waiting for his train at Lavallette, he had noticed Henry Stevens in the railroad station "about a quarter after seven."

Mrs. Sarah M. Wilson, who lived next door to the Stevenses, had spoken to the defendant on the porch of her house "at about 10:30 P.M." on September 14. On Friday morning she had seen him on the beach at seven o'clock.

Q. And when next after that did you see him?
A. I saw him about half past nine or ten in the morning.

He was standing back of his garage, where he was cleaning some fish.

At one that afternoon he had called for her and her two college-bound daughters and driven them to Point Pleasant.

After Elaine and Alice Wilson had confirmed their mother's testimony, Senator Case called a Mrs. Emma Holzlohner to the stand. In August 1924, Mrs. Holzlohner had been visiting her daughter, Mrs. Bertha Tegen, who then shared the Phillips farmhouse with Anna Hoag. She remembered that during her visit a man had knocked at the door one morning and asked for directions to Raritan Township. "I was a stranger there," Mrs. Holzlohner said, "and I told him I didn't know."

Q. And did you call Mrs. Hoag, or something like that?
A. Yes, I did. She just came around from the hen house, and I asked her could she direct this man to Raritan Township, and she said she didn't know.

The stranger had sat on the porch for a few minutes and then gone to the well for a drink of water. Case spun around. "Henry Stevens," he barked, "stand, please." Was that the man, the lawyer asked, whom Mrs. Holzlohner had seen that day? "No, sir," she replied definitely. "He was taller than Mr. Stevens, and very pale-looking, with a little gray mustache."

Mrs. Tegen was even more explicit than her mother about the incident. "This man knocked at the door, and Mother went to the door and he asked for Raritan Township, and Mother did not know. She asked me and I did not know either, so Mrs. Hoag was coming up from the barn and we asked her whether she knew where Raritan Township was and she said no, but that she would direct him to the Raritan car, which she did.

"It was a very warm day, and he sat down and started talking to Mother. When it was near time to go, he asked for a drink of water and I directed him to the pump, and when he went to go out he came back for his coat and then went out, and I did not see him go out." No, Henry Stevens was not the man she had seen that day.

With Mrs. Hoag's damaging testimony that Stevens had been the nervous visitor who had asked her for directions that August afternoon at least countered by that of his last two witnesses, Case decided to try his hand at repairing other holes in the dike. Remembering that Mr. and Mrs. John S. Dickson, the Plainfield couple who on the first day of the trial had stated that a stuttering, epileptic Willie Stevens had stopped at their house on September 14, 1922, the lawyer called Dr. Lawrence Runyon, the Hall family physician.

Bald-headed Dr. Runyon, who had known Willie for thirty years, insisted that his eccentric patient had never suffered from epilepsy.

Q. Can you tell whether he is a stutterer?

A. He has never stuttered in my presence, to my knowledge.

On cross-examination, Runyon claimed that while Willie was not "absolutely normal," he was more than capable of taking care of himself. "He is brighter than the average person," he said. "He reads books that are above average and knows the answers, and makes a good many people look like fools."

Tuesday morning was devoted to three fingerprint experts for the defense who presented a solid front in denying that the smudge on State's Exhibit 17, the dead clergyman's calling card, bore any resemblance to Willie Stevens' prints. According to one of them, the disputed print might have been the result of "an afterthought." From the scowl on Simpson's face it was obvious that the euphemism had not been lost on him.

The courtroom regulars, who had begun to fidget under

the seemingly endless talk of whorls, ridges, and bifurca-
tions, were relieved to discover that it would not continue
during the afternoon session.[1]

The defense's first witness of the afternoon was Asbury Park
attorney John R. Phillips. Under McCarter's deft questioning,
he testified that he had known Edward H. Schwartz, one of
Simpson's fingerprint experts, for six years. Three or four
months after the murders Schwartz had shown Phillips one of
Hall's calling cards.

Q. At that time was the card smudged?

A. The card was a white card with no smudges on it.

The card was the one, Schwartz told the lawyer, that had
been found near the minister's left foot.

Last August, Phillips had visited Schwartz at his Monmouth County home. At that time the fingerprint expert had
claimed that he was better qualified in his specialty than
either Lieutenant Drewen or Commissioner Faurot. "Did he
then ask you," McCarter demanded, "if you knew of any of
the lawyers connected with the defense in this Hall matter
that was pending, he would like to be retained by them?"
He most certainly did, Phillips replied.

Q. And did he say that there were certain things about
the print on that card that negatived the claim of the state
with reference to it?

A. Yes, sir, words to that effect.

Phillips was followed by James F. Mason, Mott's former
chief investigator, who now headed the Essex County Detective Bureau. According to Mason, one of Hall's calling cards
had been turned over to him on November 1, 1922.

Q. Did you do anything upon the card?

A. Yes, sir. I put my initials in the upper left-hand corner.

Fully aware that State's Exhibit 17 contained no initials,
McCarter asked Mason when he had given the card to Lieu-

1 Simpson decided to postpone his cross-examination of the defense's
experts until he had had an opportunity to study the transcript of their
direct testimony.

tenant Schwartz. "It was the next morning," the detective replied.

As Mason left the stand, there was a brief huddle at the defense table.

Suddenly Case stood up.

"Mr. William Stevens to the stand," he ordered.

Willie, who looked delighted at being called, walked briskly to the witness chair.

Wearing a brown silk tie whose small knot nestled under his wing collar, the defendant looked neater than he had at any time during the trial. His wiry black hair was carefully brushed, and as he waited for Case's first question he kept smoothing out his bushy black mustache with the eraser end of the yellow pencil he had brought into court every day. "He looks like a successful delicatessen dealer," Damon Runyon noted.

As Willie peered curiously through his thick-lensed spectacles at the sea of faces in front of him, Parker attempted to end the hubbub that had been generated by the announcement of the celebrated witness's name. It took several minutes of furious gavel pounding by the presiding justice before the courtroom was quiet once more.

The silence, however, did not last long. At Willie's first answers the spectators burst into such spontaneous laughter that even Parker could not resist a smile.

"Mr. Stevens, how old are you?" Case began. "I am forty-four," the witness replied in the slow, gravely serious voice he was to employ during his eighty minutes on the stand. The lawyer hurriedly consulted his notes. "Isn't that fifty-four?" he asked. Willie smiled broadly. "Oh, yes," he answered quietly.

As soon as the laughter subsided, Case, who did not seem particularly disturbed by the outburst, calmly continued his examination.

When had Willie last fired his Iver-Johnson revolver?

At least fourteen years ago.

How had his relations with his brother-in-law been?

Very cordial.

Had he ever worn a gold watch and chain?

Never in his life.

Had he ever suffered from epilepsy?

No, sir, he had not.

Had he known Mrs. Mills?

Just by sight.

On the night of the murders Hall had left the house after supper. "I don't really have to go out tonight," the minister had said, "but I am simply going out to see about a payment on the bill for the operation."

Willie had then gone to his room and locked his door.

Q. Why did you lock it?

A. On account of the terrible odor of the smoke, tobacco smoke. It seemed that everyone in the house objected to the smell of Willie's old briar pipe.

He had gone to bed "between half past eight and half past nine," but because of the warmth of the night had been unable to fall asleep until he had kicked off some of his covers.

Q. After you had gotten to sleep, did anything happen?

A. I was awakened by my sister knocking at my door and I immediately arose and went to the door, and she said, "I want you to come down to the church, as Edward has not been home; I am very much worried," or words to that effect.

He and his sister had left the house by the Redmond Street gate at what Mrs. Hall had told him was "about half past two."

When they arrived at the church, they saw that the building was dark. "Then Mrs. Hall said, 'We might as well go down and see if it could not be possible that he was at the Mills house.' We went down there."

Q. Did she say any reason why he might have been there?

A. She did. There might have been somebody sick there.

Seeing no lights in the Mills apartment, they had returned

home. "My sister said, 'You might as well go to bed. You can do no more good.' With that I went upstairs to bed."

He had first learned of his brother-in-law's death on Saturday afternoon. "I remember I was in the parlor, reading a copy of the New York *Times*," he said deliberately. "I heard someone coming up the steps and I glanced up, and I heard my aunt, Mrs. Charles J. Carpender, say, 'Well, you might as well know it, Edward has been shot!' "

Q. And what happened then?

A. Well, I simply let the paper go that way and I put my head down and cried.

Mrs. Hall and Henry Carpender looked tense when Case indicated to Simpson that the witness was at his disposal. But if Willie was feeling any fear as the special prosecutor bore down on him, his face gave no indication of it. When Simpson stopped in front of him, the defendant's lips curved in a gentle, disarming smile. It was only when one looked at Willie's pudgy hands, which gripped the arms of the witness chair with such force that the knuckles whitened with strain, that the extent of his nervousness became apparent.

Simpson's voice was carefully restrained as he probed for the weak spots in Willie's direct examination. Did he remember telling Prosecutor Stricker that his sister had awakened him at 1:30 A.M.? He had no recollection of that. Had Mrs. Hall seemed agitated on the way to the church that night? Not necessarily.

Q. She was alarmed, wasn't she, about [the rector's] disappearance?

A. She did not seem to be raving or agitated.

Q. Was she alarmed at his disappearance?

A. She was worried.

Had any effort been made to determine whether Hall had been in the Mills apartment? No, sir. Since the lights were out, it had been assumed that the minister was not there. Didn't Mr. Witness think it was "rather fishy" to get up in the middle of the night in order to look for the missing clergyman and not at least knock at the Millses' front door?

Willie hesitated. "Can you answer that broad question, Mr. Stevens?" Justice Parker inquired solicitously. "The only way I can answer it, your Honor," Willie said, "is that I don't see that it is at all fishy."

Simpson thought otherwise. "If you were my brother and I were looking for you," he continued, "and I went to a place where I thought you were and I knew it was the last place you were and I did not knock on the door and try to find out whether you were there, wouldn't you think that was a fish story I was trying to tell?" Willie stood his ground. "No, sir, I do not," he answered firmly.

No, he had never seen one of his brother-in-law's calling cards. Simpson placed State's Exhibit 17 on the rail in front of the witness. "May I handle it?" Willie asked timorously. "Surely," the special prosecutor replied.

Q. You did not take a calling card like this with your left hand behind it, your thumb in front like that, and put it at the feet of Dr. Hall after he was murdered?

A. Positively no.

As the cross-examination continued, it soon became apparent that Willie was not going to be any pushover for his astute adversary. When Simpson asked him to repeat, for the third time, his movements on the night of the murder, the prosecutor insisted that there was method in his madness. "I am not doing this with the idea of wasting time," he explained to Parker, "but to show whether or not, by reason of the peculiar mentality of Mr. Stevens, he has not been taught this story and learned it by rote."

Willie raised his hand. "May I say a word?" he asked. "Certainly, say all you want," Simpson replied expansively. "All I have to say is I was never taught, as you insinuate, whatsoever," the witness said gravely. "That is my best recollection from the time I started out with my sister to this present minute."

Willie's statement was far more effective than all his

lawyers' objections to Simpson's line of inquiry because the
special prosecutor immediately drifted off to other matters.
If the defendant had locked himself in his room at approximately nine o'clock on the night of September 14, 1922, it
would be impossible, would it not, for anyone to see him
through the door? Naturally.

Q. Now, with that locked door, nobody could see whether
you were in the house unless they came up and knocked on
the door and asked or called for you?

A. They could see the light in the room.

"Outside of the light, there was no way of knowing
whether you were there or not?" Simpson demanded. Willie
thought for a moment. "If a person sees me go upstairs, isn't
that a conclusion that I was in my room?" he countered. The
defendant's unassailable logic carried the round.

"Absolutely," the special prosecutor replied lamely.

Willie was still on the stand when Parker adjourned for
the day. The next morning Simpson roared back to the attack. Wasn't it a fact, he demanded, that Willie frequently
delivered notes from the rector to Mrs. Mills? Absolutely
not. The only time he had ever visited the Carman Street
apartment was when his sister asked him to speak to Mr.
Mills about some window boxes he was making for her.

Q. You did not see Mrs. Mills then?

A. I did not.

Was Willie absolutely certain that he had never suffered
from epilepsy? He was. Then, Simpson purred, he could not
possibly have any objection to being examined by one of
the state's physicians. For a moment Willie looked helplessly
at the battery of defense attorneys clustered around the
counsel table. Then his face brightened. "I would rather
consult my attorneys,"[2] he answered.

Q. You would rather consult your lawyers before you
say yes or no?

[2] Willie's examination never took place, as Simpson did not press the
question again.

A. Yes, sir. Is that permissible?

"Certainly," the prosecutor replied sheepishly. "You show very good judgment."

Willie beamed. "Thank you," he said gratefully.

By ten thirty Simpson had run out of questions, and Willie walked back to rejoin his co-defendants in front of the rail. "You were wonderful, Willie," Mrs. Hall said as her brother settled himself in his chair. There was universal agreement that Willie, for all his eccentricities, had conducted himself with all the aplomb of a courtroom veteran. Not only had he held his own with Senator Simpson, but on several occasions he had more than justified the prosecutor's jocular reference to him as "a sort of genius."

They were still murmuring about Willie's exemplary performance when Case called his next witness. Raymond Smith Dugan, a lanky Princeton University astronomy professor, was asked to discuss the moon that had risen over De Russey's Lane on September 14, 1922. According to his calculations, "the time of moonrise was 11:23 Eastern Standard Time, P.M."[3]

Q. Can you tell us what phase the moon was in when it came up that night?

A. It was just perceptibly crescent; it was a little less than half-moon.

Those who had expected that Mrs. Hall would take the stand before the Thanksgiving Day recess were doomed to disappointment. Case spent the remainder of the day calling witnesses who, while hardly spectacular, added support to the defense theories.

Marie Demarest's daughter, for example, testified that she had been with her mother when, the latter claimed, she had seen Ralph Gorsline and Minnie Clark watching the murdered couple in Buccleuch Park. "Did you see anything of the kind?" Case asked her. "I did not," the girl replied. The

3 If Dugan was correct, the waning moon hadn't risen until twelve twenty-three Eastern Daylight Saving Time. According to Mrs. Gibson, she had started on her second trip to the Phillips farm "about a quarter or twenty minutes to twelve," at which time "it was bright moonlight."

special officer assigned to patrol the park had never seen the minister "sitting on any bench with Mrs. Mills."

A clergyman who had attended Hall's funeral on the Monday after the murders had not noticed any scratches on the widow's face.

Q. How close to her were you?

A. I don't suppose I was more than two or three feet away, say two feet.

One of Mrs. Hall's neighbors had paid a sympathy call on her shortly after the bodies were discovered. "There were no scratches on her face," she assured Case.

Robert Erling's story that he had seen Mrs. Gibson astride her mule in De Russey's Lane on the night of the murders was next to be undermined. Jenny Lemford Waller, the young lady with whom the millwright had spent the evening of September 14, denied that they had stopped in De Russey's Lane at any time that night.

Q. Did you see anything of a woman stopping and looking in the car?

A. No.

Q. Did you see anything of any woman on a mule at all?

A. No.

Ferd David was recalled by Senator Case. The huge Middlesex detective had examined "several visiting cards of Mr. Hall's" that Totten had turned over to him in September 1922.

Q. Did you find any evidence of fingerprints on any of the cards?

A. We did not find any.

Case changed course abruptly. Did Detective David remember that Mrs. Gibson had been brought to his office on October 17, 1922, and asked to identify Mrs. Hall and her brothers as the persons she had seen in De Russey's Lane on the night of the murders? He did.

Q. Did Mrs. Gibson on that occasion say to you that she could not identify any of these defendants?

A. She did.

Case beamed. "Cross-examine," he said.

"Have you ever qualified in court as a fingerprint expert?" Simpson barked. "No, sir," David replied curtly. Could the witness remember when he had received the minister's eyeglasses? "I believe it was on Monday, the eighteenth of September, or Tuesday, September 19, 1922."

Q. Is it true that at one time, in the presence of several newspapermen, you came out rubbing the glasses with your thumb, saying, "Those are not fingerprints, those are flyspecks," for the purpose of erasing any fingerprints that might have been on the glasses?

A. Absolutely no.

Former Sheriff Conkling took David's place in the witness chair. He recalled that in July 1923 he had met Mrs. Gibson on Main Street in Somerville.

Q. Referring to this occasion, did you then say to Mrs. Gibson, "Jane, do you think the Stevens family had anything to do with the murders?" and did she reply, "I do not"?

A. She did.

Senator Simpson was brief. Had the ex-sheriff ever told the prosecution's investigators about this conversation? No, he had not because they had never asked him about it. The prosecutor's ample eyebrows arched in disbelief. "You did not tell them?" he asked incredulously. "No, sir," Conkling replied laconically.

Edwin R. Carpender was next. One of Mrs. Hall's many first cousins, he had made the official identification of the minister's body at the site of the murders. Later that Saturday, after making the necessary arrangements for the funeral, he had picked up a suit and a set of underwear from the Hall house. When Mrs. Hall told him that she would like her husband to be buried in his vestments, Carpender had driven to Minnie Clark's house to obtain the key to the church.

With Mrs. Clark's assistance, he had located a stole, a

cassock, and a white surplice, and he had placed them in a box Mrs. Hall had given him for that purpose. He had then driven directly to Hubbard's undertaking parlor.

Q. Did you at any time take any papers or personal effects except the vestments from the church?

A. No, sir.

Q. Did you at any time take any of the papers or personal effects of Mr. Hall except his funeral clothing from the Hall house?

A. No, sir.

In fact, the top of his green Mercer sports car had been down, and anybody could have seen that there was nothing on its back seat but the box of clothing.

Wasn't it a fact, Simpson began, that Mr. Carpender had asked the editor of the New Brunswick *Home News* to suppress the story of the murders? "I asked him if he could keep it out of the papers over Sunday," the witness retorted. Had he given instructions to Mr. Hubbard to bring the body to New Brunswick on Saturday? He had.

Q. Had you received any instructions from Mrs. Hall to do that, or did you do it on your own authority?

A. I received them from her.

Carpender's stately wife, Elovine, said that Mrs. Hall had called her on the morning of Saturday, September 16, and asked her to come to the house. "She told me that Edward had gone out on Thursday night for a short while and had never come home again, and that she was almost frantic with worry." That afternoon Mrs. Carpender had informed Mrs. Hall that the missing man's body had been found.

"How did Mrs. Hall receive the news?" Case asked solicitously.

"Why, she broke down completely for a few moments," Mrs. Carpender replied.

Thanksgiving Day dawned sunny and cold, with the temperature dropping to the freezing point by 9 A.M. Simpson took advantage of the holiday to schedule an early morning meeting in his Jersey City office. In addition to his chief investigators, the prosecutor had summoned Messrs. Faurot and Schwartz to discuss the testimony of the three fingerprint experts presented by the defense. When the conference ended, Simpson informed the reporters who filled his anteroom that forty Newark policemen had been assigned to check on the alibis of Willie and Henry Stevens.

Mrs. Hall had Thanksgiving dinner with her co-defendants in the Somerville jail. The menu was standard for the day—fruit cup, roast turkey with chestnut dressing, candied sweet potatoes, creamed onions, cranberry jelly, and plum pudding with hard sauce.

The widow, who appeared to be in excellent spirits, left shortly after dinner and returned to New Brunswick. She spent the rest of the day cheerfully welcoming scores of friends who dropped in to wish her well. If there was any uneasiness in the defense camp, it was well camouflaged.

When court resumed on Friday morning, the defense's three fingerprint experts, whose cross-examinations had been delayed in order to give Simpson time to study their direct testimony, took the stand. One conceded that an identifiable print could be obtained from a paper surface as much as ten days later. The other two admitted, under Simpson's persistent questioning, that they had examined the minister's calling card for only "a few minutes."

George M. Sipel, a firm believer in the Calvin Coolidge brand of brevity, averaged only three words apiece in answering Case's eighteen questions. The Middlebush farmer said that on November 13, 1922, Mrs. Gibson had offered him one hundred dollars to tell the police that he had seen her riding her mule in De Russey's Lane on the night of the murders. She had also asked him to say that he had noticed two men and a woman standing next to an automobile which was parked "to the left of the road."

Simpson had just started his cross-examination of Sipel when Case interrupted him.

"May this witness stand aside for the time being and another witness be sworn before recess?" he asked Parker. When the justice nodded his assent, Tim Pfeiffer opened a small door behind the bench to admit a swarthy bespectacled man. The spectators suddenly came to life when they realized that the new witness, who had been smuggled into the courtroom through Parker's chambers, was none other than the elusive Felix De Martini.

After the private detective was sworn, Parker looked up at the courtroom clock. "There will not be any time to examine Mr. De Martini before lunch," he announced. "We will take a recess until half past one."

Simpson, who had been shocked by De Martini's sudden appearance, held up his hand. "This man is under oath," he pleaded, "and I think he ought to be warned by the court to have nothing to say to the counsel on the other side."

Parker obliged the stunned prosecutor by assigning a policeman to guard the new witness during the recess. The defense lawyers were smiling broadly as they left for lunch. By having De Martini sworn before Simpson could arrest him as an accessory after the fact, they had insured the detective's freedom until he had finished testifying.

The afternoon session started out with the reading into the record of a series of letters written by Sipel to Mrs. Hall in late 1922 and early 1923. In substance, they were thinly disguised appeals for money. "I am a businessman," he had written in one, "and I wish to state I was dragged into this through the untruthfulness of the state's star witness, and it has practically put my business at a standstill."

On January 28, 1923, he had made his intentions somewhat plainer. "I leave it to your judgment, Mrs. Hall, whether you don't think I ought to at least be reimbursed for the loss I suffered during your proceedings and very plainly done you a great deal of good." Three days later he had warned her to "attend to this matter at once."

At long last it was De Martini's turn. Remembering that both Mrs. Demarest and Mrs. Gibson had testified that De Martini had visited their homes and tried to bribe or frighten them into changing their stories, Case decided to limit his examination to these issues. "Did you, either in the month of October, 1922, or at any other time, call upon Mrs. Marie Demarest?" he asked. "I never knew there was such a woman by that name in existence," De Martini snapped.

Q. Did you ever go to Mrs. Gibson's house to see her?

A. No, sir. I never spoke to that woman.

"Mr. De Martini," Simpson began, "if you were so eager to solve the case, why didn't you contact Mrs. Gibson, who claimed to be an eyewitness?" Because he had always thought that her story "sounded ridiculous."

Q. What was ridiculous in her description of the homicide?

A. Because at the time she came out and made that statement, if she had been genuine I should have believed she would have come and told the authorities much before the time.

If Mrs. Gibson's story was of no moment to him, why had he bothered to station one of his operatives at the plant where her husband worked? The private detective had a ready answer. "I put him in because I had some information that a man named Reinhardt[4] had not been working on the fourteenth, fifteenth, and sixteenth of September, and in the meantime I had learned Mr. Easton was working there, and I told him to pick up what information he could."

Just how had Mr. De Martini earned the five thousand dollars he had charged Mrs. Hall for his services? First of all, he had shadowed Jim Mills for several weeks. "Then I visited the scene of De Russey's Lane and made a general

4 A relative, apparently, of Eleanor Mills.

canvas to see if I could locate anybody that had seen anything or heard the shots in order to establish the time."

Q. Did you get anybody to tell you what time the shots
were fired?

A. Well, the times vary. Some would say between nine
and ten, some would say about nine thirty, some would say
about ten fifteen. It varies.

Was it true, as one of his former operatives had previously
testified, that De Martini had warned him "to keep away
from all officials"? It was not. He had discharged this man
in 1924 when the latter had turned in a faulty report in a
Connecticut case.

Simpson lifted his head sharply.

"Did you have somebody say to him that if he was a witness he had better look out, that he would be bumped off,
or words to that effect?" he barked.

"No!" the witness shouted angrily.

"That's all for the present," the prosecutor retorted.

Case spent the rest of the day examining witnesses who
claimed that Mrs. Gibson was regarded in the community
as a chronic liar. One man, who had known her for ten years,
said that "her reputation for truth and veracity was bad."
The assessor of Franklin Township had heard several people
discuss her penchant for tall stories. A Rutgers French in-
structor who lived near the Pig Woman's farm agreed fully
with his predecessors.

The day was not destined to end quietly, however. As soon
as the last of Mrs. Gibson's detractors had left the courtroom, De Martini was brought back in by two deputies. The
private detective, who had just been arrested in the courthouse rotunda, was arraigned before Judge Cleary on a
charge of accessory after the fact.

State Senator J. Henry Harrison of Newark, De Martini's
attorney, asked that Cleary parole the detective in his custody. The judge smiled. "I know you," he said, "but I do

not know the defendant." Bail was then set at three thousand dollars, and a bond for that amount was promptly posted.

Saturday, the nineteenth day of the trial, was also its coldest, with the mercury hovering four degrees below freezing when court opened at 10 A.M. Despite the frigid weather, however, the courtroom was filled long before the day's session began.

There had been persistent rumors during Friday that Mrs. Hall would take the stand the next morning, and would-be spectators, mainly women, had begun to arrive at the white stone courthouse more than three hours before trial time. By nine o'clock the rotunda was so filled with chattering females, armed with sandwiches, thermos bottles, and collapsible canvas chairs that court attendants found it impossible to keep the corridors of the building clear.

The morning's chief witness, however, proved to be Timothy Pfeiffer. The tall, gaunt lawyer, who had been associated with the case since September 26, 1922, testified that he had hired De Martini a week after Mrs. Hall had retained him.

Q. And for what purpose did you employ him?

A. To find out who committed the murder, wherever it led.

Outside of fees paid to De Martini and his operatives, no money had been given or promised by Mrs. Hall to George Sipel or anyone else.

Pfeiffer claimed that he had done everything in his power to co-operate with the authorities in charge of the case. "One of the first things I did after September 26, 1922," he recalled, "was to call Mr. Stricker. I made an appointment to see him at his office in Perth Amboy. I said that if there was anything I could do acting as attorney for Mrs. Hall and her family in the solution of the crime I should be glad to do so.

"Mr. Stricker wanted to know if he could examine Mrs. Hall and any other persons who might be connected with her. I said that he could any time he wanted, that I would not even demand that I be present at the time when they were examined." In March 1923 he had turned over all of De Martini's reports to Attorney General McCran.

Simpson caused a minor stir in the courtroom when, his voice dripping with sarcasm, he asked Pfeiffer if De Martini's efforts had uncovered the "real murderers" of Hall and Mrs. Mills. "I think he came to a closer approximation than you have," the lawyer replied tartly.

Q. Who did he find out were the murderers?

A. I decline to answer that unless the court compels me to.

Q. That is a fair question.

A. We have made no accusations against anybody in this case.

Parker agreed with the witness that it would be unfair to reveal the names of those suspected by De Martini, and the prosecutor's intriguing question was never to be answered.

Pfeiffer took full responsibility for advising Mrs. Hall not to make any public statement for more than a month after the murders. If his client was really innocent, Simpson thundered, why had the lawyer kept her from talking to reporters? "I am not in the habit of trying my case in the newspapers," Pfeiffer retorted pointedly.

Q. Then you don't think an innocent woman should make any statement to the newspapers?

A. I don't think it is desirable to.

He hadn't even permitted the widow to speak to Charlotte Mills because he suspected the girl was busy feeding stories to the New York *American*.

It was not until two o'clock that McCarter indicated to Bailiff Bunn that he was at last ready for Mrs. Hall. When the widow heard her name called out, she stood up slowly, placed her black pocketbook carefully behind her, and walked toward the witness chair. Dressed all in black, except for a white collar and a small pearl necklace, she waited patiently for the court clerk to administer the oath. Her lips tightened as Mc-

Carter, with a kindly smile on his florid face, left the counsel table and stationed himself directly in front of her.

"Mrs. Hall, where were you born?" he began gently. "In Aiken, South Carolina," was the quiet response. Her family had moved to New Brunswick when she was two months old and settled down in the big house on Nichol Avenue. In 1911, at the age of thirty-seven, she had been saved from almost certain spinsterhood by the young pastor of St. John's.

Q. I want to ask you this question, Mrs. Hall; whether during your husband's life, so far as you knew or observed, your husband was a devoted husband?

A. Absolutely.

Yes, she had known Eleanor Mills. "I saw her quite frequently at the church," she said, "in connection with work done in the church, and for a short time she was in my Sunday school class."

Q. She was an active worker in the church, was she?

A. Yes.

With the possible exception of Minnie Clark, Mrs. Mills had been St. John's most energetic parishioner.

It had been Mrs. Hall who drove Mrs. Mills to the Middlesex General Hospital for the latter's kidney operation in February 1922.

Q. While she was there, did you visit her?

A. A good many times.

Q. Do you remember how she got home after she was convalescent?

A. I took her home in the car.

In fact, she had contributed generously to the choir singer's hospital and medical expenses.

In August 1922 she and her husband had gone to Islesford, Maine, for their summer vacation. "We spent our time over on Mount Desert, climbing the mountains and walking about there a great deal, out in the boats a great deal."

Q. At that time had you noticed any change whatever in his demeanor or conduct toward you?

A. None whatever.

She knew that the clergyman had received some letters at Islesford from Mrs. Mills because he had shown them to her. "They were, as near as I can remember," she told McCarter, "descriptions of evening services at church."

On the day before the murders the Halls had taken Mrs. Mills and Mrs. Clark on a picnic to Lake Hopatcong as a reward for their efforts on behalf of the church. The next afternoon, while Hall was visiting a nearby hospital, Mrs. Mills had telephoned. "She asked if Mr. Hall were home and I said no, and I said, 'Do you want to leave any message?' and she said, 'You tell him there is something about the doctor's bill I do not understand,' and I said I would tell him." She had told her husband about the call as soon as he returned home.

After supper that evening she had been sitting on the porch when she heard the telephone ring. When it rang a second time, she had hurried to the first-floor extension, which was located at the foot of the stairs. Just as she lifted the receiver to her ear, she had heard Louise Geist speaking on the upstairs extension.

Q. Did you hear your husband engaged in the act of talking over the phone?

A. No.

She had immediately returned to the porch, where she remained until she joined Frances Voorhees, her husband's niece, in the library.

"We were sitting at the table," she continued, "playing some card game, and in a little while Mr. Hall came down and stood in the doorway for a moment and said he was going out to see about the bill."

Q. About what time do you think that was, Mrs. Hall?

A. I think it must have been between seven and half past.

After putting Frances to bed at nine o'clock, she had returned to the library. Two hours later she had gone to bed, where she had read for a while before falling into a fitful sleep.

In the middle of the night she had awakened and gone downstairs. "I looked around the house just to see if there was anywhere that I had missed Mr. Hall coming in, and about half past two I was perfectly frantic about it—and I did not know what could have happened—and then I went and called my brother William and told him Mr. Hall had not come in and told him the hour, and that I did not know where he could be; but the only thing I could think of was to go down and see if by any chance he had stopped at the church and possibly fallen asleep there."

After waking Willie she had returned to her room, where she had donned "a gray coat and a brown felt hat."

Q. Is that the coat that was subsequently dyed?

A. No, it was not. That was a brown coat.

She and her brother had gone first to the church. Seeing no lights in the building, they had walked to Carman Street. "I could not think of anything else to do," she explained, "and as Mr. Hall had spoken of going to the Millses', at least going to see about the bill, I thought there was some possible chance that someone was ill there and he might have gone there."

When they saw that the second-floor apartment was dark, they had returned home. "You entered the front door?" Mc-Carter asked. "Yes," was the soft reply. "I went to my room and again prepared for bed."

She had been unable, however, to sleep for the rest of the night. "About seven o'clock I called police headquarters and asked if there had been any accidents, and thinking—the one thought in my mind was that there might have been an automobile accident and my husband might have been injured and unable to communicate with me, and I asked that question; and they said that nothing had been reported." She had not bothered to give her name to the desk sergeant because she "didn't think it was necessary."

At seven o'clock she had driven to St. John's, where she talked to Jim Mills. "I asked him first if there had been anybody ill at his house," she said. "He said, 'No.' And I said, 'Did Mr. Hall say where he was going when he went to your house last night?' He said that he did not know that Mr. Hall had been there, and I said, 'Well, he has not been home all night.' And Mr. Mills said, 'My wife has been away all night.' "

Mrs. Bonner and Mrs. Voorhees, her husband's sisters, had arrived in New Brunswick at noon. During the drive from the railroad station Mrs. Hall had explained to the two women that their brother had been missing since Thursday evening. "Then I stopped by the Mills house, saw James Mills on the porch, went up, and I said, 'Have you heard anything?' and he said, 'No.' I said, 'I have not heard anything either,' and that was the extent of our conversation." An hour later she had telephoned to Senator Florence and asked the lawyer to come to her house.

Florence, who had once represented her aunt's estate, had arrived "between three and four."

Q. Did you give him any instructions?

A. I told him about my husband's absence and asked him if he would get in communication with the police, if he considered that the proper thing to do.

The lawyer had advised her that the police should be notified about the minister's strange disappearance and had left at once to do so.

She had first learned of her husband's death at one the next afternoon. As soon as she had composed herself, she had asked Edwin Carpender to take some of the clergyman's clothes to Hubbard's funeral parlor.

Q. Did you request that the body be brought home?

A. No, I asked if it would be. They said they thought it advisable not to.

McCarter wound up with a flourish. "Now, Mrs. Hall," he asked slowly and deliberately, "did you kill your husband or Mrs. Mills?" The witness's eyes opened wide. "I did not, Mr. McCarter," she said quietly.

Q. Did you play any part whatever in that dreadful tragedy?

A. I did not.

Q. Did you participate in any way in it?

A. I did not.

Q. Were you in or about De Russey's Lane or Phillips farm or in that neighborhood, or in the neighborhood of what is known as the crab apple tree on the evening of September 14, 1922?

A. I was not.

McCarter turned to Simpson. "You may inquire," he said.

In distinct contrast to his relatively gentle treatment of her brothers, the prosecutor was bitingly sardonic as he began his cross-examination. "If your husband had told you that he was going to the Mills apartment," he began, "why didn't you take the trouble of sending Willie upstairs to knock at the door?" Because she had seen no lights on the second floor.

Q. You did not expect him to carry a lamp in his hand, did you?

A. No.

"You went to the place where you thought he had gone," the prosecutor exploded, "and you never sent your brother upstairs, or knocked at the door, or made a single inquiry, did you?" Mrs. Hall's "No" was barely audible.

The next order of business on Simpson's agenda was the widow's telephone call to the New Brunswick police early Friday morning. Why had she called the police? To find out if her husband had been in an accident. "But you said to the police, 'Have there been any casualties?' " the prosecutor reminded her. "Doesn't that mean accidents?" she asked.

"Did you say, 'Have there been any casualties?' " Simpson demanded. "I don't remember," Mrs. Hall replied uncertainly.

Q. Weren't you looking to see if the dead bodies had been found? Isn't that the reason you used the word "casualties"?

A. I don't know as I did use the word. I do not remember.

No, she had not bothered to check with the two New Brunswick hospitals. "If my husband had been in any accident and taken to a hospital," she explained, "I would have been notified. He was well known."

Q. How do you know that there would not have been carelessness or lack of interest or mistaken identity or he would not have been so hurt that they could not identify him?

A. I was quite sure there would not be anything of the kind.

Mrs. Hall looked relieved when Parker's gavel signified the end of the trial's fourth week. When she arrived home, however, her spirits had revived sufficiently for her to ask one of her cousins to find out who had won the Army-Navy football game, which was being played in the Midwest for the first time. In Chicago, where 110,000 people had crowded into Soldier Field to witness the contest, the two service teams had battled to a 21–21 tie in freezing weather.

On Sunday the defense announced that it had only two more witnesses to call before resting. With the testimony of 157 persons—87 'for the state and 70 for the defense—already in the record, it was obvious that the record-breaking trial was reaching its conclusion.

Despite the notoriety and cash bonanza it had brought to Somerville, most of the town's citizens seemed weary of the spectacle. "I don't know how much the sensational trial has increased business activity here," Mayor Thomas A. Flockhart told a reporter, "but I am sure that all of us will welcome heartily its conclusion so that we can settle down to normal life again."

Chapter 27

THE TRIAL—FINAL WEEK

(Monday, November 29, through Friday, December 3, 1926)

On Monday, Mrs. Hall returned to the stand. Looking tenser than she had on Saturday, she was dressed in the same somber clothing she had worn during her first appearance. Simpson, dazzlingly attired in a broad-striped shirt, wanted to know where Mrs. Hall had gone to telephone one of her husband's sisters on Friday morning. She had called from Hoagland's Drug Store, "about ten o'clock."

Q. And you did not telephone from your own house, but you telephoned from a booth outside?

A. Yes.

Except for her one call to police headquarters earlier that morning, she had made no attempt to contact the authorities. "Mr. Florence communicated with them," she explained patiently. "I said to him some investigation must be made, my husband had disappeared and I did not know where he was and I didn't know what else to do."

Q. Why did you let all Friday go by without telling the police?

A. Well, it was the most natural thing to speak to his family and then later, when we had called in a lawyer, to put such investigation in his hands.

When she first saw Jim Mills on Friday morning, why had she assumed that her husband and the sexton's wife had

gone away together? Because Mills had told her that Eleanor
was also missing.

Q. You immediately put her with Dr. Hall when you
found she was away, too, although you did not have any suspicion of them?

A. I went there because he had said he was going to speak
to her that evening, and I thought I could get some information from her family.

If she told Mills that she was afraid the couple had been
injured, her only thought had been "that there had been
some automobile accident, they might have been killed or
injured in some way right nearby."

As the morning wore on, Simpson kept harrying his pliant
witness like a terrier with a cornered mouse. In the main, he
was interested in pounding away at the fact that for a
solicitous wife, she had done very little to locate the missing
rector.

At last Parker cut him off. "Mr. Simpson," he said, "you
have been over that ground three or four times. There must
be some reasonable limit to cross-examination, especially the
repetition." Mrs. Hall's grateful smile punctuated the justice's ruling.

Undaunted, Simpson turned to other matters. Why had
she been so sure on Saturday that her husband was dead?
Because he had not come home for two successive nights.
"The only thing I could think of," she told her diminutive
tormentor, "was that he must be dead."

Q. Did you think that he had been murdered or that he
was just dead?

A. I did not go beyond thinking that he must be dead.

Did Mrs. Hall remember that Beekman and Totten had
come to her house on the Sunday following the murders?
She did. And after she had described her movements from
Thursday through Saturday to the two officials, without al-
luding to her trip to the church with Willie, didn't Totten
tell her he had a report that someone had seen her returning

to her house early Friday morning? Yes, but she had not intended to withhold that information.

"I was in a very much agitated state of mind," she explained, "and I told everything I could think of as I thought of it. As Mr. Totten asked me various questions I answered them, and when it came to this he said to me, 'Do you know a woman was seen going in your place early Friday morning?' and I said, 'Yes, I was that woman.' "

With a meaningful look in the general direction of the jury box, Simpson walked back to the counsel table and picked up a bulky manila folder. It contained, he revealed, more than a hundred letters written by Mrs. Hall to Henry Stevens after February 1923. "Isn't it a fact," he emphasized, "that in not one of these letters you uttered one phrase of regret for this terrible tragedy which you say emptied your life of everything worthwhile?"

Mrs. Hall's eyes filled with tears. "I have no recollection of what I have said in all the letters," she murmured.

It was almost noon when Simpson ground to a close with a few desultory questions about Mrs. Hall's refusal to see Charlotte after the bodies had been found. As soon as the special prosecutor's curt "That is all" brought her long ordeal to an end, the widow rose and walked quickly to her seat. As she sat down, Willie leaned over and kissed her on the cheek.

Hall's two sisters, Fannie H. Voorhees and Theodora H. Bonner, inaugurated the afternoon session. Mrs. Voorhees said that Mrs. Hall had called her at eight thirty on Friday morning to tell her the rector was missing. Immediately after learning this she had contacted Mrs. Bonner, and with her had taken the first available train to New Brunswick. Mrs. Bonner added that it had been her suggestion to send for Senator Florence, and that when he arrived the lawyer had been instructed to notify the police.

As Mrs. Bonner returned to her seat behind the rail, Mc-

Carter conferred briefly with his six associates. The white-haired attorney then approached the bench.

"The defense rests," he said quietly.

Simpson's rebuttal witnesses were led off by Mary Elverson, a Toms River court stenographer. Mrs. Elverson, it seemed, had recorded the examinations of Arthur L. Applegate and Thaddeus S. Mellinger, two of Henry Stevens' alibi witnesses, on September 3, 1926. After a monumental legal battle between Simpson and Case over its admissibility Mrs. Elverson's transcript was received as State's Exhibit 147.

In substance, it indicated that Applegate had said he had no independent recollection of the date on which he had caught his big bluefish, and that either detectives or reporters had suggested to him that the incident might have taken place on the evening of September 14. As far as Mellinger was concerned, the memorable fish had been weighed on Friday, and not Thursday night.

August Hartkorn, an examiner of questioned documents with almost forty years' experience, specialized in studying "individuality in handwriting and the manner of its production." Simpson handed him Henry Stevens' diary for 1922. Had he examined the entries for September 14? He had.

Q. What can you say in describing the entry?

A. The entry consists of four lines. The first line reads, "Three blues." The second line, "Art, one blue, six pounds," third line, "At Max's. In aft." and "One blue, four pounds," the fourth line.

He was certain that the entry had been made with three different pencils.

In looking through the entire diary Mr. Hartkorn had been unable to find another entry in which three pencils were used. In addition, he swore that the style of writing employed by Stevens on September 14 showed marked peculiarities.

"I have found here," he elaborated, "that the line 'Three

blues' and 'Art, one blue, six pounds,' and 'one blue, four pounds,' are made with deliberation, carefully written, whereas 'At Max's in the afternoon,'—there is no attention paid to the base line of writing such as I find in the surrounding entries."

If the glowing smile on Simpson's face was any indication, Hartkorn had conclusively proved that only the reference to the anonymous Max had been entered on the fourteenth.

The next morning McCarter attempted to force Hartkorn to concede that only the last two items in the entry for September 14 might have been written the following day. But the handwriting expert, who had been testifying in courts for almost four decades, was not one to succumb easily to even the most determined of defense attorneys. When he refused to follow McCarter's lead, the lawyer subsided meekly.

Simpson next called eight persons, all but one of whom swore that Mrs. Gibson was not one to distort the truth. The exception was a physician who had treated the Pig Woman from 1919 to 1923. His answers caught the special prosecutor by surprise.

Q. Would you say whether or not her reputation for truth and veracity is good or bad?

A. Well, from what people say to me, I would say that it was about fifty–fifty.

Simpson exploded. "You are given to me as a reputation witness," he shouted, "and you bowl me over by saying that her reputation for truth and veracity is not so good, and I am trying to find out how you got on the stand." The spectators howled when the doctor replied, "Lord, I don't know; I cannot guess."

Shortly after court had adjourned for the day, the prosecutor held a press conference in Bergen's office. "As soon as the defense finishes its cross-examination of the state's rebuttal witnesses tomorrow," he announced, "I shall move for a mistrial in the case. We have a number of affidavits in proof of our contention that some members of the jury have been guilty of improprieties."

Copies of a letter he had written to Governor Moore the preceding day were distributed to the reporters. He had minced no words in describing what he termed "the disgusting condition of affairs in Somerville." As far as he was concerned, the jury was hopelessly prejudiced against the prosecution.

"Some of them sleep during the evidence, they receive telephone calls without any guard, and also receive visitors who talk to them without any guard or sheriff's officers. I have reports that the jurors are so stupid and unintelligent —that is, one or two of them—that they have openly boasted they didn't care what the evidence was, but they would find against the state."

The defense team immediately downgraded Simpson's threatened action. "We also understand," one lawyer said, "that the so-called 'facts' upon which the motion of Senator Simpson will be made were manufactured by representatives of the *Daily Mirror,* the Hearst tabloid newspaper with which the prosecution has been so intimately associated since the *Mirror* instigated the investigation for its own selfish purposes."

On Wednesday morning the special prosecutor was as good as his word. As soon as Justice Parker had gaveled the trial's twenty-second—and coldest—day into being, he approached the bench. His first request was that the jury be excused. As soon as it had left the room, Simpson moved for a mistrial "on the ground of the misconduct of the jury."

He based his motion on (1) the proclivity of some of the jurors to doze while witnesses for the state were on the stand, (2) the failure of the sheriff to guard the jury properly, and (3) the open hostility of some of the panel's members, one of whom had referred to him publicly as "a goddamn lying little son of a bitch."

To support his charges, he proceeded to read fifteen brief affidavits to Parker. That of one, a newspaper reporter, was typical. "I have been at the Hall-Mills trial every day," he swore, "and on several occasions have noticed jurymen number 2 and number 5 nodding and apparently giving no attention to the testimony; to such an extent has this gone on that I have several times made note of it in the stories that I have sent daily to my paper, because it seemed as if the jurors were asleep."

When Parker promised a quick ruling, Simpson resumed his rebuttal by calling a Jersey City police officer. Although Felix De Martini had denied earlier that he had ever seen Mrs. Demarest before the trial began, she had testified that the detective had once spoken to her in a Brooklyn courthouse elevator during his extradition proceeding. The policeman, who had also been present in the elevator, said that De Martini had indeed greeted Mrs. Demarest by name on that occasion.

After several other occupants of the elevator had confirmed Mrs. Demarest's story, Simpson was down to his last two witnesses. A reporter for the Philadelphia *Evening Ledger* had spoken to Arthur Applegate when the latter was being questioned in Toms River, in early September.

Q. Did Arthur Applegate tell you that he could not tell definitely the date when the bluefish was weighed?

A. He did.

The newsman was succeeded by Elsie Barnhardt, Mrs. Mills' sister, who insisted that De Martini, despite his testimony to the contrary, had once told her he had called on Mrs. Gibson.

"That is the state's rebuttal," Simpson informed the bench as the elephantine Mrs. Barnhardt returned to her seat behind the rail.

The defense's surrebuttal was mercifully brief. Eldridge W. Stein, a handwriting expert, concluded that the phrase "Art, one blue, six pounds," in Henry Stevens' diary for September 14, 1922, had been written before the sentence

"At Max's in the afternoon," which immediately followed it. Although he agreed that at least three pencils had been used to make the entries, he thought that all four had been written "very freely."

In other words, there was nothing to indicate that the entry about Applegate's fish had been made on any day other than September 14.

"Mr. Stein," Simpson purred on cross, "how long have you examined the Stevens diary?"

"An hour or so."

"And did that examination occur in your studio?"

"No, sir."

"Where did it take place?"

"Here in the courthouse, last Friday."

"No further questions," the prosecutor snorted disdainfully.

Two newspapermen had the dubious distinction of being the last of the 178 witnesses whose testimony was to fill 5,098 pages of the record. They had also been riding with Mrs. Demarest and De Martini in what must have been the most populated elevator in Brooklyn in early October. Neither man had heard the private detective speak to Mrs. Demarest during the entire ride.

As the last reporter left the stand, Case approached the bench. "If your Honors please," he said with an air of finality, "the defense rests."

Parker turned to Simpson. "Is there anything else?" he asked. "No, nothing else," the prosecutor replied. The justice brought down his gavel. "We'll adjourn for lunch," he said.

When court resumed at one thirty, Parker announced that there would be no mistrial. "The court," he said, "has considered these affidavits and concluded to deny the motion without calling upon the defense to rebut them." Without pausing, the jurist indicated to McCarter that it was time for the defense to begin its summation.

Four weeks to the day since the trial began, the stocky, pink-cheeked McCarter, dressed in a conservative gray suit, rose and walked toward the jury box.

"Gentlemen of the jury," he began softly, "I am about to start what we lawyers call a summing up. It is not going to be an eloquent speech. It is going to be an effort on our part to bring out in a logical way the enormous mass of facts that have been during this month somewhat disconnectedly presented to you for your consideration. I shall studiously endeavor in my review of the facts to be accurate, to quote the testimony from memory as accurately as I can."

For the next two hours and fifteen minutes, with only an occasional display of emotion, he sought to impress the jurors with the innocence of his three clients. The only person in the courtroom who did not hang on his every word was Mrs. Hall. Since her cross-examination by Simpson she had taken very little interest in the progress of the trial, and it was the consensus of the press section that her four-hour stint on the stand had completely sapped her strength. Starkly pale, she gazed listlessly into space, seemingly unconcerned with the flow of oratory upon the persuasiveness of which her life might depend.

First of all, McCarter asked, what kind of people were Frances Hall and her two brothers? "Have they been thugs; have they criminal records; are they thieves?" he demanded. "No, they are refined, genteel, law-abiding people, the very highest type of character, churchgoing, Christians, who up to this time have enjoyed the perfect admiration and respect of their friends and neighbors." It was extremely unlikely, he said, that people of such unimpeachable background would resort to murder to solve any personal problems that they might have had.

Mrs. Hall's strong interest in her husband's church quite naturally brought her into contact with Eleanor Mills, one of its most active workers. "Mrs. Mills seems to have been a woman who had a drab home life," he surmised. "Her hus-

band was poor. That certainly was no crime, but she had ambition, she was good-looking. She found, as many people do
who have little money and an uninteresting home life, interest in church work."

That the two women were close can hardly be doubted
when one recalls that it was the minister's wife who took
Mrs. Mills to the hospital for her kidney operation in early
1922 and paid her bills there. "Surely one would think," he
said, "that those events show that in January and February
1922 there was the warmest interest in and devotion to Mrs.
Mills by Mrs. Hall."

And there wasn't the slightest shred of evidence that, as
late as August of that year, Mrs. Hall knew of the romance
between her husband and the choir singer. In fact, the day
before the murders the Halls took Mrs. Mills on a picnic to
Lake Hopatcong as a reward for her church work.

McCarter meticulously re-created the events of the night
of September 14–15, 1922, starting with the arrival of Frances Voorhees, the rector's ten-year-old niece, and concluding
with Mrs. Hall's telephone call about "casualties" to the
New Brunswick police. "Mr. Simpson seems to think there
is something mystic about the word 'casualties,' but if you
look in the dictionary you will find that casualty means accident, and I don't care whether she said accident or casualty.
She was almost crazy.

"She was almost crazy," he repeated, "and why should she
tell who it was? Here was a prominent clergyman, a man
high in social and church life. Is she going to say that this
man is out and has not come home, until she knows what is
the matter, until she finds out that an accident has or has not
happened? Of course, she knows all the hospitals know him;
why should she ring them up?"

Then in a perfectly natural move, she called her sisters-
in-law and asked them to come to New Brunswick, he went
on. After conferring together the three women had agreed
that a lawyer ought to be consulted. Accordingly, Senator

Florence had been requested to notify the police of the rector's disappearance.

Finally the bodies were found. "I don't know why the state has failed to bring here the people who discovered these bodies,"[1] McCarter said. "I don't know why, but it is significant that the people who discovered them are not brought here." In any event, Mrs. Hall was advised by undertaker Hubbard that because of the decomposition of her husband's body it would be better if she did not view it before the funeral.

Then, after a thorough investigation by Beekman, Stricker, and Mott, the Somerset County Grand Jury refused to indict anybody. During the next four years, outside of two trips to Europe, Mrs. Hall remained in New Brunswick. "Is she afraid of anything?" he asked his audience. "The matter has been sleeping—why not go to Lake Como and live there? Perhaps that would be a safer atmosphere. That is what she would naturally think if guilty."

Suddenly at midnight on July 26, 1926, prompted by Phil Payne, the satanic editor of the *Daily Mirror,* the police swooped down and arrested Mrs. Hall, McCarter continued. "Madam, you are under arrest for the murder of your husband four years ago," she was told. "We could not even wait until tomorrow morning. We will take you to Somerville and take you up to some justice of the peace, and after we have done with you there we will land you in the jail and we will have Payne's photographers, who are following you, take your photograph as you go in."

For the remainder of the afternoon McCarter reviewed the evidence presented by the prosecution. Starting with the Dicksons, the trial's first witnesses, he analyzed and attempted to destroy any testimony that was unfavorable to his three clients. For example, Mrs. Demarest's story of seeing the murdered couple sitting on a bench in Buccleuch Park was denied by her own daughter.

1 Pearl Bahmer and Raymond Schneider.

It was true enough that Mrs. Hall had sent a coat and a scarf to a Philadelphia dyer shortly after the crime, but she and members of her family had used the same firm for years.

As for Henry Dickman and his fantastic charge that Prosecutor Beekman had paid him to leave New Jersey, he left it to the jurors to decide whether they would give more credence to the word of a convicted deserter than to that of "a strong, honest, virile man of Somerset County."

Mrs. Demarest's statement that Felix De Martini had tried to bribe her in 1923 was, to put it mildly, preposterous. First of all, what purpose would there have been in bribing a woman whose name had not come into the case until 1926? Secondly, would any man in his right mind, after attempting without success to suppress evidence, give his real name? "Oh, it is so absurd!" he cried.

Up to now McCarter had alluded only to the circumstantial evidence against his clients. Finally he turned to the main supports of Simpson's case: Willie's fingerprint on Hall's calling card, and Mrs. Gibson's testimony.

Using one of his own cards to illustrate his point, he asked the jury to speculate how long a fingerprint would remain on a similar piece of pasteboard after it had lain on the ground for almost two days. His voice hardened. "I charge with all the solemnity that is involved in it that that card is a fraud," he declared.

"Gentlemen of the jury," he continued gravely, "mind you, their theory is that this card, a genuine card, was to be given to Payne for the administration of justice, and the discovery of a crime. For any consideration? Oh, no, no, no. Payne and the *Mirror* are not interested financially in this matter. They are doing this that justice may be vindicated."

When the lawyer's voice indicated that he was about to shift to the subject of Mrs. Gibson, Justice Parker cut him short. "It is almost four o'clock, Mr. McCarter," he said.

"The rest of your summation will have to go over until tomorrow."

McCarter finished on Thursday morning. Although Senator Case was going to discuss the Pig Woman in great detail, McCarter as chief defense attorney also had something to say about her. He hoped that the jury would not be swayed by the fact that Mrs. Gibson had testified from a hospital bed. "I stigmatize the thing as humbug," he declared.

Jim Mills, he pointed out, was at least as good a suspect as Mrs. Hall. "If knowledge of these things is important, then what are you going to do with him?" he asked. "A husband whose wife for two years has occupied the room in the attic and refused to sleep with him. A husband who has been told more than once, 'I care more for the little finger of Mr. Hall than I do for your whole body.' A husband who on that very night had a quarrel with his wife. A husband who has read the letters that he found in his wife's scarf the night before her death."

"I am not here to vindicate or scold that dead couple," McCarter said quietly. "They have their own account to make with their Creator, but I am here as a man with red blood in his veins to question the innocence of a husband who placidly admits his wife to be absent for forty hours without raising a finger to find out where she is or what has happened to her, except to say to Mrs. Hall, 'Perhaps they have eloped.'"

And to top it off, he added, after the discovery of the bodies, Mills promptly sold the letters that prove that his wife was an adulteress to a newspaper "for five hundred filthy dollars."

"It lies with you, gentlemen of the jury," he concluded, "to put an end to this persecution, to free this family from the stigma of this heartless accusation and to let these law-abiding citizens, these defendants, realize that you, at least, are not of this motley crowd who, under the guise of ferreting out crime, are seeking and acquiring wealth and hoping to gain political ascendancy."

He turned and quickly walked back to his seat at the counsel table, pausing only to stare coldly at Phil Payne before he sat down next to Case, who rose to continue the summation.

Case started off with a scathing attack on Simpson for not producing Ray Schneider. It was probably Schneider, he asserted, who had been responsible for the calling card that was found near the dead minister's left foot. "When he came there that morning, he sought what there was of value on the bodies, and he took the watch and he took the fob and he took the money, except the loose change, and he took the card case. And when he opened the card case, seeking for the money, the cards fell on the ground, and where they lit they stayed."

Never failing to remind his listeners that he, like them, was a Somerset resident, Case consistently attacked the "outsiders" who had invaded his county to treat it as though it were Sodom on the Raritan. "What necessity is there," he asked, "that Jersey City should supplant Somerville, that Hudson County should supplant Somerset County?" The reason was simple—an insidious combination of unscrupulous newspapermen and ambitious politicians—Democrats, of course—were determined, for their own selfish purposes, to pin the double murder on four innocent souls.

Case was on his feet for almost four hours. Far more biting than the gentle McCarter, he castigated every official connected with the prosecution. The state troopers who had searched Henry Stevens' house in Lavallette were nothing more than common thieves. Simpson's investigators had stolen the letters written by Mrs. Hall to her brother Henry in the summer and fall of 1923. Worst of all, the prosecutor had tried to inflame the minds of the jury with the gruesome replica of Mrs. Mills' head.

As for the witnesses produced by the state, they were even more despicable. Henry Dickman was a deserter from the New Jersey State Police, the Army, and the Navy, as well as a chronic liar who had been willing to trade slander and calumny for a free trip to the east coast. Frank Caprio, with his long criminal record, was nothing more than a professional perjurer. Phil Payne was willing to sacrifice four blameless lives for a circulation increase.

Mrs. Gibson said that one of the persons she saw in De Russey's Lane was "a big white-haired woman." The lawyer waved Mrs. Hall to her feet.

"Now, would you call this woman big?" he demanded. "Her hair is only graying now, gentlemen, and four years ago she was younger. By the moonlight she saw this face that she months afterward recognized. Ah, gentlemen, I thank God that many of you whose lives are so placed that you travel in the darkness of night, you know what can be seen by the moonlight. You can't recognize your best friend at that distance in the moonlight."

What kind of a woman, anyhow, was the state's chief witness? She said her name was Easton, yet she took title to her farm as Jane Gibson. She claimed that she was married to Mr. Easton in 1919, but she couldn't remember the church or city in which the ceremony took place. "Gentlemen, do you believe she was ever married to Mr. Easton?" he asked sharply. "Do you believe that any woman of morals ever forgets who married her or where she was married? Oh, no! Gentlemen, it is upon her testimony that you are asked to send these people to the chair!"

What did her neighbors think of this lady upon whose story the state was relying? "People around her community come in and they tell you that her reputation for veracity is bad," he pointed out. "They come here, gentlemen, and swear on their solemn oaths that this woman, who has been their neighbor for a dozen or fourteen years, is not worthy of your belief."

Of course, Senator Simpson paraded some people to the stand to testify to the contrary. But who were they? In the main, New Brunswick tradesmen who dealt with her sporadically and did not know her well. Her doctor, the only one of the state's character witnesses who could claim any long-standing acquaintance with her, said that her reputation for truth was bad.

According to Mrs. Gibson, the minister and the choir singer had been shot at close range during a struggle with their assailants. But Dr. Schultze, who performed the autopsies, said that there were no powder burns on either body. "Therefore," Case concluded, "it could not have been as the state contends. If it had been so, there would have been powder marks."

In addition, Officer Garrigan, one of the first policemen to arrive at the scene, swore that he had seen no footprints near the bodies. Sheriff Conkling reported that he had not found any signs of the titanic struggle Mrs. Gibson had so graphically described. Furthermore, except for directly under Mrs. Mills' head, there had been no blood in the area.

"I do not know how it convinces you," Case said, "but it convinces me that these bodies were shot as they sat, that there was no struggle. They occupied in death the position that they occupied in life when the assault was committed, except that they fell back prostrate instead of sitting there on the grass."

It was three forty-five when Case drew to a close. "Oh, gentlemen," he sighed wearily, "this is a serious moment in your lives and theirs." He gestured toward Mrs. Hall. "First they take away her husband, then they take away the ideals that she had held of her husband. Now they are trying to take away her life." He walked over to stand behind Willie Stevens. "Then this man sitting by her side, whom she has mothered, carried along, taken care of, has been behind the bars for months."

He turned and put his hands on Henry Stevens' shoulder.

"And this man here, as clean and white a man as ever lived. Oh, the infamy of it all, that for some ambition, for some increase in the circulation of a newspaper, that these people should be placed behind the bars, out of the sunlight for months. Let her and let them go on believing in the Bible and living the best they can the lives it tells us we should live."

As he left the courtroom, Mills was furious at McCarter's insinuations that he might have killed his wife and her lover. "They can't get anything on me," he whined. "Nobody has been set upon the way I have. I could tell you some things about the way they threatened me and tried to put the murders on me. If I had known anything about my wife's death, I would have broken under the strain of this long ago."

Thursday night was bitter-cold. The mercury, which dropped to 15 degrees above zero by six o'clock on Friday morning, had climbed only nine degrees by the time court opened. Precisely at ten thirty Simpson, whose red face attested to a thirty-two-mile drive in the subfreezing temperature, began the summation for the state. The special prosecutor, who made no secret of his suspicion of the jurors, started out by reminding them that it was their sworn duty to respect their oaths "and determine this case on the evidence."

And what was the evidence? First of all, Mrs. Hall must have known of her husband's love affair with Mrs. Mills. If not, she was the only person in New Brunswick who didn't. "Here is the cunning woman," he sneered, "thoughtful, experienced, a good judge of human nature, with pride of family, and yet she says that she never dreams that this man has changed. Do you believe such nonsense as that?"

It was not difficult, he reasoned, to reconstruct what must have taken place on the night of September 14. Mrs. Hall, despite all her denials, had overheard the telephone conversation between her husband and her rival. Once she had learned where the couple intended to meet that evening, she had called her brother Henry in Lavallette and asked him to come to New Brunswick at once.

He was willing to concede that when the defendants had started out for De Russey's Lane that night they had not intended to commit murder. "They started out to catch these people and confront them with these letters," he declared. "Henry Stevens was with her, no doubt about that. Willie Stevens was not the man, in my opinion, who did this job. It was a crackerjack marksman who did this job.

"Then there was a fight, because voices were heard, 'God damn you, let go of me,' and before that, 'Explain these letters!' and a shot—not to kill Hall. That shot was in the accident—was in the fight—and Hall had his head down."

Simpson walked over to where Mrs. Hall was sitting. "Hell hath no fury like a woman scorned," he incorrectly attributed to Byron. "The fires of hate and jealousy are raging in this woman's heart. Here is this woman who bought and paid for her husband. Of course she is jealous of the other woman. Why shouldn't she be? She was full of jealous hate. Look at her eyes."

What could be more suspicious than Mrs. Hall's actions on Friday and Saturday? he said. She called the police and didn't give her name. She didn't contact her brother Henry or check at any of the local hospitals. Yet she told Jim Mills that she was certain his wife and her husband had been the victims of foul play.

And after the minister's body was found and brought to New Brunswick, she never bothered once to visit Hubbard's and look at it. "Are these the acts of an innocent woman who has lost her husband?" he asked. "Are these the acts of a woman who has her life ruined?"

A simple review of the evidence ought to convince any fair-minded jury that the defendants were guilty. Mrs. Gibson, who, in his opinion, was "a very big character," placed them at the scene of the crime. Willie Stevens' fingerprint appeared on the minister's calling card. Mrs. Demarest said that she had seen Henry Stevens in New Brunswick on the morning after the murders.

The Dicksons swore that Willie Stevens had stopped at their house in North Plainfield on the evening of September 14, 1922, and inquired for the Parker Home. According to Garvin, Gorsline had identified Henry Stevens as being in De Russey's Lane on that fateful night. Lastly, there were the scratches on Mrs. Hall's face and the clothing that had been sent to Philadelphia to be dyed.

If Mrs. Gibson was lying, why hadn't McCarter called Nellie Russell to the stand to contradict her? "They did not call Gorsline," he added. "They did not call Minnie Clark. They did not call a number of witnesses who could help you." The fact of the matter was that the Pig Woman had been telling the truth. It was her courage and stamina that had led to the opening of a murder case that had been "hushed up for four long years."

The special prosecutor drew to a close at noon. "I have faith in the spirit of justice," he concluded, "and I don't think there was ever a finer phrase than that said by that old man who lived before the Saviour was born, who said, 'That deep base of the world and that high throne above the world where Thou art, unknown and hard of surmise, chain of things that be, or reason of our reason, God, to Thee I lift my praise, seeing the silent road that bringeth justice ere the end be tried.'"

His effort over, Simpson bowed gracefully to the jurors. As he walked back to the counsel table, Bergen rose and shook his hand. At the press bench Damon Runyon was busy preparing his next day's lead. "No man ever faced a jury with less regard for what it thought than Simpson," he wrote, "yet he made a clear summation of the state's case."

After a brief pause for lunch the trial came to a close with a thirty-five-minute charge by Justice Parker, in which the broad-shouldered jurist simply and dispassionately explained the applicable principles of criminal law.

It was exactly one fifty-two when three bailiffs escorted Foreman Dunster and his fellow jurors to the deliberation room on the second floor of the courthouse. A minute later Mrs. Hall and her two brothers, accompanied by Warden Major, left through the tunnel that led to the county jail. As soon as Parker and Cleary had retired to their chambers, the courtroom began to empty, and by two o'clock it was comparatively deserted.

Simpson had left for Jersey City after delivering his summation. Bergen, who was to represent the state during the last hours of the trial, returned to his office to await the verdict. Two of McCarter's assistants remained in the courtroom, while the rest of the defense lawyers relaxed in their sumptuous South Somerville headquarters.

As the long afternoon wore on and it became apparent that a quick decision would not be forthcoming, most of the reporters headed for nearby restaurants, leaving behind a small task force to watch for the jury's entrance. The only activity in the courtroom was supplied by the delivery boys who kept the handful of newsmen in the press section supplied with coffee and sandwiches.

By six thirty the suspense was almost unbearable. Suddenly Bill Pangborn, Somerville's only surviving Civil War veteran and one of the jury's custodians, poked his white-haired head in the courtroom door and nodded to Clerk Walter Crater. In a matter of minutes the all but deserted courtroom was completely filled as word that the jury was about to come in quickly spread to reporters, lawyers, and spectators.

Warden Major, who had been standing near the tunnel entrance, disappeared inside it. Several minutes later he emerged and led the three defendants to their seats behind the counsel table, where all of the defense attorneys except Case were already stationed. Just as Mrs. Hall and her brothers sat down, Prosecutor Bergen arrived in the court-room.

It was exactly six forty-eight when Bailiff Bunn rose and intoned his last "Oyez, oyez," of the trial as Parker and Cleary mounted the bench. "The officers will keep the door closed as the verdict is received," Justice Parker ordered. "When the verdict is received, officers will see to it that any member of the audience who makes any demonstration be brought before the court to be dealt with for contempt of court."

He turned to Crater. "You may bring the jury in," he directed.

Just as the impassive jurors filed into the room, Case, who had been having his dinner at a distant restaurant, rushed to his seat. After Dunster and his colleagues had entered the jury box, Parker quickly got down to the business at hand. "Gentlemen," he said quietly, "the court will ask you to render your verdict, separately as to each defendant, so that you will be asked as to each defendant whether you find that defendant guilty or not guilty."

"Gentlemen of the jury, have you agreed upon your verdict?" Crater asked.

"We have," the jurors said.

"Who shall say for you?" the clerk continued.

"The foreman," the panel replied in unison.

"Mr. Foreman, how do you say you find the defendant Henry Stevens, guilty or not guilty?"

Dunster hesitated for a seemingly interminable moment.

"Not guilty!" he finally blurted out.

In quick succession he announced that both Willie Stevens and Mrs. Hall had also been acquitted. His task done, the stout juryman permitted himself the luxury of a glowing smile.

When Henry Stevens heard the jury's verdict, his erect shoulders sagged and tears filled his eyes. "Where is Ethel?" he asked brokenly as he wiped his eyes with a handkerchief.

His wife, who was sitting directly behind him, reached over and patted his shoulder gently.

Although Mrs. Hall maintained the dignified mien that had characterized her appearance since the start of the trial, her brother Willie broke out into a broad grin as the verdict in his case was announced, and insisted on shaking hands with all six of his lawyers.

As the reporters fought to get out of the crowded court-room, Crater brought the formalities to a close. "Gentlemen of the jury," he said solemnly, "hearken to your verdict as the court has ordered it recorded: you find the defendant Henry Stevens not guilty; you find the defendant William Stevens not guilty; you find the defendant Mrs. Hall not guilty; in manner and form, and so say you all?"

The jurors fairly shouted their response. "We do!" they chorused.

There was a subtle smile on Parker's lined face as he dismissed the jury. "Gentlemen, you have dealt very patiently with a very long case," he said. "The court wishes to express its appreciation of the patience and the diligence with which you have handled the matter. You are excused for the term with the thanks of the court."

As soon as the jurors left the courtroom, they were surrounded by waiting newsmen, who quickly ascertained that it had taken three ballots to acquit the trio. In the main, the members of the panel had not believed Mrs. Gibson. "I would remain here for thirty years rather than vote a verdict of guilty on such evidence," one of them explained.

Since they were still under indictment for Hall's murder, the three defendants were immediately taken back to the county jail by Warden Major. As soon as they had left the courtroom, Case asked Parker to admit them to bail. In view of Simpson's absence, the justice ruled, it would be necessary for defense counsel to send the special prosecutor a telegram indicating that bail had been demanded.

"If he says he wants to have notice," he concluded, "he

will get notice. That will probably mean that these people will have to remain one more night in the county jail." Court was then adjourned to the next morning at ten o'clock.

The attorneys for the defense were unanimous in their condemnation of Simpson for not waiting in Somerville for the jury's verdict. "Simpson," one of them said, "got Prosecutor Bergen in this morning to try to show that Hudson County was not running the prosecution. But of course Bergen would not do when it came to freeing two men who have been acquitted."

Mrs. Stevens was less diplomatic. "I wish Senator Simpson had had enough sportsmanship to stay and get a dose of his own medicine," she said angrily. "Henry would not have to stay in jail if he had been there."

In Jersey City, Simpson was philosophical. "It's just what I expected," he told reporters. "The action of the jury justifies my application to the Supreme Court for a foreign jury for a trial of this case. I will recommend to Governor Moore that the three defendants be tried for the murder of Reverend Edward W. Hall. As for the question of admitting the defendants to bail, I do not feel there should be any favoritism shown to them."

It seemed hardly likely that either of the special prosecutor's recommendations would bear fruit. Attorney General Edward Katzenbach hinted at his evening press conference that the open charges against Mrs. Hall and her brothers would be dropped. "I am personally of the opinion," he said, "that a final disposition of the remaining indictments against them and against Mr. Henry Carpender cannot be too speedily accomplished."

He revealed that he had just sent telegrams to both Simpson and Justice Parker, stating that there was no official opposition to the granting of bail.

Reactions to the acquittals were varied. In general, Somerville was enthusiastic, and wherever they went, the jurors were congratulated by their fellow citizens. Mayor Flockhart, who called the verdicts "gratifying," urged his constituents to forget the excitement of the past month and "settle down to your daily round of current duties." One member of the Somerset Board of Freeholders regretted that "the case was still surrounded by as much mystery as four years ago."

Charlotte Mills had nothing but scorn for the jury. "I am not surprised," she cried bitterly. "Money can buy anything."

Reverend Ernest Pugh of Somerville's Episcopal church criticized what he called "the contemptible methods of Alexander Simpson." He hoped that "this will be the last case in our New Jersey courts where a prosecution will be lowered to the standard of a degrading public show."

The New York *Times*, on the other hand, lambasted both legal staffs. "It is hard to see that the counsel on either side got much glory," it editorialized, "and the proceedings have not given the Jerseyites reason for pride. They should forget the method in the result. Jersey Justice can at least acquit the innocent if it cannot always find the guilty."

As Mrs. Hall returned to New Brunswick, she was all smiles. "I am so happy, so happy," she chortled. "I cannot tell you how happy I am." Despite her well-known aversion to cameras, she posed willingly on her front steps for the hordes of photographers who had been waiting patiently for several hours.

Her old friend Sally Peters, who had just arrived from New York, was so excited that she kept clapping her hands for joy. Tim Pfeiffer, his normally grave countenance aglow with excitement, came in to offer his congratulations. "We had perfect faith in New Jersey justice," he said simply.

Chapter 28

ODDS AND ENDS

(December 4, 1926, to October 13, 1962)

At ten the next morning, as Somerville girded itself for an early snowstorm that was rapidly sweeping eastward from the Ohio Valley, the last legal maneuver in the Hall-Mills case took place in an almost deserted courtroom.

In a five-minute proceeding Justice Parker granted Attorney General Katzenbach's motion to dismiss all the remaining charges against Mrs. Hall, her brothers, and Henry Carpender. "The court has considered the matter in conference with the attorney general," the jurist said, "and under the circumstances, concludes that the motion should be granted. The defendants are, therefore, all discharged from custody."

As soon as the justice had left the bench, the few spectators crowded around the defendants. Included in the group of well-wishers were Foreman Dunster and four of his fellow jurors. "Our hopes were high," Henry Stevens told the foreman, "for we had faith we would get a fair deal from you." When he asked Dunster to visit him in Lavallette, the foreman, with a wry smile, promised that he would "when the bluefish are biting."

Mrs. Hall also had words of praise for the foreman. "God bless you," she said fervently. "I am so happy, and I want to thank you so much." Dunster looked around in helpless embarrassment. "I only did my duty," he murmured.

The reason for Katzenbach's presence in Somerville was quickly ascertained. In Jersey City, Simpson informed curious reporters that shortly before court time he had resigned his commission as an assistant attorney general. In his letter of resignation he had suggested to the governor that "you embalm 'Jersey Justice' and send her to the British Museum."

The former prosecutor closed his press conference with one last news item. "I intend to get in touch with State Senator William H. Bright, who represents the Cape May district," he said. "I will ask him to introduce a resolution when the Legislature meets next week, calling for an investigation of the administration of justice in Somerset County."[1]

By nightfall the temperature had dropped sharply, reaching a low of 12 degrees at ten o'clock. The snow started early the next morning, and it was quickly apparent that New Jersey was in for a heavy fall. As Mrs. Hall watched the drifts piling up on Nichol Avenue, she said that she was sorry for the handful of chilled photographers who were huddled together on the wind-swept sidewalk.

To their surprise, she finally opened her front door and invited them into the house. "They told me that they had to wait there on the chance of getting a picture of me," she said later. "They said they would not have to wait if I would give them the pictures inside, and so I did."

Because of the precarious state of her health Mrs. Gibson had not yet been told of the three acquittals. Late Sunday afternoon her physicians decided to release the news to her. "Acquitted?" she asked incredulously. "Well, can you beat that?" Five minutes later, lulled by the sight of the falling snow that had already reached a depth of five inches beneath her window, she closed her eyes.

---

[1] Bright never got around to complying with his colleague's request.

Early that evening a Jersey City reporter called the hospital. He wanted to know how the Pig Woman had reacted to the news. "She's sleeping like a baby," was the floor nurse's response.

For the next month the case managed to cling to the daily news columns as the embattled freeholders of Somerset County fought to escape some of the estimated $150,000 cost of the trial.[2] On December 10, Judge Cleary, on Bergen's recommendation, dropped the charges still pending against Felix De Martini and Minnie Clark.

Two days after Christmas, Charlotte Mills, who already exhibited the nervous condition that was to plague her for the rest of her life, appeared on the stage of Hoboken's Rialto Theatre, where *Who is Guilty?*, a play based on the tragedy, was playing to packed houses. "My mother was a good woman," Charlotte told her enthralled audience. "Please try not to think badly of her."

On March 15, 1927,[3] Mrs. Hall, Henry Carpender, and Willie Stevens sued the *Daily Mirror* for libel, asking a half million dollars each. Five months later they began similar actions against William Randolph Hearst and the *Evening Journal*. Just before Christmas 1928 it was announced that both sets of suits had been settled out of court for an undisclosed sum which was rumored to be somewhere between $50,000 and $150,000.[4]

Ten days after the lawsuit against the *Journal* had been filed, Louise Geist Riehl, whose husband had been denied a

2 They were partially successful. Despite Simpson's prophecy that Somerset County would have to pay "every cent," he informed Case on December 17 that the Jersey City policemen who assisted in the investigation would be paid by their home city.

3 Five days later, in Queens Village, New York, Henry Judd Gray and Ruth Snyder bludgeoned and chloroformed the latter's husband to death, thereby inaugurating second hyphenated-name murder trial of the Jazz Age.

4 With an uncharacteristic lack of gallantry, the New York *Times*, which had printed hundreds of thousands of words about the case, buried its brief story of the settlement on page 20.

divorce in June, asked the Court of Chancery to grant one to her.[5]

In April 1928, Aaron M. Blattman, a New York finger-print expert, sued Mrs. Hall and her brothers in the United States District Court in Trenton. Asking damages of $56,000, Blattman claimed that the defense had agreed to pay him three thousand dollars if he could prove that the fingerprint on the minister's calling card was a forgery, and a similar sum to have the right to publish his findings at the end of the trial, a privilege which he valued at $50,000.[6]

Over the years there were occasional reports hinting at a solution of the crime. On May 23, 1927, two days after Lindbergh's epochal flight to Paris, Secretary of State Kellogg forwarded a letter to Governor Moore which had been received by the American consul at Antilla, Cuba, from a local druggist.

The writer, it seems, had overheard a barroom conversation between two Germans and an Italian in which the former said that they had been hired by a wealthy German woman who was in love with Hall to kill the clergyman and his paramour. Moore, to whom the case had become a distinct political liability, said that the information in the druggist's letter was too sketchy to justify any action on his part.

In April 1928 a minor stir was caused when an Oklahoma convict confessed that he had killed the New Jersey couple. The prisoner, who was serving a term for forgery, said that he had been paid six thousand dollars by a dentist he had met when he was serving time in the Connecticut State Reformatory. The dentist, who subsequently moved to Elizabeth, New Jersey, had told him that he wanted Hall and Mrs. Mills murdered because he was related to one of them and they had disgraced their families. The story was so full of discrepancies that it was soon forgotten.

[5] She later remarried, and died in childbirth in 1936.
[6] The case was eventually settled for $750.

On May 27, 1929, Bergen received an intriguing telegram from the chief of police of Plymouth, Michigan. According to the police chief, an inmate of the Detroit City Jail had told him that he had witnessed the murders. If Bergen was interested, the chief would be only too happy to furnish more details. The Somerset prosecutor stated that he would be grateful for any information about the Hall-Mills case.

On June 8 a bulky envelope containing a five-page report of an interview with the Michigan prisoner arrived in Somerville. The anonymous jailbird's story was so patently tailored to fit the crime that Bergen didn't even bother to check it out. "It's pure bunk," he said.

The first of the major participants in the case to die was the *Mirror's* flamboyant Phil Payne. On September 6, 1927, Payne took off from Old Orchard Beach, Maine, on a nonstop flight to Rome. The plane, which was named *The Old Glory*, was flown by veteran pilot Lloyd O. Bertaud, and the flight was sponsored by William Randolph Hearst.

Six hours after take-off two distress signals were received from the aircraft. On September 9, *The Old Glory* was given up for lost, and three days later the S.S. *Kyle*, a steamship chartered by Hearst, located the wreckage of the plane six hundred miles due east of Newfoundland. No trace of its occupants was ever found.

Mrs. Gibson finally succumbed to cancer on February 7, 1930. She had been admitted to Jersey City Hospital eleven days earlier, but because of her weakened condition it had been impossible to give her needed blood transfusions. She sank into a coma early on the evening of February 6 and died without ever regaining consciousness.

Her husband, the mysterious Mr. Easton, was notified of her death by the hospital and removed the body to the Hamilton Avenue farmhouse. Mrs. Hall, who at the time was confined to a New Brunswick hospital for a minor operation, denied that she had sent a telegram to the dying woman, offering her forgiveness for her testimony at the trial. "There's absolutely no truth in that story," she emphasized.

Willie Stevens just managed to outlast his co-defendants,[7] surviving his sister by eleven days. Mrs. Hall, who had, with the exception of her church and welfare work, withdrawn completely from New Brunswick society after her acquittal, died on December 19, 1942. Several weeks before her death she had donated the wrought-iron fence which surrounded her property to the wartime scrap metal drive.

Willie, invalided by a severe heart attack in 1934, succumbed on December 30. During the last eight years of his life he never left the house on Nichol Avenue[8] except for an occasional drive in a chauffeured limousine.

In 1930, Alexander Simpson ran against Dwight Morrow for a seat in the United States Senate. He was decisively defeated and practiced law in his beloved Jersey City until his death in 1953.

One year earlier Charlotte Mills, after a lonely and frustrated life, had died in New York City at the age of forty-six. Her brother, Danny, lives today in a modest bungalow in Milltown, a suburb due south of New Brunswick, where he makes a home for his eighty-seven-year-old father, who works as a part-time sexton at the Pitman Methodist Church, two blocks away from unchanged St. John's.

The most recent death, that of Felix De Martini, occurred on October 13, 1962, when the former private detective succumbed to old age at his home in the Cypress Hills section of Brooklyn.

A year and three days later the *Mirror,* which has never succeeded in catching up with the *News,* ceased publication and sold out to its arch rival.

Today, more than forty years after the murders, the Hall-Mills case is still an open account on the books of the

---

[7] Henry Carpender died in 1934 and Henry Stevens five years later.

[8] Today the house is the home of the Dean of Douglass College.

Somerset County prosecutor. Arthur Sutphen Meredith,[9] the present occupant of that office, maintains that given enough credible evidence, he would be willing to present it to a latter-day grand jury. But it is hardly likely that the youthful prosecutor will ever find himself compelled to do so. For time and tide are against him.

Not only have many of the exhibits disappeared or disintegrated into dust, but with the exception of Tim Pfeiffer, Francis Bergen, and Jim Mills,[10] all the principals of the tragedy have passed from the scene. De Russey's Lane has been replaced by a broad macadam thoroughfare bearing the impressive name of Franklin Boulevard, and the old Phillips farm is now the site of a sprawling housing development.

Even the shades of the pretty choir singer and her clerical lover might now have some difficulty in locating the place where on a balmy September night they were dispatched into eternity.

[9] A grandson of Justice of the Peace William R. Sutphen, and the new owner of Clarence Case's Somerville home.

[10] As energetic as ever, Pfeiffer is today a partner in one of New York's largest law firms; Bergen has retired from practice, and unlike Pfeiffer, will not discuss the case with anyone.

PART IV

Chapter 29

ONE MAN'S SOLUTION

Who murdered the minister and his paramour? With little new evidence likely to develop, it is still possible, even at a distance of more than forty years, to speculate as to some of the candidates. Eight spring at once to mind. They are as follows:

1. Mrs. Hall, aided by relatives or paid assassins.
2. Jim Mills.
3. A jealous rival of Mrs. Mills.
4. Mrs. Gibson.
5. A lunatic.
6. Thieves.
7. Ray Schneider, who thought he had found Pearl Bahmer and her father in an incestuous relationship.
8. A posse of vigilantes.

In all likelihood, Mrs. Hall had nothing whatever to do with the crimes. Granted that she undoubtedly knew of the alliance between her husband and Mrs. Mills and had ample motive to harm them both, the testimony at the trial clearly indicates that she was in her house at the very time[1] the murders took place. Moreover, her actions on Friday night, Saturday, and Sunday morning were those of a distraught rather than a guilty woman.

1 At 10:15 P.M., according to earwitness Gorsline.

Finally, she was not, either by temperament or background, a murderess. Even to salve her own immense pride in her family's good name, she was not capable, by any stretch of the imagination, of taking or hiring someone to take a human life. It is probable that she would have ignored Hall's philandering for the rest of her life, so long as the image of a correct and happy marriage was maintained.

Even assuming, for the sake of argument, that the thought of murder had crossed her mind, she could not have given it serious consideration as an antidote to her domestic woes. An intelligent, farsighted woman, she must have known that her husband's violent death would inevitably subject her and her relationship with him to the glare of sensational publicity. It is indeed improbable that she would have deliberately chosen the greater of two evils. In addition, her almost pathological desire for privacy would have prevented her from setting the stage for its certain loss. Mrs. Hall may have been many things, but she was neither an impulsive fool nor a naïve simpleton.[2]

It is also equally clear that her brothers were not involved. The testimony placing Willie in Plainfield on Thursday night and Henry in New Brunswick the next morning is, to say the least, incredible. There was also evidence that Willie was in his bedroom shortly before the time the murders took place. As for Henry, there seems to be little doubt that he was fishing on the beach at Lavallette at the very time when according to Mrs. Gibson, he was shooting his brother-in-law and Mrs. Mills some fifty miles away.

Finally, it is inconceivable that either man, and particularly Willie, could have been involved in a brutal slaying. The Stevenses were hardly the types to solve their problems with blood.

[2] Moreover, it is unlikely that, Senator Simpson to the contrary, she hated Mrs. Mills. Just a month before the murders she sent a postcard to the choir singer from Islesford. "I wish you were here to see it all," she wrote. "Affectionately, F.N.H." This card, which was suppressed by the prosecution, was discovered by this writer in the office of the Somerset County prosecutor in October 1962.

Henry Carpender had an airtight alibi. He and his wife had been dining with friends until well after the time established for the murders. Furthermore, it is indeed improbable that the dignified stockbroker could have been persuaded to join an assassination plot.

But there is strong documentary evidence in existence which all but destroys Mrs. Gibson's story that she witnessed the four defendants in the act of murdering Mrs. Mills and St. John's pastor. When she returned from her first trip up De Russey's Lane on the night of September 14, the Pig Woman had made a note on the diary calendar which hung on her living room wall. "Followed thief—lost him in open wagon—lost moc—Farmer fired 4 shots," the entry read.

Yet more than a month later she described the murders in great detail and identified the eventual defendants as the persons who had collaborated to kill the two victims. "Farmer" had suddenly been transformed into three men and a woman who were anything but rustic in their dress and actions.

The information on Mrs. Gibson's wall calendar was neither made public nor given to the defense counsel. The very existence of the September 14 notation came to light on October 8, 1962, when a package of faded calendar leaves was found by this writer and Somerset Prosecutor Meredith in an envelope at the bottom of a cardboard box in the latter's office in Somerville. The calendar was wrapped in a piece of crumbling yellow paper which bore the signature of James Mason, Mott's chief investigator, and the date November 28, 1922.

When informed of the discovery on the very day it was made, Tim Pfeiffer said that as far as he knew, no defense attorney had ever been aware of the contradictory notation. "While I don't like to malign the dead," he said, "it would be just like Simpson to suppress such vital evidence of Mrs. Hall's innocence."

On September 17, Mrs. Gibson learned of the discovery of the bodies. Her calendar entry for that day reads, "Must have been what I heard and saw on 14th." From that day on she made every effort to attribute the shots fired by the unidentified "Farmer" to Mrs. Hall and her relatives.

Yet despite urgent telephone calls to Totten on September 20 and 23, and October 7, 8, 9, and 12, as well as a visit from the Somerset detective on September 24, it was not until October 20 that she succeeded in convincing the authorities that her story had merit. By this time it had grown into a complicated tale of a furious nocturnal struggle between two women and four men, punctuated by imprecations, gunshots, bloodcurdling screams, and conveniently revealing flashlight beams.

The last appearance of the "Farmer," who on September 14, 1922, had fired "4 shots," occurred when Mrs. Gibson appeared before the first grand jury that November. Then she said she had first thought that a farmer had been involved in the shooting, but that on second thought, it must have been Mrs. Hall and her homicidal relatives.

Four years later, when she testified before the second grand jury, and at the trial itself, she did not refer to any "Farmer." But by then her wall calendar was safely ensconced in the office of Prosecutor Bergen, where it was destined to remain hidden for almost thirty-six years. The state could hardly afford to have its star witness contradicted by her own written word.

Despite the defense's implication that Jim Mills might have committed the murders, almost nobody believed that he was capable of violence. A man of extremely limited talents, who looked upon the world about him with dull and uncomprehending eyes, he was thoroughly dominated, first by his wife and then by his daughter. It is highly likely that not only was he completely unconcerned by his wife's romance with Hall, but that he welcomed the limited economic benefits it brought.

Furthermore, the hapless sexton was seen on the porch of his apartment at nine o'clock on the night of the murders by his downstairs neighbor and he was still there when his

son, Danny, returned an hour and a half later. And if he had
conspired with Mrs. Hall, he would hardly have co-operated
so fully with both Mott and Simpson in their attempts to
put her in the electric chair.

Shortly after the discovery of the bodies Prosecutor Beekman intimated that one of St. John's female communicants
who was either jealous of Mrs. Mills' intimacy with the rector or resentful of her prominent role in church affairs had
engineered the double slaying. This theory, which even
Beekman eventually abandoned, has no evidence whatever to
support it. Not only did every member of the church have
an iron-clad alibi for the night of September 14, 1922, but
even the most resolute Agatha Christie fan would have difficulty in bridging the gap between cause and effect. Eleanor
Mills might have aroused annoyance, even dislike, in many
an Episcopal heart, but hardly that degree of hatred necessary to generate a pair of ghoulish murders.

It was Senator Case who suggested, somewhat facetiously,
in his summation that it was not beyond the realm of possibility that Mrs. Gibson had murdered the couple. What
her motive might have been Case failed to say, but the spectacle of the Pig Woman, who did not own a pistol, shooting
the minister and the choir singer and then cutting Mrs.
Mills' throat from ear to ear cannot be taken seriously. In
fact, the theory is negated by much of the very evidence introduced by the defense as to Mrs. Gibson's character, her
whereabouts on the night of the murders, and her efforts to
capitalize on her connection with the case.

It is possible, of course, that a lunatic was responsible for
the double murders. Significantly, when Case suggested that
Mrs. Gibson might be the guilty party, he based part of his
argument on the claim that her mind was not normal. But
if a deranged person had stumbled on the couple and killed
them in a fit of mad fury, it is highly likely that he or she
would have been captured in a matter of days.

Moreover, it is extremely difficult to believe that a mur-

derer of such mentality would have carefully arranged the
bodies in the affectionate pose in which they were found,
scattered Mrs. Mills' love letters over them, and propped the
minister's calling card against his foot. And is it likely that
a madman, after taking these steps, would then pocket Hall's
money and expensive watch?

The absence of the money and the watch, however, gives
some justification to the robbery theory. Lovers' lane hold-
ups were just as common in 1922 as they are today. But
would a thief have bothered to murder his victims and then
taken the time to arrange their bodies in such an elaborate
fashion? And what possible benefit could he have received
from cutting Mrs. Mills' throat after she was clearly dead
from three bullets in her brain? Furthermore, the minister's
unique gold hunting watch would certainly have shown up
over the years if his murderer had killed him for profit.

It is more than probable that Nicholas Bahmer had sexual
relations with his precocious daughter. But it is quite clear
that Ray Schneider met the incestuous couple on the night
of the murders and that he knew they did not go to the
Phillips farm. Schneider, moreover, despite his obvious jealousy of Pearl's other admirers, was hardly the type to murder
his rivals. Witness his quick retreat in the spring of 1922
when one of them threatened to whip him with his own
pistol.

The eighth possibility—that the couple were victims of
vigilante action—is the only one with any claim to logic and
reason. If one is willing to give serious consideration to the
arguments in support of this theory, he might well ask: Who
in the late summer of 1922 would have been most likely to
participate in the slaying of the clergyman and his mistress?
The answer to this question, even though arrived at somewhat circumstantially, seems obvious—members of one of
the many New Jersey branches of the Ku Klux Klan murdered the pair for their flagrant violation of the order's rigid
standards of sexual morality.

The proper development of this thesis must be prefaced by a brief history of the Second Invisible Empire, Knights of the Ku Klux Klan. On Thanksgiving night in 1915, William Joseph Simmons, an itinerant preacher who had a knack for creating and exploiting fraternal orders, brought the organization into being on Stone Mountain, just outside of Atlanta, Georgia. Although it took its name from the first Klan, which had been disbanded in 1869 after helping to restore the governments of southern states to local white control, its appeal was not sectional, and it began to spread northward shortly after its formation.

But its first five years of life were not marked by rapid growth, and by 1920 it faced bankruptcy. Rather than admit defeat, Simmons engaged Edward Young Clarke, a public relations specialist, to organize and run a membership drive that would draw new revenues into the Klan's empty coffers. Clarke was so successful that in October 1921, Simmons could boast to a Congressional committee that his organization had almost one hundred thousand adherents.

By 1922, largely as a result of Clarke's ingenuity and national postwar hysteria, the number of Klansmen had swelled to more than a million, and the Invisible Empire was influencing elections in many states. According to Simmons, at least seventy-five Congressmen elected that fall owed their seats to Klan support. The Klan's growing importance in American life was indicated by the publication in late 1921 of twenty-one articles on its activities by the influential New York *World*.

All new Klansmen were required to swear that they would, among other things, "most zealously and voluntarily shield and preserve, by any and all justifiable means and methods, the sacred constitutional rights and privileges of free public schools, free speech, free press, separation of church and state, liberty, white supremacy, just laws and the pursuit of happiness against any encroachment of any nature, by any person or persons, political party or parties, religious sect or people, native or naturalized or foreigner of any race, color, creed, lineage or tongue whatever."

Both above and below the Mason-Dixon line, this all-purpose oath was interpreted as authorizing members of the Klan to regulate community morality by fair means or foul. In late 1921, Henry P. Fry, a former Klansman from east Tennessee who had resigned in protest against the organization's growing lawlessness, wrote, "A large number of outrages, consisting of lawless acts of various kinds, have been reported in the newspapers as having been committed since early 1921. Women have been stripped of their clothing and covered with tar and feathers. Some men have been boldly kidnaped in broad daylight and driven in automobiles to obscure places and there flogged, and then have been whipped and mutilated for alleged immorality."

In the spring of 1921, Fry was present when three newly organized Klans in east Tennessee received their charters. "My people want to know what to do when they get their charters," he informed the state's King Kleagle, who was officiating at the ceremony. "What shall I tell them?" The answer, slightly muffled by the speaker's mask, could not have been more explicit. "Tell them to clean up their towns!"

All over the United States during 1921 and 1922, Klansmen were trying to do just that. On March 7, 1921, A. V. Hopkins, a Houston, Texas, merchant, was tarred and feathered for supposedly annoying high school girls. One month later, in the same city, automobile salesman J. W. McGee was severely whipped for the same offense.

In Fort Worth, on July 1, 1921, a young man was given twenty lashes for mistreating his wife. In the middle of that same month Mrs. Beulah Johnson, a resident of Tenaha, Texas, was kidnaped, stripped of her clothing, and tarred and feathered because she had been accused of bigamy. On the same day a Bay City banker suspected of infidelity was beaten into unconsciousness.

The next afternoon Reverend Philip S. Irvin, the arch-deacon of the English Episcopal church in Miami, Florida, was tarred and feathered, sewn into a sack, and dumped from a moving car into the street in front of his church for allegedly being too affectionate with some of his distaff parishioners.

In the spring of 1922 three Klansmen tried to kidnap Dr. William A. Muttera, a chiropractor of Morris, Illinois, who was reported to have molested a young woman patient. When he succeeded in fighting them off, the would-be abductors jumped into their car and raced back to Chicago. As they entered the city, they were arrested for speeding sixty-eight miles an hour. Police who searched the vehicle uncovered two revolvers and a cat-o'-nine-tails.

On the evening of September 13, 1922, William Hollings-worth, a Waynesboro, Pennsylvania, laborer, was kidnaped from his home by a band of masked men. Taken to a deserted field near the Maryland border, he was accused by his abductors of having treated his mother cruelly. When he denied the charges, a K was branded into each cheek and his forehead with acid. One side of his mustache was shaved off, his hair was cut in a grotesque fashion, and he was severely beaten before his attackers vanished into the night.

Four months later fifteen masked and robed men invaded the home of Mrs. R. H. Harrison, a thirty-year-old widow who lived with her young daughter in Goose Creek, Texas. Mrs. Harrison and R. A. Armand, a gentleman caller, were driven four miles out of town, where they were both viciously flogged. After the beating the widow's head was shaved and tar was rubbed into the gaping wounds on Armand's back in order to accentuate the pain.

"Two or three members of the party kept insisting that Mr. Armand and I be killed right there," Mrs. Harrison later told the police. " 'Kill them both and throw their bodies in the bayou,' they said. I heard threats to mutilate both of us. I expected death every instant."

In addition to its enforcement of sexual morality, the Klan conducted an energetic campaign to prevent divorce. In June 1923, Dr. Eugene Schreiber, a Macon, Georgia, physician who was about to shed his wife, was ordered to leave town within twenty-four hours or be killed. Early the next year Mrs. Fredericka Pace and Lynwood L. Bright, her lover, were kidnaped near Macon and driven into the country, where Bright, who had asked his wife for a divorce so that he would be free to marry Mrs. Pace, was beaten into insensibility in the latter's presence. Before he lapsed into unconsciousness, Bright was warned that he would be murdered unless he left Georgia at once.

Mainly in the South, many colored and some white men were mutilated for sexual transgressions. In some cases this mutilation consisted in amputation of the penis; in others, removal of the testicles; and in still others, branding of the scrotal sack or lower abdomen with the dreaded triple K.

For erring women the penalties, while not so brutal, were severe enough. In most instances the Klansmen contented themselves with stripping, flogging, shaving heads, and the traditional tarring and feathering. Occasionally, however, victims were raped by their tormentors or had their breasts branded.

In some areas violators of the moral code were given advance notice of proposed vigilante action. On July 22, 1921, a Klan letter, warning certain married men "to spend more time with their own wives," was published in an east Texas newspaper. A month earlier Mobile, Alabama, had been covered with ominous signs. "Law Violators, this is the first and last time that we will warn you," they proclaimed in boldface type. "Bad woman, you must obey the law, or you must leave the city. This county shall be clean. Married men, you must look after your families and quit carousing; violation of this warning means unhealthy steps for you. . . ."

By the summer of 1922 the Klan had become an integral part of the New Jersey scene. Most of its members in the northern part of the state were contained in the thirty-mile industrial complex between Paterson and New Brunswick. On April 15 three flaming crosses on nearby Garrett Mountain were witnessed by the inhabitants of Paterson. The incident, which was repeated three months later, was followed by crosses in Jersey City, Hackensack, and Perth Amboy.

During the latter part of the year Klansmen interrupted religious services in churches throughout the area in order to make donations of small sums of money to sympathetic ministers or to terrorize those whose sermons were antagonistic to the order. It was a rare Sunday indeed when a band of white-sheeted masked men failed to invade at least one house of worship.

On May 2, 1923, less than eight months after the murders, one of the largest initiations in Klan history took place on Hobbs farm, just a few miles west of De Russey's Lane. Protected by armed sentinels who patrolled the farm's boundaries at twelve-foot intervals, the ceremony took place at midnight in the presence of twelve thousand Klansmen from all over the state. For hours before the initiation thousands of cars, their license plates obscured by handkerchiefs, and identifying white ribbons tied to their radiators, moved in a seemingly endless line onto the farm.[3]

Klan efforts to enforce the moral code were much the same in New Jersey as they were in other parts of the country. On September 16, 1922, the day on which Pearl Bahmer and Ray Schneider had stumbled on the bodies, a south Jersey man was branded on the back with the initials KKK for reportedly abusing his mother. Four months later the owner of the Garden City Hotel in Atlantic City was threatened with physical harm if he didn't stop dealing with bootleggers. The following week Cape May husbands were warned that they would be severely punished if they continued to beat their wives.

[3] The following winter five crosses were burned in Middlesex County alone.

In the spring of 1923 a West Belmar resident was told that he could expect to be whipped and knifed if he didn't return fifty dollars which, the Klan had been informed, he had stolen from his mother. In late 1926, Plainfield theater owners were ordered to stop showing films on Sunday or face the consequences, while a Warren Point man who, in a drunken frenzy, had beaten his father and sister was tied to a stake and horsewhipped by a band of masked men.

In the fall of 1926 the small frame house of Harry Woolbert, a crippled painter of Somers Point, New Jersey, was burned to the ground by masked men. When Woolbert tried to escape, he was thrust back into the flames by his tormentors. He was then driven, more dead than alive, to a nearby field, where he was beaten with clubs and left unconscious on the ground. He was found three days later and taken to Atlantic City Hospital in critical condition. It was rumored that the painter's unorthodox sex life had led to his punishment by the Klansmen.

Although there was no evidence that prior to September 14, 1922, the Klan in New Jersey had used murder to punish deviators from its approved code of morals, blood had been shed in many other states. On March 12, 1923, forty Klansmen interrupted services at Newark's Grace Methodist Episcopal Church to give their Exalted Cyclops an opportunity to deny that any members of their organization had been involved in scores of brutal murders in Louisiana, where the Klan's lawlessness had become so widespread that its governor had been forced to appeal to President Harding for federal intervention.

But murder, pillage, and mayhem were much closer to New Jersey than the Pelican State. Just nine days before the murders the severed left hand of a white man was received in the mail by A. Philip Randolph,[4] the editor of *The Messenger*, a Negro magazine. The letter accompanying the gruesome package was on Klan stationery. "Now be careful

---

[4] Now president of the Brotherhood of Sleeping Car Porters.

how you publish this letter in your magazine," it warned, "or we may have to send your hand to someone else. Don't think we can't get you and your crowd. Although you are in New York City, it is just as easy as if you were in Georgia."

Because of its fundamentalist leanings and its bold appeal to racial and religious intolerance, the Klan, both in New Jersey and elsewhere, found the Protestant Episcopal Church one of its most implacable and outspoken enemies. Not only were Episcopal ministers urging their communicants to speak out against the marauding Klansmen, but they refused to accept money from masked contributors, and even, in some areas, posted guards around their churches to prevent Sunday services from being interrupted by sheeted invaders.

Shortly after the murders the Diocese of Indianapolis issued a denunciation of Simmons and his cohorts. "We feel that we should record our strong disapproval and condemnation of the Ku Klux Klan as a menace to peace and order and to social security and well-being," it declared. "The so-called enforcement of law and the attempted regulation of morality by bands of hooded and masked men can accomplish no good."

Clergymen who disapproved publicly of Klan activities were frequently threatened, and upon occasion, physically abused. On June 30, 1924, for example, Reverend Oren Van Loon, pastor of the Berkeley Community Church in a Detroit suburb, who had been outspoken in his condemnation of secret societies, was kidnaped. Two weeks later he was found wandering in a dazed condition on a Battle Creek street. When he was undressed by an intern at a local hospital, it was found that the letters KKK, two inches high, had been burned into his right shoulder with a hot iron.

Thus Edward Wheeler Hall and Eleanor Reinhardt Mills were prime targets for the type of retaliation practiced by the Klan. In addition to their open and notorious adultery and their well-publicized plans to elope, they were both active in the affairs of a wealthy and influential Protestant Episcopal church.

There was still another reason to hate Eleanor Mills—she was of German extraction. Since America's entry into World War I the Klan had become bitterly anti-German. Long after the Armistice it continued its efforts to halt the teaching of German in the public schools. As late as the summer of 1923 it was still threatening the Paterson, New Jersey, School Board for keeping the language in the curriculum.

Hours after the murders had become known, Prosecutors Beekman and Stricker began to receive letters and telephone calls accusing the Klan. One week later Beekman admitted that many people had asked him to explore this possibility. "We have no evidence to that effect," he stated. "We have heard reports of that kind and we have devoted part of our investigation to such theories, but nothing has been developed to justify such a belief."[5]

On October 23, 1922, Florence North announced that as a result of her suggestion that vigilantes might have been responsible for the crime, she had received several threatening letters from the Klan. "If you do not stop your silly activities and keep on exploiting your silly ideas," one of them read, "the Ku Klux Klan will give you a taste of the same medicine we gave to Mrs. Mills, so beware or you will see the fiery cross some night and get your due reward."

Because of the Klan's large membership in northern New Jersey, local officials, while not openly sympathetic to the organization, were careful to avoid any public show of hostility. On July 23, 1922, 625 men were initiated into the order behind the sheriff's house in Paramus. On the second anniversary of the murders Ferd David, the Middlesex County detective, announced that he hoped the Klan would join with the police in their efforts to solve the crime. "I

---

[5] The United States Secret Service, however, was sufficiently impressed by these reports to send a special agent into the area. Unfortunately, no record of his findings is in existence.

would welcome the assistance of the Klan," he proclaimed.

As late as October 1926, Senator Simpson was expressing his admiration for the masked men, five of whose names appeared on the struck jury list. Even in its dotage the Invisible Empire had just too many votes in northern New Jersey to be ignored.

The elaborate positioning of the bodies was wholly in keeping with Klan practices. The placing of Mrs. Mills' head on her lover's arm was a graphic demonstration of the couple's adulterous relationship. The calling card propped against Hall's left leg dramatized the fact that the murdered man was an Episcopal clergyman. The scattering of the love letters around the two corpses emphasized the fiery nature of the love affair that undoubtedly led to the murders.

The cutting of Mrs. Mills' throat and the removal of her windpipe, larynx, and tongue were as symbolic as the amputation of the genitalia of an Alabama Negro accused of raping a white woman. The severing of a soprano's vocal cords makes its point every bit as forcefully as the ending of a man's sexual life.[6]

It is possible, of course, that the Klansmen concerned did not intend to kill the couple. Some of the medical testimony indicated that the clergyman might have put up a struggle, and this resistance could have caused his death as well as that of his mistress. If Mrs. Gibson is worthy of any belief, some sort of scuffle took place near the crab apple tree. Moreover, several witnesses who lived in the vicinity of the Phillips farm testified that the four shots had been directly preceded by a woman's scream. It is conceivable that Mrs. Mills might have stampeded her assailants into murder.

The Klan could hardly have been unaware of the scandal at St. John's. For at least two years Hall and Mrs. Mills had made no secret of their relationship. Not only did the minis-

---

6 Rumors still persist that Hall's penis had been amputated and placed in the choir singer's mouth. The autopsy reports, however, do not mention any such mutilation of the minister's body.

ter visit the Mills apartment almost daily, but Eleanor had told her husband and most of her family that she and Hall were going to run away together as soon as Charlotte finished high school. Many people had seen the couple in Buccleuch Park, and their regular trips to "our road" at the Phillips farm were notorious.

Letters were freely exchanged, telephone calls, with the kind assistance of Miss Opie, were made on a more or less regular basis, and upon occasion even the church was used as a love nest. As the testimony at the trial clearly indicated, the romance was an open secret insofar as the Hall servants, the members of the choir, and many parishioners were concerned. Klan ears, which were more than sensitive to such gossip, could not have failed to hear rumors about the juiciest extracurricular affair in New Jersey.

However, as far as the Klan theory is concerned, how can the presence of Mrs. Mills' love letters which were scattered around the bodies be explained? If the unfortunate couple were murdered by Klansmen, how did they obtain this intimate correspondence?

The answer is simple. The letters were written by Mrs. Mills to Hall while he was on vacation in Islesford, Maine, in the summer of 1922. He did not return to New Brunswick until the end of August, and during his four-week absence Eleanor assuaged her loneliness by writing letters which she never intended to mail. On the night of September 14 she had decided to deliver them to her lover.

In January 1923, Jim Mills told Ellis Parker that on the day before his wife's murder he had seen these same letters wrapped in one of her scarves. As he described them, "they were sheets of tablets, never been in the mail, were not dated or signed." Mrs. Agnes Blust, who was one of the last persons to see Mrs. Mills alive on the night of her death, testified at the trial that the choir singer had been carrying "something brown in her arms."

According to Detective Totten, Eleanor's tan scarf had

been wrapped around the gaping wound in her neck when the body was found. Her murderers could not have failed to find her private letters and to see in them an effective way of dramatizing a flagrant violation of the Seventh Commandment.

It is conceded that the case against the Klan is a wholly circumstantial one. But legal history is filled with convictions based on such evidence. At the very least, the widespread belief in Klan involvement merited a thorough investigation of the Invisible Empire's many branches in northern New Jersey.

Instead, the authorities, in what was undoubtedly the most bungled murder case in the annals of American crime, attempted first to pin the double slaying on a clearly innocent youth, and then allowed themselves to be pressured by a circulation-hungry newspaper into accusing a respected local family on evidence that a previous grand jury had rejected and that was obviously insufficient to convict.

Why was the possibility that the Klan was responsible all but ignored by Beekman and Stricker despite the many tips received by them? In addition to the political reasons that have already been suggested, both prosecutors could not have been unaware of the difficulty of isolating and identifying members of a lynch mob. This is particularly true when it is composed of masked men who have taken an oath never to disclose either the order's activities or the names of its members.

Lastly, a charge of Klan responsibility would have been ridiculed by most people in Somerset and Middlesex counties as either an attempt to besmirch the organization or as a blatant effort to protect the real murderers. Only Klansmen might have taken the accusation seriously.

For those who insist on proof positive, the theory propounded on these pages can never be wholly satisfying. However, it seems infinitely more logical than any of those advanced by the state between September 16, 1922, and December 4, 1926. Undoubtedly there are former Klansmen still living in the New Brunswick area who could cast light on the murders, but shielded as they were by masks, a solemn oath, and secret membership lists, their erstwhile association with the sheeted order may never be established. In addition, the knowledge that there is no statute of limitations for murder in New Jersey would certainly curb the tongues of even the more loquacious survivors.

DRAMATIS PERSONAE

ARTHUR APPLEGATE	A Lavallette resident who supported Henry Stevens' alibi.
MAZIE APPLEGATE	Arthur Applegate's wife, who corroborated her husband's testimony.
NICHOLAS BAHMER	Pearl Bahmer's father.
PEARL BAHMER	A fifteen-year-old New Brunswick girl who, with Raymond Schneider, discovered the bodies of Reverend Hall and Mrs. Mills on September 16, 1922.
ELSIE BARNHARDT	One of Eleanor Mills' sisters.
ANNA K. BEARMAN	Mrs. Hall's first cousin who, shortly after the murders, sent some of the widow's clothing to Philadelphia to be dyed.
AZARIAH BEEKMAN	Somerset County prosecutor at the time of the murders.
MARCUS W. BEEKMAN	Azariah Beekman's brother.
FRANCIS L. BERGEN	Somerset County prosecutor during the 1926 investigation.
AGNES BLUST	A New Brunswick housewife who was one of the last people to see Eleanor Mills alive on the night of September 14, 1922.
THEODORA BONNER	One of Reverend Hall's sisters.

JAMES L. BOWERS	Beekman's immediate successor as Somerset County prosecutor.
ALFRED BUTLER	A New Brunswick taxi driver.
FRANK CAPRIO	A private detective who investigated the murders for Prosecutor Beekman in 1922.
ALBERT J. CARDINAL	A New Brunswick *Daily Home News* reporter who was the first newsman to visit the scene of the murders after the discovery of the bodies.
EDWIN R. CARPENDER	A first cousin of Mrs. Hall's who was in charge of the funeral arrangements for the rector.
ELOVINE CARPENDER	The wife of Edwin R. Carpender and the one who first informed Mrs. Hall of her husband's death.
HENRY DE LA BRUYÈRE CARPENDER	A first cousin of Mrs. Hall's who was indicted with her for the murders.
CLARENCE E. CASE	Assistant chief defense counsel in 1926.
SALOME CERENNER	Mrs. Gibson's mother.
MINNIE CLARK	Marie Demarest's cousin and a Sunday school teacher at St. John's.
FRANK L. CLEARY	The Somerset County judge who, with Justice Charles W. Parker, presided at the trial.
BOGART F. CONKLING	Somerset County sheriff at the time of the murders.
EDWARD I. CRONK	New Brunswick health officer at the time of the murders.
JAMES CURRAN	A New Brunswick patrolman who was one of the first policemen to arrive at the scene of the murders on September 16, 1922.
PETER F. DALY	Middlesex County judge at the time of the murders.
FERDINAND DAVID	Middlesex County detective from 1922 to 1926.

FELIX DE MARTINI	The chief private detective employed by the defense.
FRANK M. DEINER	A reporter for New Brunswick *Daily Home News*.
MARIE DEMAREST	A member of St. John's choir who testified for the prosecution.
HENRY L. DICKMAN	A deserter from the New Jersey State Police Constabulary who testified for the prosecution.
CHARLOTTE DICKSON	John Dickson's wife, who corroborated her husband's testimony.
JOHN S. DICKSON	A Plainfield accountant who claimed to have seen Willie Stevens on the night of the murders.
FREDERICK DREWEN	A fingerprint expert of the Jersey City Police Department who testified for the prosecution.
FRANK A. DUNSTER	Foreman of the trial jury.
WILLIAM EASTON	Mrs. Gibson's husband, according to everyone but the Pig Woman herself.
WALTER E. EDGE	United States Senator from New Jersey in 1922.
EDWARD I. EDWARDS	Governor of New Jersey at the time of the murders.
GRACE EDWARDS	Edward Stryker's niece who notified the police of the discovery of the bodies.
ROBERT ERLING	A New Brunswick millwright who said that on the night of the murders he had seen Jane Gibson riding her mule in De Russey's Lane.
ANNA EVANSON	Henry Stevens' cook at Lavallette, who supported his alibi.
JOSEPH A. FAUROT	A former New York City deputy police commissioner who testified for the prosecution as a fingerprint expert.
THOMAS A. FLOCKHART	Mayor of Somerville in 1926.

WILLIAM E. FLORENCE	An attorney and former state senator from Middlesex County who, at Mrs. Hall's request, informed the New Brunswick police on September 15, 1922, of the minister's mysterious disappearance.
MRS. A. C. FRALEY	A Somerset woman whose home was the closest to the scene of the murders.
EDWARD GARRIGAN	A New Brunswick patrolman who was one of the first policemen to arrive at the scene of the murders.
WILLIAM GARVIN	The former manager of the New York office of the William Burns Detective Agency, who insisted that Ralph Gorsline had visited him three weeks after the murders.
JANE GIBSON	A Somerset pig farmer who claimed that she had seen Mrs. Hall and three of her relatives murdering the minister and the choir singer near De Russey's Lane on September 14, 1922.
RUSSELL GILDERSLEEVE	A former lay reader at St. John's who testified for the prosecution.
CALVIN H. GODDARD	A firearms expert who testified for the prosecution.
RALPH GORSLINE	A St. John vestryman and choir member who was in De Russey's Lane on the night of the murders.
WILLIAM GREALIS	A delivery boy for Willie Stevens' tailor.
WILLIAM S. GUMMERE	Chief Justice of New Jersey in 1926.
FRANK HAGUE	Mayor of Jersey City in 1926 and for a long time thereafter.
EDWARD WHEELER HALL	Rector of New Brunswick's Protestant Episcopal Church of St. John the Evangelist, who, with Mrs. James

F. Mills, was murdered near De Russey's Lane on September 14, 1922.

FRANCES NOEL HALL · The widow of Reverend Edward Wheeler Hall, who was eventually indicted for the murder.

PAUL F. B. HAMFORSZKY · Former New Brunswick clergyman who disappeared on the eve of the trial.

AUGUST HARTKORN · A prosecution witness handwriting expert.

CLIFFORD HAYES · A New Brunswick youth who was mistakenly charged with the murders in 1922.

PATRICK HAYES · The Hoboken chief of police who was Special Prosecutor Simpson's chief aide during the 1926 investigation.

RUNKLE HEGEMAN · A Somerville physician who assisted at the 1922 autopsy on Eleanor Mills' body.

ANNA L. HOAG · A Somerset woman who heard shots at ten o'clock on the night of the murders and who later shared the Phillips farm with Mrs. Bertha Tegen.

CARLTON P. HOAGLAND · The Somerset publisher who was the foreman of the April 1926 grand jury.

EMMA HOLZLOHNER · The mother of Mrs. John M. (Bertha) Tegen, the co-tenant, with Mrs. Anna L. Hoag, of the Phillips farm in 1924.

JOHN V. HUBBARD · The New Brunswick undertaker who buried both bodies.

CHRIST HUEBNER · The special guard at Buccleuch Park.

EDWARD L. KATZENBACH · New Jersey attorney general in 1926.

LEON KAUFMANN · A sixteen-year-old New Brunswick boy who spent the evening of the murders with Clifford Hayes and Raymond Schneider.

ELIZABETH E. KELLY — The woman who occupied the ground floor of the house in which the Millses lived.

FRANK F. KIRBY — A Middlesex detective who was responsible for persuading Raymond Schneider to accuse Clifford Hayes of the murders.

HARRY A. KOLB — A New Brunswick milkman who delivered to the Hall house in 1922.

JOHN J. LAMB — A captain in the New Jersey State Police who was in charge of the Somerville detachment during the 1926 investigation.

A. ANDERSON LAWTON — A New Brunswick physician who assisted Special Prosecutor Simpson in 1926.

MARIE M. LEE — One of Eleanor Mills' four sisters.

E. LEON LOBLEIN — The New Brunswick veterinarian who identified Hall's body on September 16, 1922.

WILLIAM H. LONG — The Somerset County physician who accompanied Detective Totten to the scene of the murders on September 16, 1922.

JAMES P. MAJOR — Warden of the Somerset County Jail from 1908 to 1926.

JAMES F. MASON — The Essex County detective who was Mott's chief aide during the 1922 investigation.

ROBERT H. McCARTER — Chief defense counsel in 1926.

THOMAS F. McCRAN — New Jersey attorney general at the time of the murders.

JOHN J. MEANEY — The motorman on the Easton Avenue trolley on the night of the murders.

THADDEUS MELLINGER — A summer resident of Lavallette who supported Henry Stevens' alibi.

CHARLOTTE MILLS	The daughter of James and Eleanor Mills, who was sixteen years old at the time of her mother's death.
DANIEL MILLS	The son of James and Eleanor Mills, who was twelve years old at the time of his mother's death.
ELEANOR REINHARDT MILLS	A member of St. John's choir who was murdered near De Russey's Lane on September 14, 1922.
JAMES FRANCIS MILLS	Eleanor Mills' husband.
A. HARRY MOORE	Governor of New Jersey during the 1926 investigation of the murders.
WILBUR A. MOTT	The special prosecutor who conducted the first investigation of the murders in 1922.
IRA NIXON	A fellow employee of Elisha K. Soper's who contradicted his testimony at the trial.
FLORENCE M. NORTH	Charlotte Mills' attorney in 1922.
MILLIE OPIE	A dressmaker and milliner who lived next door to the Millses.
CHARLES W. PARKER	The Supreme Court justice who presided at the trial.
ELLIS H. PARKER	Burlington County detective at the time of the murders, and one of New Jersey's most successful criminologists.
CEDRIC A. PAULUS	Mrs. Hall's chauffeur in 1926.
PHILIP A. PAYNE	Editor of the New York *Daily Mirror* in 1926.
SALLY PETERS	Maid of honor at the Halls' wedding and Mrs. Hall's confidante from September 1922 to December 1926.
J. MERVIN PETTIT	Hall's successor at St. John's.
TIMOTHY N. PFEIFFER	Mrs. Hall's personal attorney in 1922 and 1926.
WILLIAM PHILLIPS	A watchman at the New Jersey College for Women who saw an unidentified woman enter the Hall

house early on the morning of September 15, 1922.

JOHN PIARD
A Lavallette summer resident who supported Henry Stevens' alibi.

CATHERINE RASTALL
A member of St. John's choir who was in De Russey's Lane on the night of the murders.

J. KEARNEY RICE, JR.
The Highland Park resident who claimed that Henry Carpender was at his house on the night of the murders.

ARTHUR S. RIEHL
Louise Geist's husband, whose petition for an annulment of his marriage inspired the second investigation of the murders.

LOUISE GEIST RIEHL
A maid in the Hall house at the time of the murders.

LAWRENCE RUNYON
Willie Stevens' physician.

NELLIE LO RUSSELL
A neighbor of Mrs. Gibson's who completely contradicted the latter's story of what happened on the night of the murders.

RAYMOND SCHNEIDER
The New Brunswick youth who, with Pearl Bahmer, discovered the bodies on September 16, 1922.

OTTO H. SCHULTZE
The New York County Medical Examiner who assisted at the 1926 autopsies.

EDWARD H. SCHWARTZ
Superintendent of the Bureau of Records of the Newark Police Department.

H. NORMAN SCHWARTZKOPF
Superintendent of the New Jersey State Constabulary.

GEORGE SILZER
Governor of New Jersey from 1922 to 1924.

ALEXANDER SIMPSON
A Hudson County state senator and the special prosecutor during the 1926 investigation.

GEORGE SIPEL	A Middlebush farmer who testified for the defense in 1926.
ARTHUR L. SMITH	The New Brunswick surgeon who assisted at the 1922 autopsies.
ELISHA K. SOPER	A Middlesex resident who drove by De Russey's Lane at midnight on September 14, 1922.
ELDRIDGE W. STEIN	A handwriting expert who was a witness for the defense.
ETHEL STEVENS	The wife of Henry Stevens.
HENRY STEVENS	Mrs. Hall's brother and one of the defendants at the trial.
WILLIAM STEVENS	The eccentric brother of Frances Hall, who was one of the four suspects indicted for the murders.
JOHN STILLWELL	The driver of Hall's hearse.
AGNES W. STORER	St. John's organist in 1922.
JOSEPH E. STRICKER	Middlesex County prosecutor at the time of the murders.
EDWARD STRYKER	The owner of a house approximately six hundred feet from the crab apple tree under which the bodies were found; it was his telephone that was used to notify the police of the murders.
SAMUEL T. SUTPHEN	The Somerville undertaker to whose funeral parlor the two bodies were taken on September 16, 1922.
WILLIAM R. SUTPHEN	The Somerset County justice of the peace who signed the warrants for the arrest of Mrs. Hall and her codefendants.
BERTHA TEGEN	A co-tenant of the Phillips farm in 1924.
AUGUSTA TENNYSON	One of Eleanor Mills' sisters.
JOHN E. TOOLAN	Middlesex County prosecutor at the time of the trial.
GEORGE D. TOTTEN	Somerset County detective at the time of the trial.

BARBARA TOUGH	A maid in the Hall house at the time of the murders.
PETER TUMULTY	Mrs. Hall's man of all work in 1922.
SANFORD W. TUNISON	Somerset County sheriff in 1926.
ENOCH T. VAN CAMP	Mayor of Lavallette in 1922.
FANNIE H. VOORHEES	One of Hall's sisters.
FRANCES VOORHEES	Hall's ten-year-old niece, who was visiting him on the last day of his life.
JENNIE WALLER	The girl who accompanied Robert Erling to De Russey's Lane on the night of the murders.
RUSSELL E. WATSON	A member of the defense's legal staff in 1926.
SARAH M. WILSON	A Lavallette summer resident whose home adjoined that of Henry Stevens.